Country Home

STAY FOR SUPPER

MEREDITH® BOOKS
Des Moines, Iowa

MEREDITH® BOOKS
President, Book Group: *Joseph J. Ward*
Vice President and Editorial Director: *Elizabeth P. Rice*
Executive Editor:: *Connie Schrader*
Art Director:: *Ernest Shelton*
Test Kitchen Director: *Sharon Stilwell*

STAY FOR SUPPER
Editors: *Linda Henry, Heather M. Hephner, Nancy Wall Hopkins,*
Sandra Mosley
Graphic Designer: *Lyne Neymeyer*
Project Managers: *Liz Anderson, Marsha Jahns, Jennifer Speer Ramundt*
Food Stylists: *Lynn Blanchard, Janet Herwig, Kathleen E. German,*
Mary-Helen Steindler
Photographers: *Catherine E. Money, Kathy Sanders*
Electronic Text Processor: *Paula Forest*

COUNTRY HOME®
President, Magazine Group: *William T. Kerr*
Editor, Country Home: *Jean LemMon*

MEREDITH CORPORATION CORPORATE OFFICERS:
Chairman of the Executive Committee: *E. T. Meredith III*
Chairman of the Board, President and Chief Executive Officer: *Jack D. Rehm*
Group Presidents:
Joseph J. Ward, Books
William T. Kerr, Magazines
Philip A. Jones, Broadcasting
Allen L. Sabbag, Real Estate
Vice Presidents:
Leo R. Armatis, Corporate Relations
Thomas G. Fisher, General Counsel and Secretary
Larry D. Hartsook, Finance
Michael A. Sell, Treasurer
Kathleen J. Zehr, Controller and Assistant Secretary

On the cover: *Peach Cobbler with Cinnamon–Swirl Biscuits (see recipe, page 202)*

Illustrations and Engravings: *Dover Publications, Inc., New York, New York*

All of the recipes in this book have been tested in the Country Home®
Test Kitchen to ensure that they are practical and reliable, and meet our
high standards of taste appeal. We guarantee your satisfaction with this
book for as long as you own it.

All of us at Meredith®Books are dedicated to providing you with the
information and ideas you need to create tasty foods. We welcome
your comments or suggestions. Write us at:

Meredith® Books, Cook Book
Editorial Department, RW240
1716 Locust St.
Des Moines, IA 50309-3023

INTRODUCTION

WHEN I WAS GROWING UP, farm families didn't make phone-ahead reservations before visiting. Folks just dropped by in the late afternoon, had coffee at the kitchen table, and exchanged ideas or local news. Invariably, the question would be asked, "Won't you stay for supper?" Living in the country meant good food— tomatoes sliced while they were still warm from the sun, tangy apples baked into pies that filled the kitchen with the aroma of fruit and cinnamon, and wild strawberries simmered to make preserves that have yet to be matched. At our house food was homegrown and plentiful. Meals were liberally seasoned with laughter and often were shared with

friends and family. That's why our County Home® cookbook STAY FOR SUPPER is so close to my heart. Not only is it loaded with great, down-home recipes and old-fashioned illustrations, it's been designed to help you re-create the good times, the simple times, when some of the friendliest words spoken were "Stay for supper." ■

CONTENTS

CHAPTER ONE

ROUND 'EM UP

MEATS — FROM A SUNDAY POT roast to a glazed Easter ham — are the backbone of a country meal. Many of the recipes included here, such as Mustard-Glazed New England Boiled Dinner and Chicken-Fried Steak with Gravy, conjure up memories of days gone by. But we've also included new favorites, such as Beef Tenderloins with Peppercorns and Rosemary Lamb Kabobs, that modern country cooks will want to add to their collections and pass down through the years. ■

If you have extra Baked Country Ham, use it for Country Ham with Redeye Gravy (see recipe, page 116) or as part of a traditional southern breakfast that might include biscuits, eggs, and grits.

Pictured on page 7.

BAKED COUNTRY HAM

1   12- to 14-pound country or *country-style ham*
2   teaspoons whole cloves
8   cups apple cider or *apple juice*
½   cup packed brown sugar
2   teaspoons ground cloves
     Dry sherry or *red wine vinegar*

PLACE HAM IN A LARGE CONTAINER. COVER WITH cold water and soak for 16 hours, changing water once. Pour off water. Scrub ham in warm water with a stiff brush and rinse well. Cut skin from ham and trim off fat. Insert whole cloves into ham.

Place ham, fat side up, in a large roasting pan. Insert a meat thermometer into the thickest portion of the ham, making sure it doesn't touch fat or bone. Pour apple cider or apple juice over ham.

Bake ham, covered, in a 325° oven for 4 to 4½ hours or till the meat thermometer registers 160°. Drain off pan juices.

For glaze, in a small bowl combine brown sugar and ground cloves. Add just enough sherry or vinegar to make a paste. Spread glaze over fat side of ham.

Bake ham, uncovered, about 30 minutes more or till the meat thermometer registers 170°. Let stand for 15 to 20 minutes before slicing. Makes 25 to 30 servings.

COUNTRY HAMS

COUNTRY HAMS ARE QUITE DIFFERENT FROM THE more common fully cooked hams. Country hams have a distinctive, robust flavor and are saltier and drier than other hams. The names of country hams, such as Smithfield, Virginia, Kentucky, or Tennessee, indicate where the ham was processed. The flavor of a country ham depends on the diet fed to the hog, the wood used for smoking, the curing process, and the aging process.

To prepare a country ham, soak it overnight to reduce the saltiness. Then, trim off the fat and mold (a harmless by-product of the aging process). Bake the ham until the internal temperature is 170°. To serve, slice country ham very thin.

Country hams are available in supermarkets, speciality food stores, and mail-order food catalogs. Usually they weigh 10 to 14 pounds, however some smaller hams also are available.

CRANBERRY-GLAZED HAM

1 5- to 7-pound smoked fully cooked ham, shank portion
    Whole cloves
1 6-ounce can frozen cranberry juice cocktail concentrate, thawed
¼ cup packed brown sugar
2 tablespoons prepared mustard
1 tablespoon lemon juice
⅛ teaspoon ground cinnamon
⅛ teaspoon ground cloves

CUT SKIN FROM HAM. USING A SHARP KNIFE, SCORE top of ham by cutting diagonal slashes about ¼ inch deep in a diamond pattern. Insert a whole clove in the center of each diamond.

For cranberry glaze, in a small mixing bowl combine thawed cranberry juice cocktail concentrate, brown sugar, mustard, lemon juice, cinnamon, and ground cloves. Stir together till brown sugar is dissolved.

Place ham on a rack in a shallow roasting pan. Insert a meat thermometer into the thickest portion of the ham, making sure it doesn't touch fat or bone. Bake, uncovered, in a 325° oven for 1¾ to 2¼ hours or till the meat thermometer registers 140°, basting with glaze every 30 minutes.

Heat remaining cranberry glaze and pass with the ham. Makes 18 to 25 servings.

If you have ham left over, grind some for ham balls or a ham loaf, or cube some for a casserole. Package and freeze the ham in meal-size portions. For the best flavor, use the ham within a month.

COUNTRY RIBS WITH
GINGERY BARBECUE SAUCE

2½ to 3 pounds meaty pork country-style ribs
½ cup chopped onion
1 clove garlic, minced
1 teaspoon grated gingerroot or ¼ teaspoon
   ground ginger
1 tablespoon cooking oil
1 8-ounce can tomato sauce
½ cup water
¼ cup chili sauce
2 tablespoons brown sugar
1 tablespoon vinegar
1 tablespoon Worcestershire sauce
⅛ teaspoon pepper

TRIM FAT FROM RIBS. PLACE RIBS, BONE SIDE
down, on a rack in a shallow roasting pan.
Bake, uncovered, in a 350° oven for 1 hour.
Drain well.

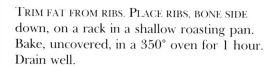

Meanwhile, for sauce, in a medium saucepan
cook the onion, garlic, and gingerroot or
ground ginger in hot oil till onion is tender.
Stir in tomato sauce, water, chili sauce, brown
sugar, vinegar, Worcestershire sauce, and
pepper. Bring to boiling; reduce heat. Simmer,
uncovered, about 30 minutes or till sauce is of
desired consistency.

Spoon sauce over ribs. Bake ribs, covered, for
30 to 60 minutes more or till well-done,
spooning sauce over ribs occasionally. Spoon
any remaining sauce over ribs before serving.
Makes 4 servings.

> GRILLING DIRECTIONS: Prepare Country
> Ribs with Gingery Barbecue Sauce, *except*
> in a covered grill arrange *medium-hot* coals
> around a drip pan (see tip, page 28).
> Test for *medium* heat above the pan. Place
> ribs on the grill rack over the drip pan
> but not over coals. Lower the grill hood.
> Grill for 1 hour. Prepare sauce as
> directed. Brush ribs with sauce. Grill ribs
> about 30 minutes more or till well-done,
> brushing occasionally with sauce. Spoon
> remaining sauce over ribs before serving.

R E D   B E A N S   A N D   R I C E

  1   cup dry red beans *(about 8 ounces)*
6½ cups cold water
  1   pound meaty smoked pork hocks
  2   cups sliced carrots *(about 4 carrots)*
  1   cup sliced celery *(about 2 stalks)*
  ½ cup chopped onion
  2   cloves garlic, minced
  2   bay leaves
1½ teaspoons snipped fresh thyme
      or ½ teaspoon dried thyme, crushed
  ½ teaspoon bottled hot pepper sauce
  4   ounces smoked sausage, chopped *(about ¾ cup)*
  3   cups hot cooked rice
      Bottled hot pepper sauce *(optional)*

RINSE BEANS. IN A DUTCH OVEN OR LARGE KETTLE combine beans and *4 cups* water. Bring to boiling; reduce heat. Simmer for 2 minutes. Remove from the heat. Cover; let stand for 1 hour. (*Or,* soak beans in water overnight in a covered pan.) Drain beans and rinse.

In the same Dutch oven or kettle combine beans, *2½ cups* water, pork hocks, carrots, celery, onion, garlic, bay leaves, thyme, and the ½ teaspoon hot pepper sauce. Bring to boiling; reduce heat. Cover and simmer about 2 hours or till beans are tender, stirring occasionally. (Add additional water during cooking, if necessary.)

Discard bay leaves. Remove pork hocks. When pork hocks are cool enough to handle, remove meat from the bones. Cut meat into bite-size pieces. Discard bones. Return meat to bean mixture; add sausage.

Simmer beans and meat, uncovered, about 15 minutes or till a thick gravy forms. (Add water, if necessary, so beans are saucy but not soupy.) Serve over rice. If desired, pass bottled hot pepper sauce. Makes 5 servings.

In the early days, creole cooks served red beans and rice on Monday, washday, because it was convenient to put the beans on to simmer and then forget about them until the end of the busy day.

BOURBON-AND-MUSTARD-GLAZED PORK CHOPS

2 tablespoons Dijon-style mustard or *brown mustard*
2 tablespoons bourbon or *frozen orange juice concentrate*
2 tablespoons molasses
1 tablespoon brown sugar
1 tablespoon cooking oil
1 tablespoon soy sauce
¼ teaspoon pepper
4 pork loin chops, cut 1¼ inches thick

FOR GLAZE, IN A SMALL MIXING BOWL STIR together mustard, bourbon or orange juice concentrate, molasses, brown sugar, cooking oil, soy sauce, and pepper. Set aside.

—■—

In a covered grill arrange *medium* coals around a drip pan (see tip, page 28). Test for *medium-slow* heat above the pan. Place chops on rack over pan but not over coals. Lower hood. Grill for 40 to 45 minutes or till no pink remains, turning once. Brush chops with glaze often during the last 10 minutes of cooking. Brush again with glaze before serving. Serves 4.

BROILING DIRECTIONS: Prepare Bourbon-and-Mustard-Glazed Pork Chops, *except* place chops on the unheated rack of a broiler pan. Broil 3 inches from the heat for 12 minutes. Turn and broil for 12 to 14 minutes more or till no pink remains. Brush chops with glaze often during last 10 minutes of broiling. Brush again with glaze before serving.

Bourbon, an American creation, first was made in 1789 in what is now Bourbon County, Kentucky. Bourbon adds a mellow flavor to sauces, soups, and meat dishes.

HERBED GARLIC CHOPS

2 tablespoons all-purpose flour
1 tablespoon snipped fresh basil or *1 teaspoon dried basil, crushed*
1 tablespoon snipped fresh oregano or *1 teaspoon dried oregano, crushed*
4 pork loin chops, cut ¾ inch thick (about 1½ pounds)
2 cloves garlic, minced
1 tablespoon cooking oil, margarine, or *butter*

IN A SHALLOW DISH COMBINE FLOUR, BASIL, oregano, ¼ teaspoon *salt*, and ¼ teaspoon *pepper*. Coat pork chops on both sides with flour mixture. Set aside.

—■—

In a large skillet cook garlic in hot oil for 30 seconds. Add chops and cook, uncovered, over medium heat for 5 minutes. Turn chops and cook, uncovered, for 5 to 7 minutes more or till no pink remains. Makes 4 servings.

When there's little time to cook, you still can have hearty country flavor. These pork chops are ready in 15 to 20 minutes.

Vegetable Salad with Parmesan Dressing

Bourbon-and-Mustard-Glazed Pork Chops

PORK CROWN ROAST

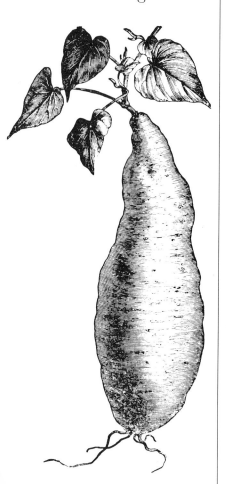

Searching for an impressive dish to serve for a dinner party or a holiday meal? Here's your answer. Pork Crown Roast looks spectacular, yet is simply slabs of ribs tied in a ring.

4 pounds pork loin back ribs (16 to 20 ribs)
1 clove garlic, halved
6 cups whole wheat bread cubes (8 slices)
2 medium sweet potatoes, peeled and coarsely shredded (2 cups)
½ cup chopped onion
½ cup chopped celery
3 tablespoons margarine or butter
¼ teaspoon salt
¼ teaspoon ground cinnamon
¼ teaspoon pepper
⅛ teaspoon ground ginger
2 cups chopped apple (about 2 medium)
½ cup chopped walnuts
⅓ to ⅔ cup apple cider or apple juice
¼ cup light corn syrup (optional)

TO FORM THE CROWN ROAST, TIE THE 2 OR 3 slabs of ribs securely together with string, bone side out, forming a circle and leaving a center 5 inches in diameter. Invert crown and place in a shallow roasting pan. Rub inside of the crown with the cut side of garlic. Insert a meat thermometer into meaty portion, making sure it doesn't touch any bone.

—■—

For stuffing, place bread cubes in a shallow roasting pan. Bake in a 350° oven about 10 minutes or till dry, stirring once. (You should have about 4 cups dried cubes.) In a large saucepan cook shredded sweet potato, onion, and celery in margarine or butter till tender. Stir in salt, cinnamon, pepper, and ginger.

—■—

In a large bowl combine bread cubes, apples, and walnuts. Add sweet potato mixture. Drizzle with enough apple cider or apple juice to moisten, tossing lightly.

—■—

Loosely spoon stuffing into the center of the pork crown. Cover stuffing with foil. (Transfer any remaining stuffing to a casserole. Cover and chill.)

—■—

Roast pork crown in a 450° oven for 20 minutes. Reduce oven temperature to 350°. If desired, brush pork with corn syrup. Roast for 1 to 1¼ hours more or till the thermometer registers 160°. During the final phase of roasting meat, bake the stuffing in the casserole, covered, for 30 to 35 minutes or till heated through.

—■—

Transfer roast to a serving platter. Remove strings. To carve, use a fork to steady the crown roast and cut between the ribs. Serve stuffing with the pork. Makes 6 to 8 servings.

PORK MEDAILLONS WITH BRANDY – CREAM SAUCE

1   2- to 2½-pound boneless pork loin roast
     Pepper
⅓   cup chicken broth
1   tablespoon chopped shallot or green onion
¼   cup whipping cream
¼   cup brandy or cognac
½   cup unsalted butter, cut into small pieces and softened
1   tablespoon lemon juice
¼   teaspoon salt
⅛   teaspoon white pepper

RUB PORK ROAST WITH PEPPER. PLACE MEAT ON A rack in a shallow roasting pan. Insert a meat thermometer into the thickest portion of the meat. Roast in a 325° oven for 1 to 1¼ hours or till the meat thermometer registers 160°.

For sauce, in a medium saucepan combine chicken broth and shallot or green onion. Bring to boiling; reduce heat. Cover and simmer for 2 minutes. Stir in whipping cream and brandy or cognac. Simmer, uncovered, over medium heat about 10 minutes or till sauce is reduced to ⅓ cup. Remove from heat. Strain sauce; return sauce to pan.

Add butter to sauce, one piece at a time, stirring constantly with a wire whisk. Stir in lemon juice, salt, and white pepper.

To serve, slice meat across the grain into 18 slices. Place 3 slices on each plate, spooning sauce atop meat. Makes 6 servings.

For a country harvest dinner, serve these tender, juicy pork roast slices with rice pilaf and steamed squash.

PORK LOIN WITH
SAUSAGE STUFFING

1 cup chopped onion
¼ pound bulk Italian sausage
½ cup snipped parsley
⅓ cup soft bread crumbs
¼ cup raisins
1½ teaspoons snipped fresh thyme,
    or ½ teaspoon dried thyme, crushed
¼ teaspoon pepper
1 to 2 tablespoons water
1 2½- to 3-pound boneless pork top loin roast
¼ cup apricot preserves

FOR STUFFING, IN A MEDIUM SKILLET COOK ONION and sausage till sausage is brown and onion is tender. Drain well. Add parsley, bread crumbs, raisins, thyme, and pepper. Drizzle with enough water to moisten, tossing lightly. Set stuffing aside.

———■———

Trim fat from meat. Cut a pocket lengthwise through the thickest portion of the meat, cutting to within ½ inch of the other side. Fill the pocket with the sausage stuffing.

———■———

Place meat on a rack in a shallow roasting pan. Insert a meat thermometer into the thickest portion of the meat. Roast in a 325° oven for 1 to 1¼ hours or till the meat thermometer registers 160°.

———■———

Meanwhile, in a small saucepan cook and stir apricot preserves till melted. About 15 minutes before meat is done, brush it with melted preserves. Cover and let stand for 15 minutes before carving. Makes 8 to 10 servings.

BIEROCKS

1   16-ounce package hot roll mix
1   pound ground beef
1   cup finely chopped onion
3   cups shredded cabbage
¼   cup water
¼   teaspoon salt
¼   to ½ teaspoon pepper
    Milk

PREPARE HOT ROLL MIX ACCORDING TO PACKAGE directions for the basic recipe through the kneading step. Cover dough and let rest.

Meanwhile, for filling, in a large skillet cook ground beef and chopped onion till meat is brown and onion is tender. Drain off fat. Stir in shredded cabbage and water. Cook about 5 minutes or till cabbage is tender. Drain. Stir in salt and pepper.

Divide dough into 6 portions. Roll each portion into a 7x5-inch rectangle.

Spoon *one-sixth* of the filling *lengthwise* down the center of a dough rectangle. Bring long edges of the dough together over the filling and pinch edges to seal. Pinch the ends of the dough to seal. Repeat with remaining filling and dough rectangles.

Place pastry bundles, seam side down, on a greased baking sheet. Let stand in a warm place for 20 minutes. Brush with milk.

Bake in a 350° oven for 25 to 30 minutes or till golden brown. Let stand for 5 to 10 minutes before serving. Makes 6 servings.

CHEESY BIEROCKS: Prepare Bierocks, *except* stir 1 cup shredded *cheddar or American cheese* into flour and yeast mixture of the hot roll mix. Add ½ teaspoon *caraway seed* to filling with salt and pepper. Sprinkle 2 tablespoons shredded *cheddar or American cheese* lengthwise down center of *each* dough rectangle before topping with filling. Fold dough over filling, seal, and bake as directed.

Across the plains of Nebraska and Kansas, bierocks (also called runzas) are popular sandwiches. The German-Russian immigrants who settled in the Midwest are credited with the idea for these log-shaped pastry bundles filled with seasoned ground beef and cabbage.

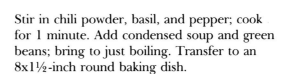

1   cup all-purpose flour
1   teaspoon baking powder
⅛   teaspoon salt
¼   cup shredded American cheese (1 ounce)
2   tablespoons shortening
⅓   cup milk
1   pound ground beef
1   cup chopped onion
¾   cup chopped celery
⅓   cup chopped green pepper
1   clove garlic, minced
1   tablespoon chili powder
1   tablespoon snipped fresh basil or 1 teaspoon dried basil, crushed
⅛   teaspoon pepper
1   10¾-ounce can condensed tomato soup
1   cup loose-pack frozen cut green beans
1   egg yolk
2   tablespoons milk

This hearty one-dish meal is a close culinary cousin to traditional hamburger pie, which is topped with mashed potatoes instead of a flaky lattice crust.

FOR CHEESE CRUST, IN A MIXING BOWL STIR together flour, baking powder, and salt. Cut in cheese and shortening. Add the ⅓ cup milk; mix well. Form dough into a ball.

■

On a lightly floured surface, roll dough into a 9-inch square about ¼ inch thick. Using a fluted pastry wheel or knife, cut crust into eighteen ½-inch-wide strips.

■

In a large skillet cook ground beef, onion, celery, green pepper, and garlic till beef is brown and vegetables are tender. Drain well.

■

Stir in chili powder, basil, and pepper; cook for 1 minute. Add condensed soup and green beans; bring to just boiling. Transfer to an 8x1½-inch round baking dish.

■

Weave crust strips atop ground beef mixture, forming a lattice crust. Trim strips at the edge of the dish and press strips down slightly. In a small bowl stir together egg yolk and the 2 tablespoons milk; brush over lattice crust.

■

Bake pie, uncovered, in a 425° oven about 15 minutes or till golden. Makes 4 servings.

SPINACH-AND-RICOTTA-STUFFED MEATLOAF

> 1 beaten egg
> ¾ cup soft bread crumbs (1 slice)
> 1 8-ounce can tomato sauce
> ¼ cup finely chopped onion
> ¼ cup finely chopped green or red sweet pepper
> ½ teaspoon garlic salt
> ¼ teaspoon pepper
> 1½ pounds ground beef
> 1 beaten egg
> 1 10-ounce package frozen chopped spinach, thawed and well drained
> 1 cup ricotta cheese
> ¼ cup grated Parmesan cheese
> 1½ teaspoons snipped fresh basil or marjoram or ½ teaspoon dried basil
>   or marjoram, crushed
> Chunky Tomato Sauce

IN A MIXING BOWL COMBINE A BEATEN EGG, THE bread crumbs, ¼ *cup* of the tomato sauce, the onion, green or red sweet pepper, garlic salt, and pepper. (Reserve remaining tomato sauce for Chunky Tomato Sauce.) Add ground beef and mix well. Set aside.

———■———

In another bowl stir together a beaten egg, spinach, ricotta cheese, Parmesan cheese, and basil or marjoram. Pat *one-third* of the meat mixture onto the bottom of a 9x5x3-inch loaf pan. Spread *half* of the spinach mixture over the meat layer. Repeat layers once. Top with a final layer of the meat mixture.

———■———

Bake in a 350° oven about 1¼ hours or till no pink remains and juices run clear. Let stand for 5 minutes. Cut into 6 slices. Serve with Chunky Tomato Sauce. Makes 6 servings.

CHUNKY TOMATO SAUCE: In a small saucepan combine the reserved tomato sauce; one 7½-ounce can *undrained tomatoes*, cut up; ⅓ cup chopped *onion*; ⅓ cup chopped *green or red sweet pepper*; ⅓ cup shredded *carrot*; 1 teaspoon *sugar*; 1½ teaspoons snipped fresh *basil or marjoram or* ½ teaspoon dried *basil or marjoram*, crushed; 1 clove *garlic*, minced; and ⅛ teaspoon ground *pepper*. Bring to boiling; reduce heat. Cover and simmer about 10 minutes or till onion and sweet pepper are tender.

RIB EYE ROAST WITH
HERB AND MUSHROOM SAUCE

1 4- to 4½-pound beef rib eye roast
1 teaspoon lemon-pepper seasoning
Herb and Mushroom Sauce

MOISTEN ROAST WITH WATER; RUB WITH LEMON-pepper seasoning. Place roast, fat side up, on a rack in a shallow roasting pan. Insert a meat thermometer into the thickest portion of the meat. Roast in a 350° oven for 1¼ to 1¾ hours for rare (140°), 1¼ to 2 hours for medium (160°), or 1½ to 2 hours for well-done (170°).

———■———

Transfer roast to a warm serving platter. Let stand, covered with foil, for 15 minutes before carving. Serve with Herb and Mushroom Sauce. Makes 12 to 14 servings.

HERB AND MUSHROOM SAUCE: In a medium saucepan melt 2 tablespoons *margarine or butter.* Add 1 cup sliced fresh *mushrooms;* ¼ cup finely chopped *onion;* 2 cloves *garlic,* minced; and 1 tablespoon snipped fresh *thyme or* ¼ teaspoon dried *thyme,* crushed. Cook for 4 to 5 minutes or till onion is tender, stirring frequently. Stir in 2 tablespoons *all-purpose flour.* Add 1 cup *half-and-half or light cream* and 1 teaspoon *instant beef bouillon granules* all at once. Cook and stir over medium heat till thickened and bubbly. Add 2 tablespoons snipped *parsley* and, if desired, 1 tablespoon *brandy.* Cook and stir 1 minute more. Makes 1⅓ cups.

MARINATED POT ROAST
WITH VEGETABLES

Originally, a Dutch oven was a three-legged iron stewpot that was placed over fireplace coals. Once the food was added to the pot, coals were heaped on the flanged lid to produce heat all around the food. The oven was just large enough to hold one shallow pan.

1 2½- to 3-pound boneless beef chuck pot roast
1 teaspoon finely shredded orange peel
1 cup orange juice
2 tablespoons olive oil or cooking oil
1 tablespoon snipped fresh basil or 1 teaspoon dried basil, crushed
¼ teaspoon pepper
2 tablespoons olive oil or cooking oil
1 cup water
1 tablespoon instant beef bouillon granules
1 clove garlic, minced
1 cup fresh pearl onions or frozen small whole onions
1 pound whole tiny new potatoes, quartered
1 10-ounce package frozen tiny whole carrots
1 9-ounce package frozen Italian-style green beans or cut green beans
2 tablespoons cornstarch
2 tablespoons cold water

TRIM FAT FROM ROAST. PLACE ROAST IN A PLASTIC bag set in a bowl or shallow dish. For marinade, combine orange peel, orange juice, 2 tablespoons oil, basil, and pepper. Pour marinade over roast and close bag. Marinate in the refrigerator for 4 to 24 hours, turning the bag occasionally to distribute marinade.

Remove roast from plastic bag, reserving marinade. Pat roast dry with paper towels. In a 4½- or 5-quart Dutch oven heat 2 tablespoons oil. Carefully add roast to hot oil. Brown roast on both sides. Drain off fat.

Add reserved marinade, the 1 cup water, bouillon granules, and garlic to the roast. Cook, covered, in a 325° oven for 1 hour.

Peel fresh pearl onions. Add pearl onions or small whole onions and potatoes to roast. Cook, covered, for 30 minutes. Add carrots and green beans; spoon juices over vegetables. Cook, covered, about 30 minutes more or till roast and vegetables are tender. Transfer roast and vegetables to a warm platter, reserving pan juices. Cover roast and vegetables with foil to keep warm.

For gravy, strain pan juices through a sieve into a large measuring cup. Using a metal spoon, skim off fat. If necessary, add enough water to pan juices to equal 2 cups. Return juices to the Dutch oven.

In a small bowl stir together cornstarch and the 2 tablespoons water; stir into the pan juices. Cook and stir till thickened and bubbly. Cook and stir 2 minutes more. Serve gravy with roast and vegetables. Makes 8 servings.

MAPLE-GLAZED POT ROAST

1 2½- to 3-pound beef chuck pot roast or boneless beef round
    rump roast
1 tablespoon cooking oil
½ cup maple syrup or maple-flavored syrup
1 teaspoon finely shredded orange peel
½ cup orange juice
2 tablespoons white wine vinegar
1 tablespoon Worcestershire sauce
½ teaspoon salt
¼ teaspoon pepper
1 bay leaf
5 medium carrots and/or parsnips, cut into 3-inch pieces
2 small onions, cut into wedges
2 stalks celery, bias-sliced into 2-inch pieces
1 medium acorn squash
¼ cup water
2 tablespoons cornstarch

TRIM FAT FROM ROAST. IN A DUTCH OVEN BROWN roast on all sides in hot oil; drain fat. Combine maple syrup or maple-flavored syrup, orange peel, orange juice, white wine vinegar, Worcestershire sauce, salt, pepper, and bay leaf. Pour over roast. Bring to boiling; reduce heat. Cover and simmer over low heat for 1¼ hours.

———■———

Add carrots and/or parsnips, onions, and celery to meat. Cover and simmer for 15 minutes. Meanwhile, rinse squash. Halve and stem squash; cut horizontally into ¾-inch-thick slices. Add squash slices to meat. Cover and simmer for 10 to 15 minutes more or till meat and vegetables are tender. Transfer meat and vegetables to a warm platter, discarding bay leaf and reserving pan juices. Cover roast and vegetables with foil to keep warm.

———■———

For gravy, measure 1¾ cups reserved pan juices, and return them to the pan. In a small bowl combine water and cornstarch; stir into juices in pan. Cook and stir till thickened and bubbly. Cook and stir for 2 minutes more. Serve gravy with roast and vegetables. Makes 8 servings.

A maple–orange glaze adds a sheen to this beef roast and flavor to these vegetables.

DEVILED SWISS STEAK

Pour the rich mushroom sauce over piles of mashed potatoes—the perfect side dish for this hearty steak.

1 pound boneless beef round steak, cut ¾ inch thick
2 tablespoons all-purpose flour
1 tablespoon dry mustard
¼ teaspoon salt
¼ teaspoon pepper
1 tablespoon cooking oil
1 cup water
1 tablespoon Worcestershire sauce
1 teaspoon instant beef bouillon granules
1 large onion, sliced and separated into rings
2 4-ounce cans whole mushrooms, drained

CUT MEAT INTO 4 SERVING-SIZE PIECES. TRIM FAT. In a shallow dish or on a sheet of waxed paper combine flour, dry mustard, salt, and pepper. Coat the meat pieces on both sides with the flour mixture.

———■———

In a large skillet brown meat pieces on both sides in hot oil. Drain off fat.

———■———

Combine water, Worcestershire sauce, and bouillon granules; pour over meat. Place onion slices and mushrooms atop meat pieces. Bring to boiling; reduce heat. Cover and simmer over low heat about 1¼ hours or till the meat is tender.

———■———

Transfer meat pieces, onion, and mushrooms to a warm serving platter. Skim fat from sauce in the pan. Spoon some of the sauce over the meat. Serve remaining sauce with the meat. Makes 4 servings.

CHICKEN-FRIED
STEAK WITH GRAVY

    1   pound beef top round steak, cut ½ inch thick
    ¾   cup fine dry bread crumbs
    1½   teaspoons snipped fresh basil or oregano
             or ½ teaspoon dried basil or oregano, crushed
    ½   teaspoon salt
    ¼   teaspoon pepper
    1   beaten egg
    1   tablespoon milk
    2   tablespoons cooking oil
    1   small onion, sliced and separated into rings
    2   tablespoons all-purpose flour
    1⅓   cups milk
         Salt
         Pepper

CUT STEAK INTO 4 SERVING-SIZE PIECES. TRIM FAT. Place meat pieces between 2 pieces of plastic wrap. Pound meat with a meat mallet to ¼-inch thickness.

———■———

In a shallow dish or on a piece of waxed paper combine bread crumbs, basil or oregano, the ½ teaspoon salt, and the ¼ teaspoon pepper. In another shallow dish stir together egg and the 1 tablespoon milk. Dip meat pieces in egg mixture, then coat with bread crumb mixture.

———■———

In a 12-inch skillet brown meat pieces in hot oil over medium heat about 3 minutes on each side. Reduce heat to low. Cover and cook for 45 to 60 minutes more or till tender. Transfer meat pieces to a platter; cover to keep warm.

———■———

For gravy, cook onion in pan drippings till tender but not brown. (Add more oil, if necessary.) Stir in flour. Add the 1⅓ cups milk all at once. Cook and stir till thickened and bubbly. Cook and stir for 1 minute more. Season to taste with salt and pepper. Serve gravy with meat. Makes 4 servings.

Many small-town cafes feature crisp, chicken-fried steak, mashed potatoes, and gravy as their blue-plate specials. In the South and Southwest, the steak usually is coated with flour and fried. In the Midwest, the steak often is coated with crumbs, browned in oil, then covered and cooked, as in this recipe.

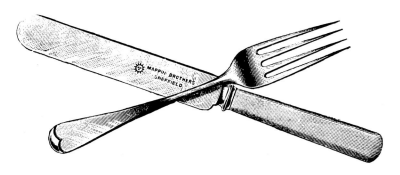

BEEF TENDERLOIN
WITH PEPPERCORNS

2 teaspoons cracked whole black peppercorns
2 beef tenderloin steaks, cut 1 inch thick
    (about 10 ounces total)
2 tablespoons margarine or butter
2 teaspoons margarine or butter
1 teaspoon all-purpose flour
    Dash salt
    Dash ground pepper
⅓ cup half-and-half, light cream, or milk
1 tablespoon horseradish mustard
    Whole pink peppercorns (optional)
    Fresh thyme (optional)

SPRINKLE CRACKED BLACK PEPPER OVER BOTH sides of steaks, pressing pepper into steaks.

———■———

In a heavy 8-inch skillet melt the 2 tablespoons margarine or butter. Add steaks to skillet and cook, uncovered, over medium-high heat for 4 minutes. (If steaks brown too quickly, reduce heat to medium.) Turn steaks over. Cook 3 to 4 minutes more for medium-rare to medium doneness. Transfer steaks to two dinner plates. Cover to keep warm.

———■———

Meanwhile, for sauce, in a small saucepan melt the 2 teaspoons margarine or butter. Stir in flour, salt, and the dash of ground pepper. Add cream or milk all at once. Cook and stir over medium heat till thickened and bubbly. Cook and stir for 1 minute more. Stir in horseradish mustard. Remove from the heat.

———■———

To serve, pour the sauce around the steaks. If desired, drizzle steaks with a little sauce and garnish with pink peppercorns and fresh thyme. Makes 2 servings.

This tenderloin steak, topped with a horseradish cream sauce, is the epitome of great country dining.

SHORT RIBS WITH SWEET-AND-SPICY MOLASSES SAUCE

3 to 4 pounds beef short ribs, cut into serving-size pieces
1 large onion, sliced and separated into rings
    Celery leaves
⅓ cup honey
¼ cup red wine vinegar
2 tablespoons molasses
1 tablespoon snipped fresh thyme or 1 teaspoon dried thyme, crushed
½ teaspoon bottled hot pepper sauce

TRIM FAT FROM RIBS. PLACE RIBS IN A 4-QUART Dutch oven. Add onion, celery leaves, 4 cups *water*, 1 teaspoon *salt*, and ¼ teaspoon *pepper*. Bring to boiling; reduce heat. Cover and simmer about 1½ hours or till tender.

——■——

Remove ribs from the Dutch oven. Skim fat from cooking liquid. Strain and reserve ½ *cup* of the cooking liquid.

——■——

For sauce, in a small mixing bowl combine reserved ½ cup cooking liquid, honey, vinegar, molasses, thyme, and hot pepper sauce.

——■——

In a covered grill arrange *medium-slow* coals around a drip pan (see tip, below). Test for *slow* heat above the drip pan.

——■——

Place cooked ribs on the grill rack over the drip pan but not over the coals. Brush with sauce. Lower the grill hood. Grill 20 to 25 minutes or till heated through, turning and brushing occasionally with sauce. Heat any remaining sauce and pass with ribs. Serves 4.

BROILING DIRECTIONS: Prepare Short Ribs with Sweet-and-Spicy Molasses Sauce, *except* after simmering short ribs, place ribs on the unheated rack of a broiler pan. Brush with sauce. Broil 4 to 5 inches from the heat for 10 to 15 minutes or till heated through, turning often and brushing with sauce. Heat any remaining sauce and serve with ribs.

JUDGING COAL TEMPERATURE

WHEN GRILLING, DETERMINE THE TEMPERATURE of the coals by holding your hand, palm side down, above the coals or the drip pan at the height the food will be cooked. Count the seconds "one thousand one, one thousand two." If you need to remove your hand after two seconds, the coals are *hot;* after three seconds, they are *medium-hot;* after four seconds they're *medium;* after five seconds, they're *medium-slow;* and after six seconds, they're *slow.*

——■——

For indirect cooking, *hot* coals will provide *medium-hot* heat over the drip pan. *Medium-hot* coals will provide *medium* heat, *medium* coals provide *medium-slow* heat, and so on.

MUSTARD-GLAZED NEW ENGLAND BOILED DINNER

2 bay leaves
2 tablespoons snipped fresh thyme
    or 2 teaspoons dried thyme, crushed
1 teaspoon whole cloves
½ teaspoon whole black peppercorns
1 3- to 3½-pound corned beef brisket
8 cups water
3 small onions, halved
4 medium carrots or parsnips, quartered crosswise
3 small potatoes (about 12 ounces)
3 stalks celery, quartered crosswise
½ of a small head cabbage, cut into 6 wedges
    Mustard Glaze

FOR THE SPICE BAG*, CUT A DOUBLE THICKNESS of 100 percent cotton cheesecloth into a 6- or 8-inch square. Place bay leaves, thyme, cloves, and peppercorns in the center of the cheesecloth. Bring up the corners of the cheesecloth and tie them with a clean string.

■

Place corned beef in a 4- to 6-quart Dutch oven. Add spice bag and the water to corned beef. Bring to boiling; reduce heat. Cover and simmer for 2½ hours.

■

Add onions, carrots or parsnips, potatoes, and celery to corned beef. Return to boiling. Cover and simmer for 10 minutes. Add cabbage wedges; simmer, covered, about 10 minutes more or till meat and vegetables are tender.

■

Meanwhile, prepare Mustard Glaze. Drain meat and vegetables; discard the spice bag. Arrange meat and all vegetables on a serving platter. Spoon Mustard Glaze over meat and vegetables. Slice the corned beef across the grain. Makes 6 to 8 servings.

■

*NOTE: If a spice packet is provided with the corned beef, use it instead of the bay leaves, thyme, cloves, and peppercorns.

> MUSTARD GLAZE: In a medium saucepan combine ⅔ cup packed *brown sugar*, ½ cup *vinegar*, ½ cup *prepared mustard*, and ½ teaspoon *garlic powder*. Bring to boiling, stirring till sugar dissolves. Cook, uncovered, for 5 minutes. If necessary, beat smooth with whisk or rotary beater. Makes about 1 cup.

Early American settlers tossed whatever meat and vegetables they had into an iron pot and cooked it over the fire for hours. Today's New England boiled dinner is similar to that meal, except that it usually is made with a corned beef brisket.

LAMB CHOPS WITH
BLUE CHEESE SAUCE

Country families often dress up plain meats with an interesting sauce, such as this blue cheese sauce. The sauce is equally good over broiled pork chops or roast beef.

8 lamb rib chops, cut ¾ to 1 inch thick
  (1¼ to 1½ pounds total)
1 tablespoon cooking oil
1 clove garlic, minced
1 tablespoon margarine or butter
1 teaspoon all-purpose flour
½ cup milk
¼ cup crumbled blue cheese (1 ounce)
1 tablespoon snipped parsley
1 small tomato, peeled, seeded, and chopped

TRIM FAT FROM LAMB CHOPS. IN A LARGE SKILLET cook chops in hot oil over medium heat for 4 minutes. Turn chops and cook for 3 to 5 minutes more for medium doneness. Transfer lamb chops to a warm serving platter. Cover to keep warm.

Meanwhile, in a small saucepan cook garlic in margarine or butter for 1 minute. Stir in flour. Add milk all at once. Cook and stir till thickened and bubbly. Cook and stir for 1 minute more. Add blue cheese; stir till cheese almost melts. Stir in parsley. Spoon sauce over lamb chops and sprinkle with chopped tomato. Makes 4 servings.

ORANGE-GLAZED LAMB CHOPS

1 tablespoon brown sugar
1 teaspoon cornstarch
½ teaspoon finely shredded orange peel
½ teaspoon grated gingerroot
  Dash ground red pepper
½ cup orange juice
1 tablespoon soy sauce
6 lamb loin chops, cut 1 inch thick (about 1¾ pounds total)
1 tablespoon snipped parsley
1 tablespoon finely chopped walnuts or pecans

FOR GLAZE, IN A SMALL SAUCEPAN COMBINE BROWN sugar, cornstarch, orange peel, gingerroot, and red pepper. Stir in orange juice and soy sauce. Cook and stir till thickened and bubbly. Cook and stir for 2 minutes more. Remove glaze from the heat.

———■———

Trim fat from lamb chops. Place chops on the unheated rack of a broiler pan. Broil 3 inches from the heat for 6 minutes. Turn and broil 5 to 6 minutes more for medium. Brush chops with orange glaze often during broiling.

———■———

To serve, sprinkle chops with parsley and nuts. Reheat remaining glaze and serve with chops. Makes 3 servings.

GRILLING DIRECTIONS: Prepare Orange-Glazed Lamb Chops, *except* place chops on an uncovered grill directly over *medium* coals (see tip, page 28). Grill for 8 minutes. Turn and grill for 6 to 8 minutes more for medium doneness. Brush chops with orange glaze often during grilling. Serve as directed.

ROSEMARY LAMB KABOBS

¾ cup white grape juice
2 tablespoons olive oil or cooking oil
2 tablespoons lime juice
1½ teaspoons snipped fresh rosemary or ½ teaspoon dried rosemary, crushed
2 cloves garlic, minced
⅛ teaspoon ground cinnamon
1 pound boneless lamb round steak or sirloin steak, cut into 1-inch cubes
2 cups baby carrots (about ½ pound)
2 medium zucchini or yellow summer squash, sliced ½ to ¾ inch thick
1 large green or red sweet pepper, cut into 1-inch pieces
Fresh rosemary (optional)

FOR MARINADE, IN A SCREW-TOP JAR COMBINE grape juice, oil, lime juice, rosemary, garlic, and cinnamon. Cover and shake well. Place lamb cubes in a plastic bag set in a shallow dish. Pour marinade over lamb; close bag. Marinate in the refrigerator for 4 hours, turning once to distribute marinade. Drain lamb cubes, reserving marinade.

—■—

Trim carrots, leaving ½ to 1 inch of stem, if desired. Scrub but *do not peel.* Cook carrots in a small amount of boiling water for 3 minutes. Add zucchini or summer squash and cook for 1 to 2 minutes more or till vegetables are crisp-tender. Drain.

—■—

On eight 8-inch skewers, alternately thread lamb cubes, whole carrots, zucchini or summer squash, and green or red sweet pepper.

—■—

Place kabobs on an uncovered grill directly over *hot* coals (see tip, page 28). Grill for 8 to 12 minutes for medium doneness, brushing with reserved marinade and turning kabobs occasionally. If desired, garnish with sprigs of fresh rosemary. Makes 4 servings.

GARLIC-MARINATED GRILLED LAMB

This full-flavored, grilled lamb is ideal for a large outdoor party. When planning the party, order the leg of lamb several days ahead because some supermarkets and meat markets do not regularly carry it. Also, ask the butcher to bone and butterfly the leg of lamb.

1 5- to 7-pound leg of lamb,
  boned and butterflied
3 cups dry red wine
½ cup chopped onion
⅓ cup olive oil
⅓ cup soy sauce
1 tablespoon lemon juice
3 cloves garlic, minced
1 teaspoon snipped fresh thyme or ¼ teaspoon dried thyme, crushed
  Horseradish-Mustard Sauce

REMOVE FELL (PAPER-THIN, REDDISH PINK LAYER) from the outer surface of the leg of lamb. Trim fat from lamb.

■

For marinade, in a large shallow dish combine wine, onion, olive oil, soy sauce, lemon juice, garlic, and thyme. Add lamb; cover. Marinate in the refrigerator for 8 to 24 hours, turning twice to distribute marinade. Drain lamb. Discard marinade.

■

To keep the lamb flat during cooking, insert two 18-inch metal skewers through meat at right angles, making a cross. (*Or*, place the lamb in a wire grill basket.)

■

In a covered grill arrange *medium* coals around a drip pan (see tip, page 28). Test for *medium-slow* heat over the drip pan. Place lamb on the grill rack over the drip pan but not over the coals. Lower the grill hood. Grill about 1¼ hours for medium doneness. Remove skewers or remove lamb from the grill basket. Let stand for 15 minutes.

■

To serve, thinly slice lamb across the grain. Pass Horseradish-Mustard Sauce with lamb. Makes 12 to 16 servings.

HORSERADISH-MUSTARD SAUCE: In a small mixer bowl beat ½ cup *whipping cream* till soft peaks form. Fold in 1 tablespoon *horseradish mustard* and 1 tablespoon *snipped fresh chives.* Serve immediately. Makes about 1 cup.

LEG OF LAMB WITH PEPPERCORNS AND MUSTARD

1   4- to 6-pound leg of lamb, boned and butterflied
1   teaspoon cracked whole black peppercorns
1   teaspoon whole green peppercorns, crushed
1   teaspoon ground white pepper
1   cup dry red wine
¼   cup olive oil or cooking oil
1   tablespoon snipped fresh rosemary or ½ teaspoon dried rosemary, crushed
3   cloves garlic, minced
3   tablespoons Dijon-style mustard or horseradish mustard

REMOVE FELL (PAPER-THIN, PINKISH RED LAYER) from outer surface of lamb. Trim fat from lamb. With boned side up, pound lamb with a meat mallet to an even thickness. Place lamb in a plastic bag set in a deep bowl.

Combine the cracked black pepper, green peppercorns, and white pepper. Set aside.

For marinade, combine *half* of the pepper mixture, the wine, oil, rosemary, and garlic. Pour mixture over lamb. Seal bag. Marinate in the refrigerator for 6 to 24 hours, turning bag occasionally to distribute marinade.

Remove lamb from the bag, reserving marinade. Spread mustard over boned side of lamb. Pat remaining pepper mixture into the mustard on the lamb. Roll up lamb; tie securely. Place, seam side down, on a rack in a shallow roasting pan. Insert a meat thermometer into the thickest portion of the lamb.

Roast in a 325° oven for 1¾ to 2½ hours or till the meat thermometer registers 150°, basting occasionally with reserved marinade. Let stand 15 minutes before carving. Remove strings. Makes 12 to 16 servings.

STEAKS OR CHOPS WITH PEPPERCORNS AND MUSTARD: Prepare Leg of Lamb with Peppercorns and Mustard, *except* substitute 4 *beef rib eye steaks* or 8 *lamb loin chops*, cut 1 inch thick, for the leg of lamb. For pepper mixture and marinade, cut the amounts of the remaining ingredients in half. Marinate steaks or chops as directed.

Place steaks or chops on the unheated rack of a broiler pan. Broil 3 inches from the heat for 5 minutes. Turn and broil for 4 minutes more. Using *1 tablespoon* total, spread Dijon-style mustard or horseradish mustard on one side of steaks or chops. Pat the remaining pepper mixture into the mustard on the steaks or chops. Broil 1 minute more or till of desired doneness. Makes 4 servings.

SUNDAY DINNER

REMEMBER WHEN THE whole family gathered on Sunday

for a delicious dinner? It was always a very special, home-cooked

meal. Now you can invoke memories of those scrumptious

foods with these recipes. Whether you choose Glazed Ham

Balls, Banana Pudding, or one of the other favorites in this chapter,

you'll enjoy comfort food that conjures up warm thoughts of

home and family. ∎

MENU

Glazed Ham Balls ▪ *New Potatoes with Lemon–Basil Sauce*

Sesame Asparagus ▪ *Parsnip–Carrot Salad*

Cranberry–Orange Streusel Muffins ▪ *Banana Pudding*

GLAZED HAM BALLS

2 beaten eggs
¾ cup finely crushed graham crackers
½ cup chopped onion
¼ cup milk
⅛ teaspoon ground cloves
    Dash pepper
1 pound ground fully cooked ham
½ pound ground pork
¾ cup catsup
2 tablespoons brown sugar
2 tablespoons vinegar
2 tablespoons light corn syrup
½ teaspoon dry mustard

IN A LARGE MIXING BOWL COMBINE EGGS, crushed crackers, onion, milk, cloves, and pepper. Add ground ham and ground pork; mix well. Shape into 12 balls, using about ⅓ *cup* mixture for *each* ball. Place ham balls in a 12x7½x2-inch baking dish.*

———■———

Bake ham balls, uncovered, in a 350° oven for 30 minutes. Meanwhile, for glaze, in a small mixing bowl combine catsup, brown sugar,

vinegar, corn syrup, and dry mustard. Pour glaze over ham balls. Bake for 15 minutes more. Makes 6 servings.

———■———

*NOTE: To make ahead, at this point cover and chill uncooked ham balls for up to 12 hours. Prepare glaze; cover and chill for up to 12 hours. Uncover ham balls and bake as directed above.

Pictured on page 37.

PARSNIP–CARROT SALAD

 2 *cups shredded parsnips (about 2 parsnips)*
 1 *cup shredded carrots (about 2 carrots)*
 1 *cup sliced celery*
 ⅓ *cup raisins*
 ½ *cup mayonnaise or salad dressing*
 1 *teaspoon finely shredded orange peel*
 ¼ *cup chopped pecans*
 Milk (optional)

IN A LARGE MIXING BOWL COMBINE PARSNIPS, carrots, celery, and raisins.

———■———

In a small bowl stir together mayonnaise or salad dressing and orange peel. Gently stir mayonnaise mixture into parsnip mixture. Cover and chill for 2 to 24 hours.

———■———

Pictured on page 37.

Spread pecans in a baking pan. Bake in a 350° oven for 5 to 10 minutes or till light brown, stirring once or twice. Cover; set aside.

———■———

To serve, stir a little milk into salad if mixture is too thick. Sprinkle with pecans. Serves 6.

TIMETABLE

1 DAY AHEAD:
- Prepare Cranberry-Orange Streusel Muffins (see recipe, page 42). Cool; wrap in foil and store in a cool place.
- Prepare Parsnip-Carrot Salad (see recipe, above), *except* do not sprinkle with pecans. Cover and chill.
- Prepare Glazed Ham Balls (see recipe, opposite). Place in a baking dish. Cover and chill.
- Prepare glaze for ham balls. Cover and chill.

———■———

2 TO 4 HOURS AHEAD:
- Prepare Banana Pudding (see recipe, page 43); chill.

1 HOUR AHEAD:
- Place Glazed Ham Balls in the oven.

———■———

30 MINUTES AHEAD:
- Prepare New Potatoes with Lemon-Basil Sauce (see recipe, page 41).

———■———

15 MINUTES AHEAD:
- Prepare Sesame Asparagus (see recipe, page 40).
- Place foil-wrapped muffins in the oven and heat about 15 minutes.
- Sprinkle toasted pecans over salad.

SESAME ASPARAGUS

1¼ pounds fresh asparagus spears or *two 10-ounce packages
frozen asparagus spears*
3 tablespoons margarine or *butter*
1 tablespoon sesame seed
⅓ cup dry bread crumbs

SNAP OFF AND DISCARD WOODY BASES FROM fresh asparagus. If desired, scrape off scales.

■

In a medium saucepan cook fresh asparagus, covered, in a small amount of boiling water for 6 to 8 minutes or till crisp-tender. (*Or,* cook frozen asparagus according to package directions.) Drain. Arrange asparagus in a shallow serving dish. Cover to keep warm.

■

In the saucepan melt margarine or butter. Add sesame seed. Cook and stir about 30 seconds or till light brown. Stir in bread crumbs. Sprinkle bread crumb mixture over asparagus. Makes 6 servings.

Pictured on page 37.

NEW POTATOES WITH
LEMON–BASIL SAUCE

1 ½ *pounds tiny whole new potatoes*
¼ *cup margarine or butter*
2 *tablespoons snipped parsley*
2 *tablespoons lemon juice*
2 *teaspoons snipped fresh basil or ½ teaspoon dried basil, crushed*
¼ *teaspoon pepper*

SCRUB NEW POTATOES THOROUGHLY WITH A stiff brush. Cut potatoes in halves or quarters. In a large saucepan cook potatoes in a small amount of boiling lightly salted water for 15 to 20 minutes or till tender. Drain potatoes.

Meanwhile, for sauce, in a small saucepan melt margarine or butter. Stir in parsley, lemon juice, basil, and pepper.

Transfer new potatoes to a serving bowl. Pour lemon-basil sauce over potatoes; toss gently to coat potatoes with sauce. Makes 6 servings.

Pictured on page 37.

CRANBERRY–ORANGE
STREUSEL MUFFINS

1 ¾ cups all-purpose flour
⅓ cup sugar
1 ½ teaspoons baking powder
¼ teaspoon baking soda
¼ teaspoon salt
1 beaten egg
½ teaspoon finely shredded orange peel
¾ cup orange juice
¼ cup cooking oil
½ cup cranberries, coarsely chopped*
   Streusel Topping

GREASE TWELVE 2½-INCH MUFFIN CUPS OR LINE with paper bake cups; set aside.

In a medium mixing bowl stir together flour, sugar, baking powder, baking soda, and salt. Make a well in the center.

In another bowl stir together egg, orange peel, orange juice, and oil. Add egg mixture all at once to flour mixture. Stir *just till moistened* (batter should be lumpy). Gently fold cranberries into batter.

Spoon batter into the prepared muffin cups, filling each ⅔ full. Sprinkle about *2 teaspoons* of the Streusel Topping over batter in *each* muffin cup. Bake in a 400° oven about 20 minutes or till golden. Remove from muffin cups and cool slightly on a wire rack. Serve warm. Makes 12.

*NOTE: If desired, substitute frozen cranberries. Do not thaw before chopping.

STREUSEL TOPPING: In a small mixing bowl combine ¼ cup *sugar*, 1 tablespoon *all-purpose flour*, ½ teaspoon ground *cinnamon*, ¼ teaspoon ground *allspice*, and ¼ teaspoon *finely shredded orange peel.* Cut in 1 tablespoon *margarine or butter* till crumbly. Makes ½ cup.

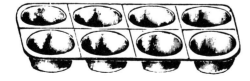

BANANA PUDDING

⅔ cup sugar
3 tablespoons cornstarch or ⅓ cup all-purpose flour
2¼ cups milk
3 egg yolks
1 tablespoon margarine or butter
1 teaspoon vanilla
3 egg whites
½ teaspoon vanilla
¼ teaspoon cream of tartar
⅓ cup sugar
4 cups vanilla wafers (about 50 wafers)
3 medium bananas, sliced (about 3 cups)

FOR PUDDING, IN A MEDIUM SAUCEPAN COMBINE the ⅔ cup sugar and the cornstarch or flour. Gradually stir in milk. Cook and stir over medium-high heat till mixture is thickened and bubbly. Reduce heat; cook and stir for 2 minutes more. Remove from the heat.

In a small mixing bowl beat egg yolks lightly with a fork. Gradually stir about *1 cup* of the hot pudding into egg yolks. Return all to the saucepan; cook till bubbly. Cook and stir for 2 minutes more. Remove pudding from the heat. Stir in margarine or butter and the 1 teaspoon vanilla.

For meringue, in a medium mixing bowl combine egg whites, the ½ teaspoon vanilla, and cream of tartar. Beat with an electric mixer on medium speed about 1 minute or till soft peaks form (tips curl). Gradually add the ⅓ cup sugar, about *1 tablespoon* at a time, beating on high speed about 4 minutes more or till mixture forms stiff, glossy peaks and sugar dissolves.

Cover the bottom of an 8x1½-inch round baking dish with *one-third* (about 16) of the vanilla wafers. Top with *half* of the banana slices and *half* of the pudding. Repeat vanilla wafer, sliced banana, and pudding layers. Stand remaining vanilla wafers on ends around the edge of the baking dish.

Immediately spread meringue over *hot* pudding, carefully sealing to edge of dish to prevent shrinkage. Bake in a 350° oven for 15 minutes. Cool on a wire rack for 1 hour. Chill for 3 to 6 hours. Cover for longer storage. Makes 6 to 8 servings.

Pictured on page 37.

TEXAS
BARBECUE

IN TEXAS, WHERE everything is big, a pit barbecue

usually serves 20 people or more. These barbecues often feature

a beef brisket wrapped in moistened burlap, buried in a

pit with hickory and mesquite, and baked for hours.

We scaled down this Texas-style feast so you can get a feel for

the eat-till-you-drop barbecues that are a Texas tradition.

Roll up your sleeves and dig in!∎

MENU

Nectarine Sunrise ▪ *Texas-Style Beef Brisket* ▪ *Sweet Pepper Slaw*

Southwestern-Style Three-Bean Salad ▪ *Corn on the Cob with Pepper Butter*

Peach–Berry Pie

NECTARINE SUNRISE

2 cups coarsely chopped, pitted nectarines and/or *peeled peaches*
1 6-ounce can frozen orange juice concentrate
⅔ cup tequila
2½ cups ice cubes
½ cup grenadine syrup
Fresh mint sprigs (optional)

IN A BLENDER CONTAINER COMBINE CHOPPED nectarines or peaches, frozen orange juice concentrate, and tequila. Cover and blend till smooth. With blender running, add ice, a few cubes at a time, through the opening in lid. Blend till slushy and mixture measures 5 cups.

Place *1 tablespoon* of the grenadine syrup in *each* of 8 stemmed glasses. Add nectarine mixture. Use a straw to slightly stir the drink in a circular motion to get a swirled effect. If desired, top each with a mint sprig. Serve at once. Makes 8 (5-ounce) servings.

TEXAS-STYLE BEEF BRISKET

1 3- to 4-pound fresh beef brisket
½ cup dry red wine
2 tablespoons red wine vinegar or cider vinegar
2 tablespoons cooking oil
2 tablespoons Worcestershire sauce
2 cloves garlic, minced
1 teaspoon prepared mustard
¼ teaspoon ground coriander
⅛ teaspoon ground red pepper
4 to 6 cups mesquite wood chips
1 teaspoon seasoned salt
½ teaspoon paprika
    Chunky Red Sauce

TRIM FAT FROM BRISKET; PLACE IN A PLASTIC BAG in a shallow dish. For marinade, combine wine, vinegar, oil, Worcestershire sauce, garlic, mustard, coriander, red pepper, and 2 tablespoons *water*. Pour marinade over meat in bag. Close bag; marinate overnight in refrigerator; turn bag occasionally. Drain meat; reserve marinade. Mix salt, paprika, and ½ teaspoon *pepper*. Rub over meat.

———■———

At least 1 hour before grilling, soak wood chips in enough water to cover. Drain wood chips. In a covered grill arrange *medium-slow* coals around a drip pan. Test for *slow* heat above the pan (see tip, page 28). Pour 1 inch of water into the drip pan. Place brisket, fat side up, on the grill rack over the drip pan but not over the coals. Brush with some of the reserved marinade. Lower grill hood. Grill for 2 to 2½ hours or till tender, brushing with reserved marinade every 30 minutes.

———■———

Add more wood chips, coals (about 8 new coals at a time), and water every 30 minutes or as necessary.

———■———

To serve, slice brisket thinly across the grain. Serve with Chunky Red Sauce. Serves 8 to 10.

CHUNKY RED SAUCE: In a saucepan mix 1¼ cups chopped *tomatoes*, 1 cup *catsup*, ¾ cup chopped *green pepper*, ¼ cup *steak sauce or Worcestershire sauce*, 2 tablespoons *brown sugar*, 2 tablespoons chopped *onion*, ½ teaspoon *garlic powder*, ¼ teaspoon ground *nutmeg*, ¼ teaspoon ground *cloves*, ¼ teaspoon ground *cinnamon*, ⅛ teaspoon ground *ginger*, and ⅛ teaspoon *pepper*. Bring to boiling; reduce heat. Simmer, covered, for 5 minutes or till green pepper is crisp-tender. Makes 2½ cups.

Pictured on page 45.

S W E E T   P E P P E R   S L A W

3 *sweet peppers (red, yellow,* and/or *green), cut into julienne strips (about 3 cups)*
3 *cups shredded cabbage*
3 *medium carrots, cut into julienne strips (about 1½ cups)*
½ *cup chopped onion*
¼ *cup salad oil*
¼ *cup tarragon vinegar or vinegar*
1 *tablespoon Dijon-style mustard*
2 *teaspoons sugar*
½ *teaspoon celery seed*

IN A BOWL MIX SWEET PEPPERS, CABBAGE, carrots, and onion. For dressing, in a screw-top jar combine oil, vinegar, mustard, sugar, celery seed, ¼ teaspoon *salt,* and ¼ teaspoon *pepper.* Cover and shake well. Pour dressing over sweet pepper mixture; toss to coat. Cover; chill 3 to 24 hours. Serves 8.

Pictured on page 45.

T I M E T A B L E

1 DAY AHEAD:
■ Marinate Texas-Style Beef Brisket (see recipe, page 47). Prepare Chunky Red Sauce (see recipe, page 47); chill.
■ Prepare Sweet Pepper Slaw (see recipe, above); chill.
■ Prepare Southwestern-Style Three-Bean Salad (see recipe, opposite); chill.
■ Prepare desired butter for Corn on the Cob with Pepper Butter (see recipes, page 50); chill.

——■——

5 TO 6 HOURS AHEAD:
■ Prepare Peach-Berry Pie (see recipe, page 51).
■ Soak wood chips.

——■——

3 HOURS AHEAD:
■ Light charcoal grill.
■ Start grilling the brisket.

——■——

30 MINUTES AHEAD:
■ Start boiling water for corn; cook corn.
■ Bring red sauce to room temperature or heat, if desired.

——■——

15 MINUTES AHEAD:
■ Prepare Nectarine Sunrise (see recipe, page 46).

SOUTHWESTERN-STYLE
THREE-BEAN SALAD

 1 *15-ounce can garbanzo beans, rinsed and drained*
 1 *15-ounce can black beans, rinsed and drained*
 1 *8-ounce can red kidney beans, rinsed and drained*
 1 *cup thinly sliced celery*
 ¾ *cup chopped red onion*
 ⅓ *cup salad oil*
 ¼ *cup vinegar*
 1 *clove garlic, minced*
 2 *tablespoons snipped fresh cilantro*
 2 *tablespoons lime juice*
 1 *tablespoon sugar*
 1 *teaspoon chili powder*
 1 *teaspoon ground cumin*
 ¼ *teaspoon salt*

IN A LARGE MIXING BOWL STIR TOGETHER garbanzo beans, black beans, red kidney beans, sliced celery, and chopped onion.

For dressing, in a screw-top jar combine salad oil, vinegar, garlic, cilantro, lime juice, sugar, chili powder, cumin, and salt. Cover and shake well.

Pour dressing over bean mixture; toss to coat. Cover and chill for 3 to 24 hours, stirring occasionally. Serve with a slotted spoon. Makes 8 servings.

CORN ON THE COB
WITH PEPPER BUTTER

8 fresh ears of corn
Pepper Butter or Cilantro–Lime Butter

REMOVE THE HUSKS FROM CORN; SCRUB WITH A stiff brush to remove silks. Rinse. Cook, covered, in a small amount of lightly salted boiling water (*or*, cook, uncovered, in enough boiling water to cover) for 5 to 7 minutes or till tender. Serve with Pepper Butter or Cilantro-Lime Butter. Makes 8 servings.

PEPPER BUTTER: Beat ⅓ cup *butter or margarine* with an electric mixer on medium speed about 30 seconds or till softened (*or*, let stand at room temperature about 30 minutes). Stir in ¼ teaspoon ground *red pepper*, ⅛ to ¼ teaspoon ground *black pepper*, and ⅛ teaspoon *garlic powder*. Transfer the butter mixture to a piece of plastic wrap. Shape the butter into a small cylinder about 3 inches long. Wrap tightly and chill till firm. To serve, unwrap and slice into rounds.

CILANTRO–LIME BUTTER: Beat ⅓ cup *butter or margarine* with an electric mixer on medium speed about 30 seconds or till softened (*or*, let stand at room temperature about 30 minutes). Stir in 1 tablespoon snipped fresh *cilantro or parsley* and 1 teaspoon finely shredded *lime peel*. Transfer the butter mixture to a piece of plastic wrap. Shape the butter into a small cylinder about 3 inches long. Wrap tightly and chill till firm. To serve, unwrap and slice into rounds.

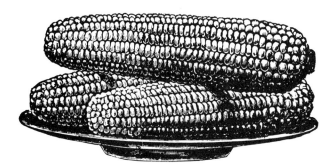

Pictured on page 45.

PEACH–BERRY PIE

½ to ¾ cup packed brown sugar
¼ cup all-purpose flour
¼ teaspoon ground cinnamon
 5 cups thinly sliced, peeled peaches or frozen unsweetened peach slices
¼ cup peach preserves
 1 tablespoon lemon juice
 1 cup red raspberries or blueberries
  Pastry for 9-Inch Double-Crust Pie
  Milk
  Pastry Cutouts

IN A BOWL COMBINE DESIRED AMOUNT OF BROWN sugar, the flour, and the cinnamon. If using frozen peaches, let stand for 15 to 30 minutes or till peaches are *partially* thawed but still icy. Stir peaches, preserves, and lemon juice into sugar mixture; toss till coated.

—■—

Spoon *half* the peach mixture into a pastry-lined 9-inch pie plate. Sprinkle with berries; cover with remaining peach mixture. Cut slits in top crust. Adjust top crust. Seal; flute edge. Brush crust with milk. Arrange Pastry Cutouts on top crust. Cover edge of pie with foil. Bake in a 375° oven 25 minutes. Remove foil. Bake 20 to 25 minutes more or till golden. Serves 8.

PASTRY CUTOUTS: Use a cookie cutter or knife to cut desired shapes from the pastry scraps. Mix 1 *egg yolk* with ¼ teaspoon *water*. Divide yolk mixture between 3 or 4 bowls. Add 2 or 3 drops of a different *food coloring* to each bowl and mix well. With a clean, small paintbrush, paint pastry cutouts.

PASTRY FOR 9-INCH DOUBLE-CRUST PIE: Combine 2 cups *all-purpose flour* and ½ teaspoon *salt*. Cut in ⅔ cup *shortening or lard* till pieces are the size of small peas. Using a total of 6 to 7 tablespoons *cold water*, sprinkle *1 tablespoon* over part of the mixture; gently toss with a fork. Push to one side of bowl. Repeat till all is moistened. Divide dough in half. Form each half into a ball. On a floured surface, flatten a ball of dough with your hands. Roll from center to edges, forming a circle about 12 inches in diameter. Wrap pastry around rolling pin. Unroll into a 9-inch pie plate. Ease pastry into pie plate, being careful not to stretch it. Trim even with rim of pie plate.

For top crust, roll out remaining dough. Cut slits in crust to allow steam to escape. Fill pastry in pie plate with desired filling. Place top crust on filling. Trim top crust ½ inch beyond edge of plate. Fold top crust under bottom crust; flute edge. Bake as directed.

Pictured on page 45.

CHAPTER TWO

FROM SEA TO SHINING SEA

WHETHER THEY CATCH IT THEMSELVES or buy it at the fish market, country cooks are hooked on fish and seafood. In this bounty of great-tasting, country-style dishes, you'll find recipes for Maine shrimp, Washington salmon, and fresh-water fish from points in between. ■

PAN-FRIED CATFISH

Crisp catfish or trout sizzling straight from the skillet, Hush Puppies (see recipe, page 143), and creamy coleslaw make a perfect combination.

Pictured on page 53.

 1 pound fresh or frozen catfish or other fish fillets (½ to 1 inch thick)
 ¼ cup sliced onion
 4 slices bacon, cut up
 ½ cup cornmeal
 ½ cup all-purpose flour
 1½ teaspoons snipped fresh rosemary or ½ teaspoon dried rosemary, crushed
 ¼ teaspoon salt
 ¼ teaspoon paprika
 ⅛ teaspoon pepper
 ½ cup buttermilk or milk
 2 tablespoons cooking oil
   Lemon wedges

THAW FISH FILLETS, IF FROZEN. RINSE FISH AND pat dry with paper towels. Measure thickness of fish. Set aside.

Cut onion slices in half. In a heavy large skillet cook onion and bacon till bacon is crisp. Using a slotted spoon, remove bacon and onion from the skillet and set aside. Discard drippings.

In a shallow dish combine cornmeal, flour, rosemary, salt, paprika, and pepper.

Dip fish fillets in buttermilk or milk, then coat with the cornmeal mixture. In the same skillet heat *1 tablespoon* of the oil. (Add more oil as necessary during cooking.) Add *half* of the fish in a single layer. (If fillets have skin, cook skin side last.) Fry over medium heat till golden on the first side. Allow 3 to 4 minutes per side for ½-inch-thick fillets (5 to 6 minutes per side for 1-inch-thick fillets). Turn carefully. Fry till coating is golden and fish flakes easily when tested with a fork. Drain on paper towels.

Transfer fish to a serving platter. Keep fried fillets warm in a 300° oven while frying remaining fish.

To serve, sprinkle bacon and onion over fish. Serve with lemon wedges. Makes 4 servings.

PAN-FRIED TROUT: Prepare Pan-Fried Catfish, *except* substitute 4 fresh or frozen pan-dressed *trout* (8 to 10 ounces each) for the fish fillets and use a 12-inch skillet. Heat the *2 tablespoons* oil in the skillet. Add *half* of the fish and fry for 5 to 7 minutes per side or till coating is golden and fish flakes easily when tested with a fork. Repeat with remaining fish, adding 2 tablespoons more *cooking oil.*

T R O U T   W I T H   S A L S A

1 pound fresh or frozen trout, flounder, sole, or perch fillets
    (½ to 1 inch thick)
¼ cup chopped onion
¼ cup chopped green pepper
2 cloves garlic, minced
3 tablespoons margarine or butter
¼ cup all-purpose flour
¼ teaspoon salt
¾ cup chopped tomato (about 1 medium)
2 tablespoons canned diced green chili peppers
1 tablespoon lime juice or lemon juice
1 to 2 teaspoons snipped fresh cilantro or parsley

THAW FISH FILLETS, IF FROZEN. RINSE FISH AND pat dry with paper towels. Measure thickness of fish. Set aside.

———■———

In a large skillet cook onion, green pepper, and garlic in *1 tablespoon* of the margarine or butter till tender but not brown. Remove vegetables from the skillet; set aside.

In a shallow bowl stir together flour and salt. Coat fish fillets with flour mixture.

———■———

In the same skillet heat the remaining margarine or butter. Add fillets to the skillet in a single layer. (If fillets have skin, cook skin side last.) Cook over medium heat till golden on the first side. Allow 3 to 4 minutes per side for ½-inch-thick fillets (5 to 6 minutes per side for 1-inch-thick fillets). Turn carefully. Cook till coating is golden and fish flakes easily when tested with a fork. Drain on paper towels. Transfer fillets to a serving platter; keep warm.

———■———

For salsa, return onion mixture to the skillet. Stir in chopped tomato, chili peppers, lime or lemon juice, and cilantro; heat through. Spoon salsa over fish. Makes 4 servings.

Inventive country cooks always are creating new dishes. For instance, Trout with Salsa features a snappy southwestern-style sauce that is ladled over trout or any favorite fish.

RED SNAPPER STUFFED WITH BARLEY PILAF

1 2- to 2½-pound fresh or *frozen dressed red snapper* or *lake trout*
⅔ cup quick-cooking barley
¾ teaspoon finely shredded orange peel
2 oranges
¾ cup seedless red or green grapes, halved
½ cup sliced celery
½ teaspoon salt
¼ teaspoon dried thyme, crushed
1 to 2 teaspoons cooking oil
Orange Sauce

THAW FISH, IF FROZEN. RINSE FISH; PAT DRY WITH paper towels. Set fish aside. Cook barley according to package directions.

For pilaf, peel and section oranges over a medium mixing bowl to catch juice. Chop orange sections and add to reserved juice in the bowl. Add cooked barley, *¼ teaspoon* of the orange peel, grapes, celery, salt, and thyme.

Place fish in a well-greased shallow baking pan. Sprinkle the cavity lightly with salt and pepper. Spoon about *1 cup* of the pilaf into the cavity; press lightly to flatten. Brush fish lightly with cooking oil. Cover loosely with foil. Transfer remaining barley pilaf to a 1-quart casserole; cover.

Bake stuffed fish and the pilaf in the casserole in a 350° oven for 30 to 40 minutes or till fish flakes easily when tested with a fork and pilaf is heated through. To serve, spoon Orange Sauce over fish. Makes 4 to 5 servings.

ORANGE SAUCE: In a small saucepan stir together the remaining ½ teaspoon finely shredded *orange peel*, ⅔ cup *orange juice*, ¼ cup *water*, 2 teaspoons *cornstarch*, and 1 teaspoon *soy sauce*. Cook and stir till thickened and bubbly. Cook and stir 2 minutes more. Remove from the heat. Makes about ¾ cup sauce.

LIME-SEASONED SALMON

1 pound fresh or *frozen salmon, whitefish, tuna,* or *sea bass*
    steaks, cut 1 inch thick
¼ cup cooking oil
¼ cup lime juice
1 tablespoon water
1 tablespoon honey
5 cups shredded mixed greens
½ cup shredded radishes
    Lime slices

THAW FISH STEAKS, IF FROZEN. RINSE FISH; PAT dry with paper towels. Place fish in a plastic bag set in a shallow dish.

—■—

For marinade, in a small mixing bowl stir together cooking oil, lime juice, water, and honey. Pour over fish. Close bag; marinate in refrigerator for 6 hours, turning bag occasionally to distribute marinade.

—■—

In a large mixing bowl toss together shredded greens and radishes; set aside. Drain fish, reserving marinade.

—■—

Place fish on a greased grill rack. Grill on an uncovered grill directly over *medium-hot* coals (see tip, page 28) for 5 minutes. Using a wide spatula, carefully turn fish over. Grill for 3 to 7 minutes more or till fish flakes easily when tested with a fork.

—■—

Meanwhile, in a small saucepan heat reserved marinade till bubbly. Pour hot marinade over greens; toss to wilt slightly. Transfer greens to a platter. Place fish on top of the greens. If desired, sprinkle with salt and pepper. Garnish with lime slices. Makes 4 servings.

BROILING DIRECTIONS: Prepare Lime-Seasoned Salmon, *except* place fish on a greased rack of an unheated broiler pan. Broil 4 inches from the heat for 5 minutes. Using a wide spatula, carefully turn fish over. Broil for 3 to 7 minutes more or till fish flakes easily when tested with a fork. Continue as directed.

Indians in the Pacific Northwest used to hang a large salmon on a pole like a flag as a sign that fresh salmon was available. Traders identified the freshest fish by their mild, fresh odor; moist, bright appearance; and firm flesh.

FISH

POACHED SALMON WITH DILL SAUCE

A traditional Fourth of July feast in early America was poached salmon with a creamy sauce, garden-fresh peas, new potatoes, and strawberry shortcake. You can enjoy a similar menu featuring Poached Salmon with Dill Sauce as the entrée.

    1 pound fresh or frozen salmon fillets or steaks
1½ cups water
    1 small onion, cut up
    1 medium carrot, cut up
    1 medium stalk celery, cut up
    2 sprigs parsley
   ½ teaspoon salt
   ½ teaspoon whole black peppercorns
    1 bay leaf
    1 clove garlic, sliced
   ⅓ cup half-and-half or light cream
    1 tablespoon cornstarch
1½ teaspoons snipped fresh dill or ½ teaspoon dried dillweed
   ½ teaspoon instant chicken bouillon granules
    1 tablespoon lemon juice
   ½ cup finely chopped seeded cucumber

THAW SALMON, IF FROZEN. MEASURE THICKNESS of salmon. In a large skillet combine water, onion, carrot, celery, parsley, salt, peppercorns, bay leaf, and garlic. Rinse salmon; add to the skillet. Bring to boiling; reduce heat. Cover and simmer for 4 to 6 minutes per ½-inch thickness of salmon or till fish flakes easily when tested with a fork. Remove salmon from the skillet; keep warm.

For sauce, strain the cooking liquid, reserving ⅓ cup liquid. In a small saucepan, stir together half-and-half or light cream, cornstarch, dill, and chicken bouillon granules. Add reserved cooking liquid and lemon juice. Cook and stir till thickened and bubbly. Cook and stir 2 minutes more. Stir in cucumber; heat through. Serve over salmon. Makes 4 servings.

FISH 'N' CHIPS

1 pound fresh or frozen cod or other fish fillets, cut ½ inch thick
1 cup all-purpose flour
¼ teaspoon baking soda
¼ teaspoon salt
1 beaten egg
¾ cup cold milk or beer
½ teaspoon finely shredded lemon peel
2 tablespoons lemon juice
¼ teaspoon ground red pepper (optional)
1½ pounds potatoes (4 medium)
  Cooking oil or shortening for deep-fat frying
¼ cup all-purpose flour
  Malt vinegar, cider vinegar, or Tartar Sauce (see recipe, page 60)

THAW FISH, IF FROZEN. FOR BATTER, IN A MEDIUM mixing bowl stir together the 1 cup flour, baking soda, and salt. In another bowl combine egg, milk or beer, lemon peel, lemon juice, and, if desired, red pepper. Add egg mixture to flour mixture all at once; stir to combine. Let batter stand at room temperature for 30 minutes.

———■———

Cut potatoes into ½-inch-wide sticks and pat dry with paper towels. Meanwhile, in a heavy 3-quart saucepan or deep-fat fryer heat 1½ to 2 inches of oil or shortening to 365°. Fry potatoes, 5 or 6 sticks at a time, in hot oil for 5 to 6 minutes or till golden. With a slotted spoon, remove potatoes from oil and drain on paper towels.

———■———

Transfer potatoes to a wire rack on a baking sheet. Keep potatoes warm in a 300° oven while frying fish.

———■———

Cut fish into 8 pieces. Pat dry with paper towels. Coat fish with the ¼ cup flour, then dip in batter. Fry fish, 2 pieces at a time, in hot oil (365°) for 1½ to 2 minutes per side or till golden brown. Remove from oil and drain on paper towels. Keep fried fillets warm in the oven while frying remaining fish.

———■———

If desired, sprinkle fish and potatoes with salt. Serve with malt or cider vinegar or Tartar Sauce. Makes 4 servings.

This unbeatable combination of crisp-coated, moist fish and fried potatoes first became popular among workers in England. When they immigrated to America, the English brought their love for fish 'n' chips with them. Now this dish is popular in the United States from shore to shore.

In some parts of the country, po'boys are called submarine or hero sandwiches. In Louisiana, they're filled with fried oysters or fried shrimp like these Po'boys.

PO'BOYS

1 pint shucked oysters or ¾ pound fresh or *frozen peeled and deveined shrimp*
½ cup all-purpose flour
½ teaspoon salt
¼ teaspoon pepper
1 beaten egg
¼ cup cooking oil or *shortening*
2 6- or 7-inch-long loaves French bread or *four 4-inch-long French-style rolls*
¼ cup Tartar Sauce, mayonnaise, or *salad dressing*
1 cup shredded lettuce
1 tomato, thinly sliced
   Bottled hot pepper sauce (optional)
   Lemon wedges (optional)

DRAIN OYSTERS. (*OR,* THAW SHRIMP, IF FROZEN.) Rinse and pat dry with paper towels. In a small bowl combine flour, salt, and pepper. Dip oysters or shrimp into beaten egg, then coat with flour mixture.

—■—

In a large skillet heat oil or shortening. Add *half* of the oysters or shrimp in a single layer. Cook over medium-high heat for 2 to 3 minutes per side or till golden. Drain on paper towels. Transfer to a wire rack on a baking sheet. Keep fried fish warm in a 300° oven while you cook remaining seafood and assemble sandwiches.

—■—

Slice French bread or rolls in half horizontally. Place French bread or roll halves on a baking sheet in a 300° oven about 3 minutes or till heated through.

—■—

Spread cut sides of bread with Tartar Sauce, mayonnaise, or salad dressing. Arrange lettuce and tomato slices on bottoms of loaves or rolls. Add oysters or shrimp. If desired, sprinkle with hot pepper sauce and squeeze lemon juice over oysters or shrimp. Add bread tops. Makes 4 servings.

TARTAR SAUCE: In a small mixing bowl stir together 1 cup *mayonnaise or salad dressing,* ¼ cup *sweet or dill pickle relish,* 1 tablespoon *chopped green onion,* 1 teaspoon *finely shredded lemon peel,* and dash bottled *hot pepper sauce.* Cover and chill at least 2 hours to blend flavors. Makes about 1⅓ cups.

Crunchy crab cakes, popular in Maryland and Delaware for centuries, are delicious served with tartar sauce and lemon wedges.

CRAB CAKES

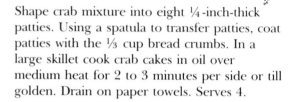

1 beaten egg
¼ cup fine dry bread crumbs
2 teaspoons Dijon-style mustard
1 teaspoon Worcestershire sauce
  Dash ground red pepper
2 6- or 6½-ounce cans crabmeat, drained, flaked, and cartilage removed
⅓ cup finely shredded carrot
2 tablespoons thinly sliced green onion
⅓ cup fine dry bread crumbs
2 tablespoons cooking oil, margarine, or butter

IN A MEDIUM MIXING BOWL COMBINE EGG, THE ¼ cup bread crumbs, mustard, Worcestershire sauce, and red pepper. Stir in the crabmeat, carrot, and green onion. Cover and chill for 45 to 60 minutes.

Shape crab mixture into eight ¼-inch-thick patties. Using a spatula to transfer patties, coat patties with the ⅓ cup bread crumbs. In a large skillet cook crab cakes in oil over medium heat for 2 to 3 minutes per side or till golden. Drain on paper towels. Serves 4.

BATTER-FRIED SHRIMP

1 pound fresh or frozen peeled and deveined large shrimp
1 cup all-purpose flour
1½ teaspoons snipped fresh basil or ½ teaspoon dried basil, crushed
⅛ teaspoon onion powder
1 beaten egg
1 tablespoon cooking oil
  Cooking oil or shortening for deep-fat frying
  Bottled cocktail sauce or Tartar Sauce (see recipe, page 60) (optional)

THAW SHRIMP, IF FROZEN. RINSE AND PAT DRY with paper towels. Set aside.

For batter, in a medium bowl combine flour, basil, onion powder, and ⅛ teaspoon *salt.* Make a well in the center of the dry ingredients. Combine egg, the 1 tablespoon oil, and ¾ cup *cold water;* add to dry ingredients. Beat with a rotary beater or wire whisk till smooth. Let rest for 10 minutes.

Meanwhile, in heavy large saucepan or deep-fat fryer heat 1½ to 2 inches cooking oil to 365°. Dip shrimp in batter to coat. Fry shrimp, a few at a time, in the hot oil for 2 to 3 minutes or till golden. Remove with a slotted spoon; drain on paper towels. Transfer to a wire rack on a baking sheet. Keep fried shrimp warm in a 300° oven while frying remaining shrimp. If desired, serve with cocktail sauce or Tartar Sauce. Makes 4 servings.

SCALLOPED OYSTERS

  1 pint shucked oysters
¼ cup sliced green onion
  2 tablespoons margarine or butter
½ cup crushed saltine crackers (about 14 crackers)
¼ cup fine dry bread crumbs
  2 tablespoons snipped parsley
½ cup milk
  1 teaspoon Worcestershire sauce
¾ teaspoon snipped fresh oregano or ¼ teaspoon dried oregano, crushed
    Dash bottled hot pepper sauce
  1 tablespoon dry sherry (optional)

DRAIN OYSTERS; SET ASIDE. IN A MEDIUM SKILLET cook green onion in margarine or butter till tender. Remove from the heat. Stir in crushed crackers, bread crumbs, and parsley.

———■———

Spread *half* of the crumb mixture in the bottom of an 8x1½-inch round baking dish or divide mixture equally among four 10-ounce custard cups. Evenly arrange oysters over crumb mixture.

———■———

In a small mixing bowl stir together milk, Worcestershire sauce, oregano, and bottled hot pepper sauce. If desired, stir in sherry. Pour mixture over oysters. Sprinkle remaining crumbs over oysters.

———■———

Bake in a 400° oven about 15 minutes or till mixture is bubbly and oysters curl around the edges. Makes 4 servings.

Scalloped oysters were named for the large scalloped shells originally used to hold the oysters as they baked. Eventually, other creamy baked dishes made with crumbs came to be called scalloped.

1 *pound fresh* or *frozen scallops*
4 *tablespoons margarine* or *butter*
2 *cups sliced fresh mushrooms*
½ *cup sliced green onion*
2 *tablespoons all-purpose flour*
¼ *teaspoon salt*
  Dash ground red pepper
1½ *cups half-and-half, light cream,* or *milk*
2 *beaten egg yolks*
3 *tablespoons Madeira* or *dry sherry*
½ *cup fine dry bread crumbs*
2 *tablespoons margarine* or *butter, melted*
2 *tablespoons snipped parsley*

THAW SCALLOPS, IF FROZEN. HALVE ANY LARGE scallops. In a large skillet cook *half* of the scallops in *1 tablespoon* of the margarine or butter over medium heat for 1 to 3 minutes or till scallops turn opaque. Using a slotted spoon, remove scallops from skillet. Repeat with remaining scallops and *1 tablespoon* of the margarine or butter. Remove scallops from the skillet. Wipe skillet with paper towels.

—■—

In the same skillet cook mushrooms and onions in remaining 2 tablespoons margarine or butter till tender. Stir in flour, salt, and red pepper. Add half-and-half, light cream, or milk all at once. Cook and stir till thickened and bubbly. Cook and stir 1 minute more.

—■—

Stir about *half* of the hot mixture into beaten egg yolks; return all to the saucepan. Cook and stir till mixture just bubbles. Reduce heat. Cook and stir 1 minute more. Remove from the heat; stir in Madeira or dry sherry.

—■—

Drain scallops; stir scallops into mushroom mixture. Spoon into four 10-ounce au gratin dishes or casseroles.

—■—

For crumb topping, in a small bowl combine bread crumbs, the 2 tablespoons melted margarine or butter, and parsley; toss gently. Sprinkle over scallop mixture. Bake in a 400° oven for 7 to 9 minutes or till crumbs are brown. Makes 4 servings.

CRAWFISH ÉTOUFFÉE

12 ounces fresh or frozen peeled crawfish tails or peeled and deveined shrimp
1 cup chopped onion
½ cup chopped celery
½ cup chopped green pepper
2 cloves garlic, minced
2 tablespoons cooking oil
2 cups chopped tomatoes (about 3 medium)
¾ cup chicken broth
1½ teaspoons snipped fresh thyme or ½ teaspoon dried thyme, crushed
¾ teaspoon snipped fresh basil or ¼ teaspoon dried basil, crushed
¼ teaspoon salt
¼ teaspoon black pepper
¼ teaspoon ground red pepper
¼ cup water
2 tablespoons all-purpose flour
3 cups hot cooked rice

THAW CRAWFISH TAILS OR SHRIMP, IF FROZEN. Rinse and pat dry with paper towels.

In a heavy large saucepan cook onion, celery, green pepper, and garlic in hot oil till vegetables are tender. Stir in tomatoes, chicken broth, thyme, basil, salt, black pepper, and red pepper. Bring to boiling; reduce heat. Cover and simmer for 20 minutes.

In a small bowl stir together water and flour; stir into vegetable mixture. Cook and stir till thickened and bubbly.

Add crawfish or shrimp to vegetable mixture. Return to boiling; reduce heat. Simmer, uncovered, about 5 minutes or till crawfish are tender or shrimp turn pink. Serve over hot cooked rice. Makes 4 servings.

Rich, savory étouffée (AY too FAY) is a Cajun specialty from the bayou country of Louisiana. It's made with either tiny lobsterlike crawfish (sometimes called crayfish or crawdads) or shrimp.

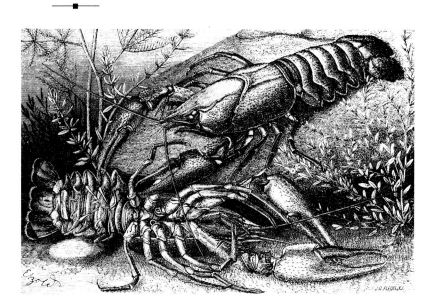

SHELLFISH

65

CHAPTER THREE

FEAST
ON
FOWL

FRY IT, ROAST IT, STUFF IT, stew it — there are as many ways to prepare poultry as there are

country cooks. To suit every taste, this collection of mouth watering poultry recipes reflects a wide

variety of soul-satisfying country meals. ■

SOUTHERN FRIED CHICKEN AND GRAVY

The exact origins of this southern classic are unknown, but fried chicken may have evolved from chicken fricassee, a dish in which chicken is fried and then stewed. Fried chicken was born when the stewing step was dropped.

Pictured on page 67.

    2 pounds meaty chicken pieces
          (breasts, thighs, and drumsticks)
    ¾ teaspoon poultry seasoning
    ½ teaspoon salt
    ⅛ teaspoon ground red pepper
    ⅛ teaspoon garlic powder (optional)
    ⅓ cup all-purpose flour*
    2 tablespoons cooking oil
    2 tablespoons all-purpose flour
    ¼ teaspoon salt
    ⅛ teaspoon pepper
    1¾ cups milk

IF DESIRED, SKIN CHICKEN. RINSE CHICKEN; PAT IT dry with paper towels. For coating mixture, combine poultry seasoning, the ½ teaspoon salt, ground red pepper, and, if desired, garlic powder. Divide coating mixture in half. Rub *half* of the coating onto the chicken pieces.

In a plastic bag combine the ⅓ cup flour and remaining coating mixture. Add chicken pieces, a few at a time, shaking to coat.

In a large skillet heat cooking oil; add chicken pieces. Cook, uncovered, over medium heat for 15 minutes, turning pieces to brown evenly. Reduce heat to medium-low. Cook, uncovered, for 35 to 40 minutes more or till chicken is no longer pink, turning once.

Transfer chicken pieces to a serving platter, reserving *2 tablespoons* drippings. Cover chicken and keep warm.

For gravy, stir the 2 tablespoons flour, the ¼ teaspoon salt, and pepper into reserved drippings. Add milk all at once. Cook and stir till thickened and bubbly. Cook and stir 1 to 2 minutes more. Serve gravy with chicken. Makes 4 servings.

*Note: If desired, substitute ¼ cup *all-purpose flour* and 2 tablespoons *fine dry bread crumbs or yellow cornmeal* for the ⅓ cup all-purpose flour.

CRISPY BATTER-FRIED
CHICKEN

1 2½- to 3-pound broiler-fryer chicken, cut up
½ cup all-purpose flour
⅓ cup wheat germ
¼ cup yellow cornmeal
1 teaspoon baking powder
1 teaspoon dry mustard
½ teaspoon onion salt
¼ teaspoon ground red pepper
1 beaten egg
⅔ cup beer or water
Cooking oil or shortening for deep-fat frying

IF DESIRED, SKIN CHICKEN. RINSE CHICKEN. IN A large saucepan cover chicken pieces with water. Bring to boiling; reduce heat. Cover and simmer for 20 minutes. Drain. Cool slightly. Pat chicken dry with paper towels.

For batter, in a mixing bowl combine flour, wheat germ, cornmeal, baking powder, mustard, onion salt, and ground red pepper. In a small bowl, stir together the beaten egg and beer or water. Add to dry ingedients; beat till almost smooth.

Meanwhile, in a heavy 3-quart saucepan or deep-fat fryer heat 1¼ inches oil or melted shortening to 365°.

Dip chicken pieces, one at a time, into batter, gently shaking off excess batter. Carefully lower chicken pieces into the hot oil. Fry 2 or 3 pieces at a time, for 2 to 3 minutes or till golden, turning once. Carefully remove and drain well. (If batter becomes too thick, add additional beer or water as necessary.) Keep fried chicken warm in a 300° oven while frying remaining pieces. Makes 6 servings.

If you like your fried chicken crispy and crunchy, here's a chicken recipe to crow about. With cornmeal and wheat germ in the batter, the coating puffs up around the chicken as it fries.

HERB AND PECAN
OVEN-FRIED CHICKEN

Try oven frying to make crispy fried chicken with fewer calories and less mess. This technique uses a hot oven and just a little fat to give chicken that skillet-fried flavor and appearance.

2 whole large chicken breasts (about 2 pounds), halved lengthwise
1 beaten egg
1 tablespoon milk
¾ cup herb-seasoned stuffing mix
⅓ cup chopped pecans
2 tablespoons snipped parsley
1 tablespoon snipped fresh basil or ½ teaspoon dried basil, crushed
⅛ teaspoon onion powder
  Dash pepper

IF DESIRED, SKIN CHICKEN. RINSE CHICKEN; PAT dry with paper towels. In a shallow bowl or pie plate stir together egg and milk. In another bowl combine stuffing mix, pecans, parsley, basil, onion powder, and pepper.

Dip breast halves into egg mixture. Coat with stuffing mixture. Place chicken pieces, meaty side up, in a 13x9x2-inch baking pan.

Bake in a 375° oven for 45 to 55 minutes or till tender and chicken is no longer pink. Makes 4 servings.

BARBECUED CHICKEN

1 2½- to 3-pound broiler-fryer chicken, quartered
Salt
Pepper
Peach Sauce or Maple Sauce

RINSE CHICKEN; PAT DRY WITH PAPER TOWELS. Break wing, hip, and drumstick joints of chicken so quarters will lie flat during cooking. Twist wing tips under back. Sprinkle with salt and pepper.

———■———

Place chicken, skin side down, on an uncovered grill directly over *medium* coals (see tip, page 28). Grill for 20 minutes. Turn pieces; grill for 15 to 25 minutes more or till tender and no longer pink. Brush often with Peach Sauce or Maple Sauce during the last 10 minutes of grilling. Heat remaining sauce and serve with chicken. Makes 4 servings.

PEACH SAUCE: In a small saucepan combine ½ cup *peach preserves*, 3 tablespoons *vinegar*, 2 teaspoons *Worcestershire sauce*, ¼ teaspoon *ground cinnamon*, and ⅛ teaspoon *ground allspice*. Heat and stir just till preserves melt.

MAPLE SAUCE: In a 1½-quart saucepan cook ¼ cup finely chopped *onion* in 1 tablespoon *margarine or butter* till onion is tender but not brown. Stir in one 8-ounce can *tomato sauce*, 3 tablespoons *maple-flavored syrup*, 1 tablespoon *prepared mustard*, ½ teaspoon *garlic salt*, and ⅛ teaspoon *ground red pepper*. Bring to boiling. Reduce heat and simmer, uncovered, about 5 minutes or till of desired basting consistency.

*B*arbecue sauces are almost as varied as the cooks who use them. Sauces for grilling can be made with ingredients ranging from tomatoes to peaches. And sauce flavorings can be just about any combination from vinegar and Worcestershire sauce to maple syrup and honey.

Sawmill gravy, a southern specialty, got its name because it was served at logging camps. The gravy was made from meat drippings and often was served on biscuits. Today, sawmill gravy usually contains bits of sausage.

BRAISED CHICKEN WITH SAWMILL GRAVY

1   2½- to 3-pound broiler-fryer chicken, cut up
¼   cup all-purpose flour
½   teaspoon garlic salt
¼   teaspoon onion powder
¼   teaspoon pepper
2   tablespoons cooking oil
¾   cup water
4   ounces bulk pork sausage
3   tablespoons all-purpose flour
½   teaspoon salt
⅛   teaspoon pepper
     Milk
3   cups hot cooked rice

IF DESIRED, SKIN CHICKEN. RINSE CHICKEN; PAT dry with paper towels. In a paper or plastic bag combine the ¼ cup flour, garlic salt, onion powder, and the ¼ teaspoon pepper. Add chicken to the bag, 2 pieces at a time, shaking to coat well.

In a 12-inch skillet heat oil; add chicken, placing meaty pieces toward center of skillet. Cook, uncovered, about 15 minutes or till chicken is lightly browned, turning pieces to brown evenly.

Carefully add water to skillet. Bring to boiling; reduce heat. Cover and simmer for 30 to 35 minutes or till chicken is tender and no longer pink. Transfer chicken to a platter; cover and keep warm. Drain juices from skillet, scraping up browned bits. If necessary, skim fat from juices. Set chicken juices aside.

Wash the skillet. In the skillet cook sausage till brown. Drain fat from pan, scraping up browned bits; reserve *2 tablespoons* sausage drippings in the skillet. (If necessary, add enough *cooking oil* to drippings to equal 2 tablespoons.) Set sausage aside.

For gravy, stir the 3 tablespoons flour, salt, and the ⅛ teaspoon pepper into reserved drippings. Cook and stir mixture over medium heat for 8 to 10 minutes or till mixture has a rich, dark brown color. Add enough milk to reserved chicken juices to equal *2 cups* (about *1⅔ cups* milk). Add milk mixture to skillet all at once. Cook and stir till thickened and bubbly. Cook and stir 2 minutes more. Crumble cooked sausage into gravy. Serve gravy with chicken and rice. Makes 6 servings.

ROSEMARY ROAST CHICKEN WITH STUFFING

1 2½- to 3-pound broiler-fryer chicken
1 tablespoon cooking oil, melted margarine, or melted butter
1 medium zucchini, halved lengthwise and thinly sliced (about 1¼ cups)
⅔ cup water
½ cup coarsely shredded carrot (about 1 carrot)
½ cup thinly sliced celery (about 1 stalk)
½ cup finely chopped onion
2 teaspoons instant chicken bouillon granules
¾ teaspoon snipped fresh rosemary or ¼ teaspoon dried rosemary, crushed
⅛ teaspoon garlic powder
⅛ teaspoon pepper
¾ cup couscous
2 tablespoons snipped parsley
1 tablespoon snipped fresh rosemary or 1 teaspoon dried rosemary, finely crushed
½ teaspoon lemon-pepper seasoning
⅛ teaspoon garlic powder

The rosemary adds a delicious flavor and piney scent to this impressive entrée.

RINSE BIRD; PAT DRY WITH PAPER TOWELS. BRUSH bird with oil, margarine, or butter. For stuffing, in a medium saucepan combine zucchini, water, carrot, celery, onion, bouillon granules, the ¾ teaspoon fresh or ¼ teaspoon dried rosemary, garlic powder, and pepper. Bring to boiling; reduce heat. Simmer, covered, for 2 minutes. Remove from heat. Stir in couscous. Cover and let stand for 5 minutes.

Spoon stuffing loosely into neck cavity of chicken. Skewer neck skin to back. Lightly spoon stuffing into body cavity. (Place any remaining stuffing in a lightly greased 1-quart casserole. Cover and refrigerate.) Twist wing tips under back. Tie legs to tail of chicken. Place chicken, breast side up, on a rack in a shallow roasting pan.

In a small mixing bowl combine parsley, the 1 tablespoon fresh or 1 teaspoon dried rosemary, lemon-pepper seasoning, and garlic powder; crush slightly. Rub mixture into the skin of the chicken.

Roast, uncovered, in a 375° oven for 1¼ to 1½ hours or till chicken is no longer pink and the drumsticks move easily in their sockets. Add the covered casserole with stuffing to the oven the last 30 minutes of roasting. Makes 6 servings.

Two southern favorites—chicken and corn bread—are paired in this home-style dish.

CHEESY CHICKEN SHORTCAKE

2 slices bacon
½ cup chopped green pepper
½ cup chopped onion
¼ cup all-purpose flour
2 teaspoons instant chicken bouillon granules
¼ teaspoon ground nutmeg
¼ teaspoon pepper
1 cup milk
¾ cup water
2 cups cubed cooked chicken or turkey
1 cup shredded cheddar or American cheese (4 ounces)
1 4-ounce can sliced mushrooms, drained
1 2-ounce jar (¼ cup) diced pimiento
4 3-inch squares Buttermilk Corn Bread (see recipe, page 142)
Fresh tarragon (optional)

IN A 3-QUART SAUCEPAN COOK BACON TILL CRISP; remove bacon, reserving drippings. Drain and crumble. Set bacon aside.

Cook green pepper and onion in reserved drippings over medium heat till tender. Stir in flour, bouillon granules, nutmeg, and pepper. Add milk and water all at once. Cook and stir till thickened and bubbly. Add chicken, cheese, mushrooms, and pimiento. Cook and stir till cheese melts and chicken is heated through.

To serve, split corn bread squares horizontally and place on individual plates. Top with chicken mixture. Sprinkle with crumbled bacon. If desired, garnish with fresh tarragon. Makes 4 servings.

ARTICHOKE–SQUASH
CHICKEN POTPIE

Wondering what to do with leftovers? Frugal colonists solved this age-old problem by making meat and vegetable pies. The pies were baked in black iron kettles or pots—hence the name potpie.

⅔ cup all-purpose flour
¼ cup yellow cornmeal
⅛ teaspoon salt
¼ cup margarine or butter
3 to 4 tablespoons water
¼ cup chopped onion
3 tablespoons margarine or butter
⅓ cup all-purpose flour
2 teaspoons instant chicken bouillon granules
1 teaspoon snipped fresh tarragon or ¼ teaspoon dried tarragon, crushed
⅛ teaspoon pepper
2 cups cubed cooked chicken or turkey
2 small zucchini or yellow summer squash, halved lengthwise and thinly sliced (about 2 cups)
1 9-ounce package frozen artichoke hearts, thawed and halved
½ cup shredded carrot (about 1 carrot)

IN A MEDIUM MIXING BOWL STIR TOGETHER THE ⅔ cup flour, cornmeal, and salt. Cut in the ¼ cup margarine or butter till pieces are the size of small peas. Sprinkle *1 tablespoon* of the water over part of the mixture; gently toss with a fork. Push to side of bowl. Repeat with remaining water till all is moistened. Form dough into a ball.

On a lightly floured surface, roll dough into a 12x6-inch rectangle; cut into eight 12x¾-inch strips. Cover and set aside.

In a large saucepan cook onion in the 3 tablespoons margarine or butter till tender but not brown. Stir in the ⅓ cup flour, bouillon granules, tarragon, and pepper. Add 1½ cups *water*. Cook and stir till thickened and bubbly. Stir in chicken or turkey, zucchini or yellow summer squash, artichoke hearts, and carrot. Return to boiling, stirring frequently.

Transfer chicken mixture to a 10x6x2-inch baking dish. *Immediately* place 5 of the pastry strips, evenly spaced, diagonally across the chicken mixture. Place the remaining 3 pastry strips, evenly spaced, on the opposite diagonal, so pastry strips form a lattice pattern. Trim off edges of pastry. Bake, uncovered, in a 450° oven for 15 to 20 minutes or till pastry is golden brown. Makes 4 servings.

SOUR CREAM
CHICKEN FRICASSEE

2 pounds meaty chicken pieces (breasts, thighs, and drumsticks)
3 tablespoons all-purpose flour
1 teaspoon paprika
¼ teaspoon salt
¼ teaspoon pepper
1 tablespoon cooking oil or shortening
1½ cups halved fresh mushrooms
1 cup thinly sliced celery
½ cup sliced green onion
1 cup chicken broth
1 large tomato, peeled, seeded, and chopped
1 teaspoon finely shredded lemon peel
1½ teaspoons snipped fresh marjoram or oregano or ½ teaspoon dried marjoram
    or oregano, crushed
⅓ cup dairy sour cream
2 tablespoons all-purpose flour
3 cups hot cooked noodles

IF DESIRED, SKIN CHICKEN. RINSE CHICKEN; PAT dry with paper towels. In a plastic or paper bag combine the 3 tablespoons flour, paprika, salt, and pepper. Add chicken to the bag, 2 or 3 pieces at a time, shaking to coat well.

———■———

In a large skillet heat cooking oil; add chicken pieces. Cook, uncovered, about 15 minutes or till lightly browned, turning pieces to brown evenly. Remove chicken; set aside.

———■———

Drain fat, reserving *2 tablespoons* of the drippings in the skillet (add more oil, if necessary). Add mushrooms, celery, and green onion to skillet. Cook and stir for 2 minutes. Stir in broth, chopped tomato, lemon peel, and marjoram or oregano.

———■———

Bring to boiling, scraping up browned bits from the bottom of the skillet. Add chicken to the skillet. Return to boiling; reduce heat. Cover and simmer for 35 to 40 minutes or till chicken is tender and no longer pink.

———■———

Transfer chicken and vegetables to a platter; keep warm. Skim fat from pan juices; measure *1 cup* of the pan juices. Discard any extra juices. In a bowl combine sour cream and the 2 tablespoons flour; gradually stir in pan juices. Return mixture to skillet. Cook and stir till thickened and bubbly. Cook and stir for 1 minute more.

———■———

To serve, spoon sauce over chicken and hot cooked noodles. Makes 4 servings.

Fricassees have been popular in the South since the last half of the 18th century. Of French origin, fricassees contain meat or poultry simmered in a cream sauce.

CHICKEN AND DUMPLINGS

Here's an old-time one-pot meal that's an American favorite. The dumplings bake right on top of the stewed chicken in a covered pot.

1   *2½- to 3-pound broiler-fryer chicken, cut up*
1   *small rutabaga, peeled and cut into ¾-inch cubes (about 2 cups)*
2   *stalks celery, cut into 1-inch pieces (about 1 cup)*
1   *small onion, cut into thin wedges*
1   *teaspoon salt*
½   *teaspoon dried sage, crushed*
½   *teaspoon dried thyme, crushed*
¼   *teaspoon pepper*
3   *cups water*
1   *cup all-purpose flour*
2   *tablespoons snipped parsley*
1   *teaspoon baking powder*
½   *teaspoon dried sage, crushed*
    Dash salt
⅓   *cup milk*
2   *tablespoons margarine or butter, melted*
1   *cup frozen peas*
½   *cup milk, half-and-half, or light cream*
¼   *cup all-purpose flour*

IF DESIRED, SKIN CHICKEN. RINSE. IN A 4½-QUART Dutch oven combine chicken, rutabaga, celery, onion, the 1 teaspoon salt, ½ teaspoon sage, thyme, and pepper. Add the water. Bring to boiling; reduce heat. Cover and simmer for 35 minutes.

——■——

Meanwhile, for dumplings, in a small bowl stir together the 1 cup flour, parsley, baking powder, ½ teaspoon sage, and the dash salt. In another bowl combine the ⅓ cup milk and melted margarine or butter. Add to dry ingredients. Stir with a fork till combined.

——■——

Stir peas into chicken mixture. Return to boiling. Drop dumpling mixture from a tablespoon into 6 mounds directly atop chicken (*do not drop batter into liquid*). Cover; simmer for 10 to 12 minutes or till a toothpick inserted near the centers of the dumplings comes out clean. (*Do not lift cover except to test for doneness.*) Using a slotted spoon, transfer chicken, dumplings, and vegetables to soup plates; cover and keep warm.

——■——

Skim fat from broth in Dutch oven; discard fat. Remove all but *2 cups* broth from Dutch oven. Slowly stir the ½ cup milk into the ¼ cup flour. Stir into broth in Dutch oven. Cook and stir till thickened and bubbly. Cook and stir 1 minute more. Spoon thickened broth onto each serving. Makes 6 servings.

BAKED CHICKEN
COUNTRY CAPTAIN

2 pounds meaty chicken pieces
　　(breasts, thighs, and drumsticks)
1 large onion, cut into thin wedges
1 small green pepper, cut into 1-inch pieces
2 tablespoons raisins
2 cloves garlic, minced
1 tablespoon cooking oil
1 tablespoon curry powder
1 16-ounce can tomatoes, cut up
½ teaspoon sugar
½ teaspoon salt
½ teaspoon ground mace
¼ teaspoon dried thyme, crushed
¼ teaspoon pepper
2 tablespoons cornstarch
2 tablespoons cold water
3 cups hot cooked rice

This curried chicken dish from East India initially became popular in America's southern seaports, where exotic spices were first available to cooks.

IF DESIRED, SKIN CHICKEN. RINSE CHICKEN; PAT dry with paper towels. Arrange chicken, onion wedges, pepper pieces, and raisins in a 12x7½x2-inch baking dish. In a small saucepan cook garlic in hot oil for 1 minute. Add curry powder. Cook and stir for 1 minute more. Stir in *undrained* tomatoes, sugar, salt, mace, thyme, and pepper. Bring to boiling; pour over ingredients in dish.

———■———

Cover and bake in a 350° oven about 1 hour or till chicken is tender. Using a slotted spoon, transfer chicken, vegetables, and raisins to a platter.

———■———

For sauce, measure pan juices; if necessary, add enough water to equal *2 cups.* Transfer to a saucepan. In a small bowl combine cornstarch and cold water; add to saucepan. Cook and stir till thickened and bubbly. Cook and stir 2 minutes more.

———■———

To serve, spoon chicken, vegetables, and raisins over hot cooked rice. Spoon some of the sauce atop chicken; serve remaining sauce. Season to taste. Makes 4 servings.

CHICKEN–RICE PATTIES

Country cooks are experts at using leftovers, and here's an example of their creativity. Leftover chicken and rice get a flavor make-over when they're oven-baked in patties and then topped with avocado and tomato slices and salsa.

2 cups finely chopped cooked chicken
¾ cup cold cooked rice
2 3-ounce packages cream cheese with chives, softened
½ teaspoon dried oregano, crushed
¼ teaspoon salt
¼ teaspoon ground cumin
   Several dashes bottled hot pepper sauce
⅓ cup margarine or butter, melted
½ cup seasoned fine dry bread crumbs
1 small tomato, cut into 8 slices
1 small avocado, seeded, peeled, and cut into 8 slices
⅔ cup salsa

IN A MIXING BOWL COMBINE CHICKEN, COLD RICE, softened cream cheese with chives, oregano, salt, cumin, and hot pepper sauce. Shape chicken mixture into eight ¾-inch-thick patties.

———■———

Dip patties in melted margarine or butter. Coat both sides of patties with bread crumbs. Place patties on a baking sheet.

———■———

Bake patties in a 450° oven about 10 minutes or till golden. Transfer to serving platter.

———■———

Top each patty with a slice of tomato and avocado. Spoon salsa atop chicken patties (if desired, heat salsa). Makes 4 servings.

CORNISH GAME HENS WITH CORN BREAD STUFFING

 4 ounces hot-style bulk pork sausage
¼ cup sliced green onion
 2 cups crumbled corn bread
¼ cup chopped toasted pecans
¼ cup chopped green pepper
 2 tablespoons dried currants or raisins
 2 teaspoons snipped fresh sage or ½ teaspoon dried sage, crushed
¼ to ⅓ cup chicken broth
 2 1- to 1½-pound Cornish game hens, halved lengthwise
 2 teaspoons cooking oil
¼ teaspoon salt
¼ teaspoon paprika
⅛ teaspoon ground cumin

FOR STUFFING, IN A LARGE SKILLET COOK SAUSAGE and onion till sausage is brown. Drain fat. Stir in corn bread, pecans, green pepper, currants or raisins, and sage. Drizzle with enough chicken broth to moisten, tossing lightly. Place stuffing in a 1-quart casserole. Cover and chill.

———■———

Rinse hen halves; pat dry with paper towels. Twist wing tips under back. Place hen halves, bone sides down, in a 13x9x2-inch baking dish. Combine cooking oil, salt, paprika, and cumin; brush oil mixture over Cornish hens.

———■———

Bake, covered, in a 375° oven for 30 minutes. Add covered casserole of stuffing to oven. Uncover hens; bake hens and stuffing about 30 minutes more or till hens are tender and no longer pink and stuffing is heated through.

———■———

To serve, divide stuffing into 4 equal mounds on individual plates. Place a hen half on top of each mound of stuffing. Makes 4 servings.

Hot-style pork sausage gives this corn bread stuffing real zing. If you'd prefer a milder stuffing, use regular pork sausage.

A P R I C O T – H O N E Y -
G L A Z E D   D U C K L I N G

If you want to, use two Cornish game hens instead of the duckling. Prepare the hens like the duckling, except do not prick their skin and roast them for only 60 minutes.

      1   4- to 5-pound domestic duckling
    1½   teaspoons snipped fresh oregano
              or ½ teaspoon dried oregano, crushed
      ½   teaspoon onion salt
      ½   teaspoon garlic salt
      ¼   teaspoon pepper
      ⅓   cup apricot preserves
      2   tablespoons honey
      ½   teaspoon finely shredded lemon peel (set aside)
      2   tablespoons lemon juice
      ½   cup chicken broth
      2   teaspoons cornstarch
      2   teaspoons soy sauce
          Wild Rice Pilaf (optional)

RINSE DUCK; PAT DRY WITH PAPER TOWELS. IN A bowl combine oregano, onion salt, garlic salt, and pepper. Sprinkle body cavity of duck with some of the oregano mixture; rub remaining mixture on skin of duck. Skewer neck skin to back; tie legs to tail. Twist wing tips under back. Prick skin all over with a fork.

———■———

Place duck, breast side up, on a rack in a shallow roasting pan. Roast in a 375° oven for 1¾ to 2¼ hours or till the drumsticks move easily in their sockets and duck is no longer pink, spooning off fat occasionally.

———■———

Meanwhile, for glaze, in a small saucepan heat apricot preserves, honey, and lemon juice just till preserves melt. Baste duck with about *half* of the glaze during the last 10 minutes of roasting.

———■———

For sauce, combine chicken broth and cornstarch; stir into remaining glaze in saucepan along with lemon peel and soy sauce. Cook and stir till thickened and bubbly. Cook and stir 1 to 2 minutes more. Serve sauce with duck. If desired, serve with Wild Rice Pilaf. Makes 4 servings.

WILD RICE PILAF: Rinse 1 cup *wild rice* in a strainer under *cold* water about 1 minute, lifting rice to rinse well. (If desired, use ½ cup *wild rice* and ½ cup *brown rice*.) In a 1½-quart saucepan combine rice, 2 cups *water*; ½ cup thinly sliced *green onion*; 2 teaspoons *instant chicken bouillon granules*; ¾ teaspoon snipped *fresh thyme or* ¼ teaspoon *dried thyme*, crushed; and ⅛ teaspoon *pepper*.

Bring rice mixture to boiling; reduce heat. Cover and simmer for 40 to 50 minutes or till rice is tender and most of the liquid is absorbed. Stir in 1 cup thinly sliced *celery* the last 15 minutes of cooking. Makes 4 servings.

Peach and Watercress Salad
(see recipe, page 147)

Apricot–Honey-Glazed Duckling

ROAST GOOSE WITH
FRUITED STUFFING

Goose was common on early American tables because the dark-meat bird was plentiful on the frontier. Today, goose is a special treat usually reserved for holidays.

1   7- to 8-pound domestic goose
¼   teaspoon salt
⅛   teaspoon pepper
2   stalks celery, quartered
1   medium onion, quartered
¼   cup apple jelly
2   teaspoons Worcestershire sauce
1   8-ounce package mixed dried fruit, coarsely chopped
8   cups dry bread cubes
1   8-ounce can whole cranberry sauce
2   tablespoons margarine or butter, melted
½   teaspoon ground cinnamon
⅛   teaspoon ground allspice
⅛   teaspoon ground ginger
    Dash pepper

RINSE GOOSE; PAT DRY WITH PAPER TOWELS. Season cavity with the salt and the ⅛ teaspoon pepper. Place celery and onion in cavity. Tuck drumsticks under the band of skin across the tail. Skewer neck skin to back. Twist wing tips under back. Prick skin well.

—■—

Place goose, breast side up, on a rack in a roasting pan. Insert a meat thermometer into the thigh meat. Roast, uncovered, in a 350° oven for 2 to 2½ hours or till meat thermometer registers 180° to 185°. Remove fat occasionally during roasting. In a small saucepan melt apple jelly; stir in Worcestershire sauce. Brush goose with jelly mixture during last 20 minutes of roasting.

—■—

Meanwhile, for stuffing, place chopped mixed dried fruit in a medium saucepan; add water to just cover fruit. Bring to boiling; reduce heat. Simmer, covered, for 5 minutes. Drain fruit, reserving liquid.

—■—

In a very large bowl combine fruit with bread cubes, cranberry sauce, melted margarine or butter, cinnamon, allspice, ginger, and the dash pepper. Drizzle with enough reserved liquid (¼ to ½ cup) to moisten, tossing lightly. Transfer stuffing to a lightly greased 2-quart casserole. Add covered casserole to oven the last 30 minutes of roasting.

—■—

Discard onion and celery from goose cavity. Let goose stand, covered, for 15 minutes before carving. Serve goose with stuffing. Makes 6 to 8 servings.

PESTO-STUFFED
TURKEY BREAST

- 1 cup firmly packed torn fresh spinach
- ½ cup firmly packed fresh basil leaves or parsley sprigs with stems removed
- ½ cup grated Parmesan cheese
- ¼ cup chopped toasted walnuts
- 1 clove garlic, quartered
- ¼ teaspoon salt
- ¼ cup olive oil or cooking oil
- 1 2½- to 3-pound fresh turkey breast portion

FOR PESTO, IN A BLENDER CONTAINER OR FOOD processor bowl combine spinach, basil or parsley, Parmesan cheese, walnuts, garlic, and salt. Cover and blend or process with several on-off turns till a paste forms, stopping the appliance several times and scraping the sides. With the appliance running slowly, gradually add oil and blend or process to the consistency of soft butter. Set pesto aside.

Rinse turkey; pat dry. Remove any bone from turkey. Slip your fingers under the skin of the turkey breast to loosen skin, leaving it attached at one long edge. Spread about ⅓ cup pesto* over the meat and under the skin. Fold the skin over pesto. Secure with toothpicks. Insert a meat thermometer into the thickest portion of the turkey breast.

Place breast, stuffed side up, on a rack in a shallow roasting pan. Roast, uncovered, in a 325° oven about 1¼ hours or till meat thermometer registers 170°. Let stand 10 minutes before carving. Makes 6 to 8 servings.

*NOTE: Divide remaining pesto into 2 portions (about ⅓ cup each) and place in small airtight containers. Refrigerate for 1 to 2 days or freeze for up to 1 month.

Use one portion of the pesto for this turkey recipe, and freeze the remaining two portions for later use. Try bringing one portion of pesto to room temperature and tossing it with 2 cups of cooked pasta. Or, use pesto in soups, sauces, and dips, or with vegetables.

COUNTRY CHRISTMAS. DINNER

AT CHRISTMASTIME, SIMPLE foods adorned with festive touches grace the tables of country cooks everywhere. And only the best is good enough for family and friends. That's why this year you should try some of our country yuletide recipes. They're sure to become some of your most requested holiday dishes. ■

MENU

Turkey with Dressing ▪ *Make-Ahead Twice-Baked Sweet Potatoes*

Garlic–Mustard Green Beans ▪ *Christmas Fruit Slaw*

Cornmeal Dinner Rolls ▪ *Cranberry–Pear Mince Pie*

MAKE-AHEAD TWICE-BAKED SWEET POTATOES

8 small sweet potatoes (5 to 6 ounces each)
¼ cup maple-flavored syrup
2 tablespoons margarine or butter
¼ teaspoon salt
¼ teaspoon ground cinnamon
⅛ teaspoon ground ginger
  Dash pepper
½ cup chopped toasted pecans
2 tablespoons maple-flavored syrup

SCRUB POTATOES. PRICK POTATOES WITH A FORK. Bake in a 375° oven for 40 to 45 minutes or till tender. Let stand about 15 minutes or till cool enough to handle. Cut a small lengthwise slice from *each* potato; discard skin from slice and place pulp in a bowl. Gently scoop out each potato, leaving a ¼-inch-thick shell. Add pulp to the bowl.

■

Add the ¼ cup syrup, margarine or butter, salt, cinnamon, ginger, and pepper to potato pulp in bowl; mash. Stir in *¼ cup* of the pecans. Spoon potato mixture into potato shells. Place in a 12x7½x2-inch baking dish. Cover and chill.

■

Before serving, remove potatoes from the refrigerator and let stand for 30 minutes; uncover. Top potatoes with the remaining ¼ cup pecans and drizzle with the 2 tablespoons maple-flavored syrup. Bake, uncovered, in a 375° oven about 25 minutes or till heated through. Makes 8 servings.

■

NOTE: If you don't make these filled potatoes ahead of time, just bake them in a 375° oven about 15 minutes or till heated through.

Pictured on page 87.

TURKEY WITH DRESSING

¾ cup wild rice
1 cup brown rice
¾ cup chopped onion
1 tablespoon instant chicken bouillon granules
1 tablespoon snipped fresh marjoram or *1 teaspoon dried marjoram, crushed*
1 tablespoon snipped fresh thyme or *1 teaspoon dried thyme, crushed*
1 cup shredded carrot
½ cup thinly sliced celery
1 10- to 12-pound turkey
   Cooking oil or *melted margarine* or *butter*
   Pan Gravy

FOR DRESSING, RINSE WILD RICE IN A STRAINER under cold water about 1 minute. Combine wild rice, brown rice, onion, bouillon, marjoram, thyme, 3½ cups *water*, and ¼ teaspoon *pepper*. Bring to boiling; reduce heat. Cover; simmer 35 minutes. Stir in carrot and celery. Cook, covered, over low heat about 10 minutes more or till rice is tender. Set aside.

Rinse bird; pat dry. Season cavity with salt and pepper. Spoon dressing loosely into neck cavity. Pull neck skin to back and fasten with a small skewer. Lightly spoon stuffing into body cavity. (Place any remaining dressing in a casserole. Cover and refrigerate.) Tuck drumsticks under tail skin. (If band of skin is not present, tie legs securely to the tail with string.) Twist wing tips under the back. Place bird, breast side up, on a rack in a shallow roasting pan. Brush with oil. Insert a meat thermometer into center of an inside thigh muscle, making sure the bulb does not touch the bone. Cover bird loosely with foil.

Roast in a 325° oven for 3 to 4 hours or till thermometer registers 180° to 185°. Cut band of skin or string between legs after 2½ hours. Uncover bird and add the dressing in the covered casserole to the oven the last 45 minutes. Let bird stand, covered, for 20 minutes before carving. Reserve pan drippings for Pan Gravy. Makes 8 servings.

PAN GRAVY: Pour pan drippings from turkey into a large measuring cup. Also scrape the browned bits into the cup. Skim and reserve fat from drippings. Place ¼ cup of the fat into a medium saucepan (discard remaining fat). Stir in ¼ cup *all-purpose flour*. Add enough *chicken broth or water* to drippings in the measuring cup to equal 2 cups. Add all at once to flour mixture. Cook and stir till bubbly. Cook and stir 1 minute more. Season with ¼ teaspoon *salt* and ⅛ teaspoon *pepper*. Makes 2 cups.

Pictured on page 87.

CHRISTMAS FRUIT SLAW

3 cups coarsely chopped apple (about 3 apples)
2 cups shredded cabbage
1¼ cups halved seedless red grapes
1¼ cups sliced celery
⅔ cup chopped walnuts or pecans, toasted
½ cup snipped pitted whole dates or raisins
⅔ cup vanilla yogurt
⅛ teaspoon ground nutmeg

TOSS CHOPPED APPLE WITH CABBAGE, GRAPES, celery, walnuts or pecans, and dates or raisins. For dressing, combine vanilla yogurt and nutmeg. Pour dressing over apple mixture; toss to coat. Cover salad and chill for 2 to 24 hours. Makes 8 servings.

TIMETABLE

1 OR MORE DAYS AHEAD:
- Thaw turkey for Turkey with Dressing (see recipe, page 89) in refrigerator, if frozen. Allow 5 hours of thawing per pound.
- Prepare Cornmeal Dinner Rolls (see recipe, page 92); freeze.

1 DAY AHEAD:
- Prepare Make-Ahead Twice-Baked Sweet Potatoes (see recipe, page 88); chill.
- Prepare dressing; chill.
- Prepare Christmas Fruit Slaw (see recipe, above); cover and chill.
- Prepare Cranberry-Pear Mince Pie (see recipe, page 93).

4 HOURS AHEAD:
- Stuff turkey and place in oven.

45 MINUTES AHEAD:
- Place casserole containing dressing in oven.
- Cook fresh greens beans, if using, for Garlic-Mustard Green Beans (see recipe, opposite).
- Begin thawing rolls.

30 MINUTES AHEAD:
- Remove sweet potatoes from refrigerator.

25 MINUTES AHEAD:
- Remove turkey and casserole with dressing from oven. Turn oven temperature to 375°.
- Place sweet potatoes in oven.
- Prepare green beans.

15 MINUTES AHEAD:
- Place rolls in oven.
- Prepare Pan Gravy (see recipe, page 89).

GARLIC – MUSTARD
GREEN BEANS

3 *9-ounce packages frozen whole* or *cut green beans* or *1½ pounds green beans*
2 *slices bacon*
¾ *cup thinly sliced onion*
2 *cloves garlic, minced*
1 *tablespoon brown mustard*
½ *teaspoon lemon-pepper seasoning* or *¼ teaspoon pepper*
⅛ *teaspoon salt*

COOK FROZEN BEANS ACCORDING TO PACKAGE directions. (*Or*, if using fresh green beans, wash and trim beans. In a large saucepan cook beans, covered, in a small amount of boiling water for 20 to 25 minutes or till crisp-tender.) Drain.

Meanwhile, in a medium skillet cook bacon till crisp. Drain, reserving drippings in skillet. Crumble bacon; set aside. Cook onion and garlic in drippings over medium heat about 3 minutes or till tender. Stir in mustard, lemon-pepper seasoning or pepper, and salt. Cook about 30 seconds more. Toss onion mixture with beans. Sprinkle bacon atop beans. Makes 8 servings.

Pictured on page 87.

C O R N M E A L   D I N N E R   R O L L S

3¼ to 3¾ cups all-purpose flour
½ cup yellow cornmeal
1 package active dry yeast
¾ cup milk
⅓ cup margarine or butter
¼ cup sugar
½ teaspoon salt
2 eggs

IN A LARGE MIXING BOWL STIR TOGETHER *1 cup* of the flour, the cornmeal, and yeast. In a saucepan heat and stir milk, margarine or butter, sugar, and salt till warm (120° to 130°) and margarine almost melts. Add to flour mixture; then add eggs. Beat with an electric mixer on low-to-medium speed for 30 seconds, scraping sides of bowl constantly. Beat on high speed for 3 minutes. Using a spoon, stir in as much of the remaining flour as you can.

———■———

Turn dough out onto a lightly floured surface. Knead in enough of the remaining flour to make a moderately stiff dough that is smooth and elastic (6 to 8 minutes total). Shape into a ball. Place in a lightly greased bowl; turn once to grease surface. Cover and let rise in a warm place till double (about 1 hour).

———■———

Punch dough down. Turn dough out onto a lightly floured surface. Divide dough in fourths. Cover and let rest 10 minutes. Divide *each* fourth of dough into 5 pieces. Shape each piece into a ball.

———■———

Lightly grease a 12-inch pizza pan or a 13x9x2-inch baking pan. Place the balls on the pizza pan or in the baking pan. Cover and let rise in a warm place till nearly double (about 30 minutes).

———■———

Bake in a 375° oven for 20 to 25 minutes or till golden brown. Remove rolls from pan; cool on a wire rack. Return rolls to pan. Wrap in moisture- and vapor-proof material. Seal, label, and freeze.

———■———

To serve, remove wrapping from rolls and thaw frozen rolls in pan at room temperature for 45 minutes to 1 hour. Cover with foil. Bake in a 375° oven about 15 minutes or till warm. Makes 20.

CRANBERRY–PEAR
MINCE PIE

1   16-ounce can pear slices
      Pastry for Lattice-Top Pie
1   27- to 29-ounce jar mincemeat or 3⅓ cups *Orange Mincemeat*
        (see recipe, page 181)
½   cup cranberries, coarsely chopped
½   cup chopped pecans, toasted
1   teaspoon milk
1   teaspoon sugar

DRAIN PEARS, RESERVING ¼ CUP SYRUP. ARRANGE pear slices in the bottom of a pastry-lined 9-inch pie plate. In a mixing bowl, stir together mincemeat, cranberries, pecans, and reserved pear syrup. Spoon mincemeat mixture over pears in pie plate. Trim bottom pastry to ½ inch beyond edge of pie plate. Top with lattice crust. Seal and flute edge. Brush lattice with milk and sprinkle with sugar. To prevent overbrowning, cover edge of pie with foil.

—■—

Bake in a 375° oven for 25 minutes. Remove the foil. Bake for 25 to 30 minutes more or till pastry is golden brown. Cool on a wire rack. Makes 8 servings.

PASTRY FOR LATTICE-TOP PIE: Prepare Pastry for 9-Inch Double-Crust Pie as directed on page 51, *except* after rolling top crust, cut pastry into ½-inch-wide strips. Transfer desired filling to pastry-lined pie plate. Trim bottom pastry to ½ inch beyond edge of plate. Weave strips on top of filling to make a lattice. Press ends of strips into rim of bottom crust. Fold edge of bottom pastry over strips; seal and flute edge. Bake as directed.

Pictured on page 87.

CHAPTER FOUR

KETTLES OF SOUPS AND STEWS

WHEN THE WINTER WINDS HOWL and the snow swirls, sit down to a comforting country supper of soul-warming soup or stew. Whether it's a thick, creamy vegetable bisque, a potful of bubbling bean soup, or a stew jam packed with meat and vegetables, these cozy and uncomplicated recipes promise to satisfy even the biggest of appetites. So get out the soup spoon– you're in for some mighty good eatin'.■

Long served at political rallies in the South, burgoo is a dish of which no two recipes are alike. Country cooks use whatever poultry, meat, and vegetables they have on hand in this spicy stew.

KENTUCKY BURGOO

4 cups water
1 16-ounce can tomatoes, cut up
¾ pound boneless beef chuck roast, cut into ¾-inch cubes
2 teaspoons instant chicken bouillon granules
1 pound meaty chicken pieces (breasts, thighs, and drumsticks), skinned if desired
2 cups cubed, peeled potatoes (about 3 medium potatoes)
1 10-ounce package frozen succotash
1 10-ounce package frozen cut okra
1 cup sliced carrots (about 2 carrots)
½ cup chopped onion
2 teaspoons curry powder
1 teaspoon sugar

IN A 4½-QUART DUTCH OVEN COMBINE THE water, *undrained* tomatoes, beef, and chicken bouillon granules. Bring to boiling; reduce heat. Cover and simmer for 30 minutes. Add chicken pieces. Return to boiling; reduce heat. Simmer, covered, about 45 minutes more or till beef and chicken are tender. Remove chicken pieces and set aside.

—■—

Stir potatoes, succotash, okra, carrots, onion, curry powder, and sugar into mixture in Dutch oven. Return to boiling; reduce heat. Simmer, covered, about 20 minutes or till vegetables are tender.

—■—

Meanwhile, when chicken is cool enough to handle, remove meat from bones; discard skin, if any, and bones. Cut the chicken into bite-size pieces. Add chicken pieces to Dutch oven. Cook about 5 minutes more or till the chicken is heated through. Makes 5 to 6 main-dish servings.

BEEF AND WILD RICE SOUP

¾   pound beef stew meat, cut into ½-inch cubes
  1   tablespoon cooking oil
  2   14½-ounce cans (3½ cups) beef broth
  1   cup sliced carrots (about 2 carrots)
½   cup sliced celery (about 1 stalk)
⅓   cup wild rice
⅓   cup sliced leek (about 1 leek) or ⅓ cup sliced green onion
        (about 5 green onions)
1½   teaspoons snipped fresh thyme or ½ teaspoon dried thyme, crushed
¼   teaspoon pepper
  1   bay leaf
½   cup water
  2   tablespoons all-purpose flour
  1   cup sliced fresh mushrooms
  2   tablespoons dry sherry (optional)

IN A LARGE SAUCEPAN OR DUTCH OVEN BROWN beef cubes in hot oil; drain fat. Add broth. Bring to boiling; reduce heat. Cover and simmer for 45 minutes. Stir in carrots, celery, *uncooked* rice, leek or green onion, thyme, pepper, and bay leaf. Return to boiling; reduce heat. Simmer, covered, about 40 minutes or till beef and rice are tender.

In a small bowl stir together the water and flour; stir into beef mixture along with mushrooms. Cook and stir till thickened and bubbly. Cook and stir 1 minute more. If desired, stir in sherry. Heat through. Remove bay leaf. Makes 4 main-dish servings.

Wild rice was the staple food of Indians in Minnesota and Wisconsin, and later of pioneers who liked to serve it in soup.

TOMATO-DILL BISQUE

Some experts credit President Thomas Jefferson, who was famous for his gardens, for using the tomato long before it was popular with the general public. One of the ways Jefferson used his garden tomatoes was to make soups like this one.

½ cup coarsely chopped onion
2 cloves garlic, minced
2 tablespoons margarine or butter
2 cups chopped, peeled tomatoes or one 14½-ounce can
    whole, peeled tomatoes, cut up
1½ cups chicken broth
1 8-ounce can tomato sauce
1 tablespoon snipped fresh dill or 1 teaspoon dried dillweed
    Dash pepper
¼ cup dairy sour cream
    Fresh dill (optional)

IN A LARGE SAUCEPAN COOK ONION AND GARLIC IN margarine or butter till tender but not brown. Stir in fresh tomatoes or *undrained* canned tomatoes, chicken broth, tomato sauce, dill, and pepper. Bring to boiling; reduce heat. Simmer, covered, for 30 minutes. Cool vegetable mixture slightly.

Place mixture, half at a time, in a blender container or food processor bowl. Cover and blend or process till smooth. (*Or*, press mixture through a food mill.) Return mixture to the saucepan; heat through. Serve with sour cream and, if desired, garnish with fresh dill. Makes 4 side-dish servings.

POTATO SOUP

During hard times, many immigrants, especially the Irish, depended on hearty soups.

2 cups cubed, peeled potatoes (about 3 medium potatoes)
⅔ cup water
½ cup finely chopped onion
1 tablespoon snipped fresh marjoram or 1 teaspoon dried marjoram, crushed
2 teaspoons instant chicken bouillon granules
⅛ teaspoon pepper
2 cups milk
2 tablespoons all-purpose flour
3 slices bacon, crisp-cooked, drained, and crumbled
1 tablespoon snipped parsley

IN A LARGE SAUCEPAN COMBINE THE CUBED potatoes, water, onion, marjoram, bouillon granules, and pepper. Bring to boiling; reduce heat. Simmer, uncovered, about 20 minutes or till the potatoes are tender. Mash potatoes slightly, but *do not drain.*

In a screw-top jar combine *½ cup* of the milk and the flour. Cover and shake well.

Stir milk mixture into potato mixture along with the remaining milk. Cook and stir till thickened and bubbly. Cook and stir 1 minute more. Stir in bacon and parsley. Serve immediately. Makes 4 to 6 side-dish servings.

POTATO–CHEESE SOUP: Prepare Potato Soup, *except* increase milk to *2¼ cups* and stir ¾ cup shredded *cheddar or Swiss cheese* (3 ounces) into the soup along with the milk. Cook and stir till cheese melts.

GREEN CHILI AND
CORN CHOWDER

½ cup chopped celery
⅓ cup chopped onion
2 cloves garlic, minced
¼ teaspoon ground cumin
¼ teaspoon dried oregano or dried marjoram, crushed
1 tablespoon cooking oil
1 14½-ounce can chicken broth
1 8¾-ounce can cream-style corn
½ cup chopped red sweet pepper
1 4-ounce can diced green chili peppers, drained
1 cup milk
2 tablespoons all-purpose flour
1 cup shredded cheddar, Monterey Jack, or American cheese (4 ounces)

IN A LARGE SAUCEPAN COOK CELERY, ONION, garlic, cumin, and oregano or marjoram in hot oil till onion is tender but not brown. Stir in chicken broth, corn, red sweet pepper, and green chili peppers. Bring to boiling; reduce heat. Simmer, covered, for 5 minutes.

In a small bowl combine milk and flour; stir into corn mixture. Cook and stir till thickened and bubbly. Add cheese; cook and stir till cheese melts. Makes 4 to 6 side-dish servings.

Chowder was a creation of the sailors and fishermen who explored the New World. Early Americans adopted the thick, hearty soup and put their own stamp on it by using native ingredients, such as corn. Green chilies are added to this corn chowder for extra flavor.

CHEESY VEGETABLE CHOWDER

Early Americans dressed up their soups with toppings, such as toasted bread shapes, chives, and dollops of whipped cream or dairy sour cream. We've followed their example by adding croutons to this chowder.

1 14½-ounce can chicken broth
1 tablespoon Worcestershire sauce
1 tablespoon snipped fresh basil or *1 teaspoon dried basil, crushed*
1 tablespoon snipped fresh thyme or *1 teaspoon dried thyme, crushed*
   Dash pepper
1 cup sliced carrots (about 2 carrots)
¼ cup chopped onion
2 cups broccoli flowerets (about ½ pound broccoli)
3 cups milk
¼ cup all-purpose flour
1½ cups shredded cheddar, Colby, or Monterey Jack cheese (6 ounces)
1 large tomato, seeded and chopped (1 cup)
   Croutons (optional)

IN A MEDIUM SAUCEPAN COMBINE BROTH, Worcestershire sauce, basil, thyme, and pepper. Bring to boiling. Stir in carrots and onion. Return to boiling; reduce heat. Cover and simmer for 15 minutes. Stir in broccoli. Return to boiling; reduce heat. Simmer, covered, for 6 to 7 minutes more or till vegetables are tender.

———■———

Meanwhile, in a small bowl combine milk and flour; stir into vegetable mixture. Cook and stir till thickened and bubbly. Cook and stir 1 minute more. Add cheese; cook and stir till cheese melts. Stir in tomato and heat through. If desired, serve with croutons. Makes 6 side-dish servings.

CIOPPINO

8   fresh or *frozen clams in shells*
8   ounces fresh or *frozen fish fillets (red snapper, perch, sea bass,* or *halibut)*
8   ounces fresh or *frozen peeled and deveined shrimp*
½   *cup sliced fresh mushrooms*
⅓   *cup chopped green* or *red sweet pepper*
¼   *cup chopped onion*
2   *cloves garlic, minced*
1   *tablespoon olive oil* or *cooking oil*
1   *16-ounce can tomatoes, cut up*
⅓   *cup dry red* or *white wine*
¼   *cup water*
2   *tablespoons snipped parsley*
2   *tablespoons tomato paste*
1   *tablespoon lemon juice*
1½ *teaspoons snipped fresh basil* or ½ *teaspoon dried basil, crushed*
1½ *teaspoons snipped fresh oregano* or ½ *teaspoon dried oregano, crushed*
1   *teaspoon sugar*
¼   *teaspoon salt*
⅛   *teaspoon crushed red pepper*

THAW CLAMS, IF FROZEN. SCRUB CLAMSHELLS under cold running water, using a stiff brush. Combine 8 cups *water* and 3 tablespoons *salt.* Add clams; soak 15 minutes. Drain and rinse. Discard water. Repeat the soaking, draining, and rinsing steps twice more.

——■——

Partially thaw fish and shrimp, if frozen. Remove and discard fish skin, if present. Cut fish into 1½-inch pieces; set aside. Cover and refrigerate fish pieces and shrimp till needed.

——■——

In a large saucepan cook mushrooms, green or red sweet pepper, onion, and garlic in hot oil till tender but not brown. Stir in *undrained* tomatoes, wine, water, parsley, tomato paste, lemon juice, basil, oregano, sugar, salt, and crushed red pepper. Bring to boiling; reduce heat. Simmer, covered, for 20 minutes. Add clams, fish pieces, and shrimp. Simmer, covered, for 5 to 10 minutes or till clams open, fish flakes easily, and shrimp are opaque. Discard any unopened clams. Makes 4 main-dish servings.

Although it has an Italian name and Italian ingredients, Cioppino (chuh PEA no) has American roots. The fish stew originated with the Italian immigrants of San Francisco in the 1930s, and is still popular at many of that city's restaurants.

LENTIL, BARLEY, AND HAM SOUP

During World War I when food supplies were limited, First Lady Edith Wilson came up with this combination of dried lentils and barley.

½ cup dry lentils
¾ cup chopped onion
½ cup chopped celery
1 clove garlic, minced
2 tablespoons margarine or butter
5 cups water
1½ teaspoons snipped fresh oregano or ½ teaspoon dried oregano, crushed
1½ teaspoons snipped fresh basil or ½ teaspoon dried basil, crushed
1 teaspoon instant chicken bouillon granules
¾ teaspoon snipped fresh rosemary or ¼ teaspoon dried rosemary, crushed
¼ teaspoon pepper
1½ cups diced fully cooked ham
1 cup thinly sliced carrots (about 2 carrots)
½ cup quick-cooking barley
1 16-ounce can tomatoes, cut up

RINSE AND DRAIN LENTILS; SET ASIDE. IN A LARGE saucepan cook the onion, celery, and garlic in margarine or butter till tender but not brown. Stir in the lentils, water, oregano, basil, bouillon granules, rosemary, and pepper. Bring to boiling; reduce heat. Simmer, covered, for 30 minutes.

Stir in the ham, carrots, and *uncooked* barley. Simmer, covered, about 20 minutes more or just till carrots are tender. Stir in the *undrained* tomatoes. Heat through. Makes 4 main-dish servings.

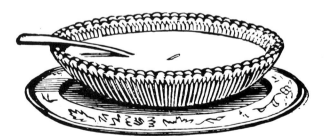

HAM AND BEAN SOUP

This soup is similar to one served every day in the United States Senate dining room. We added chopped spinach to our version.

  1 *cup dry navy beans*
  4 *cups water*
  1 *to 1½ pounds meaty smoked pork hocks or one 1- to 1½-pound*
       meaty ham bone
  1 *cup chopped onion*
 ½ *cup sliced celery*
  1 *tablespoon snipped fresh thyme or 1 teaspoon dried thyme, crushed*
 ¼ *teaspoon salt*
 ¼ *teaspoon pepper*
  2 *cups chopped, peeled rutabaga (about 1 rutabaga) or chopped, peeled potatoes*
       (about 3 potatoes)
  1 *cup sliced carrots (about 2 carrots)*
  1 *10-ounce package frozen chopped spinach, thawed and well drained*

RINSE AND DRAIN NAVY BEANS. IN A LARGE saucepan combine navy beans and the water. Bring to boiling; reduce heat. Simmer for 2 minutes. Remove from heat. Cover and let stand 1 hour. (*Or,* skip boiling the beans and soak beans overnight in a covered pan.) Drain and rinse beans.

— ■ —

In the same pan combine the navy beans, 4 cups *fresh water,* pork hocks or ham bone, onion, celery, thyme, salt, and pepper. Bring to boiling; reduce heat. Cover and simmer about 1 hour or till beans are nearly tender. Stir in rutabaga or potatoes and carrots. Return to boiling; reduce heat. Cover and simmer about 20 minutes more or till vegetables are tender. Remove pork hocks or ham bone from saucepan.

— ■ —

When cool enough to handle, cut meat off bones. Coarsely chop meat and discard the bones. Slightly mash beans and vegetables in saucepan. Return meat to saucepan; add spinach. Cook till heated through. Makes 4 to 5 main-dish servings.

CHICKEN AND HAM GUMBO

⅓ cup all-purpose flour
¼ cup cooking oil
½ cup chopped onion
¼ cup chopped celery
¼ cup chopped red or green sweet pepper
4 cloves garlic, minced
1½ teaspoons snipped fresh thyme or ½ teaspoon dried thyme, crushed
¼ teaspoon black pepper
¼ teaspoon ground red pepper
2½ cups chicken broth, heated
2 cups cubed fully-cooked ham
1½ cups chopped, peeled tomatoes (about 2 tomatoes)
4 chicken thighs (about 1⅓ pounds), skinned if desired
1½ cups sliced fresh okra (6 ounces) or one 10-ounce package frozen cut okra, thawed
2 cups hot cooked rice
2 tablespoons snipped parsley

FOR ROUX, IN A HEAVY LARGE SAUCEPAN OR Dutch oven combine flour and oil till smooth. Cook over medium-high heat for 5 minutes, stirring constantly. Reduce heat to medium-low. Cook and stir about 15 minutes more or till roux is reddish brown (similar to the color of a tarnished copper penny).

— ■ —

Stir in onion, celery, red or green sweet pepper, garlic, thyme, black pepper, and ground red pepper. Cook over medium heat for 3 to 5 minutes or till vegetables are just crisp-tender, stirring often.

— ■ —

Gradually stir in *hot* chicken broth, ham, tomatoes, and chicken thighs. Bring to boiling; reduce heat. Cover and simmer for 30 minutes. Stir in okra. Return to boiling; reduce heat. Cover and simmer for 15 to 20 minutes more or till okra and chicken are tender.

— ■ —

Remove chicken. When chicken is cool enough to handle, remove meat from bones; discard skin, if any, and bones. Cut the chicken into bite-size pieces and return to saucepan. Cook till heated through. Serve over rice. Sprinkle with parsley. Makes 4 main-dish servings.

Gumbo is a dish that reflects the influence of American Indian, Creole, Spanish, and African cultures on the South. The hearty soup or stew usually contains okra and any of a variety of meats, seafood, and vegetables.

CHAPTER FIVE

BREAKFAST ON THE FARM

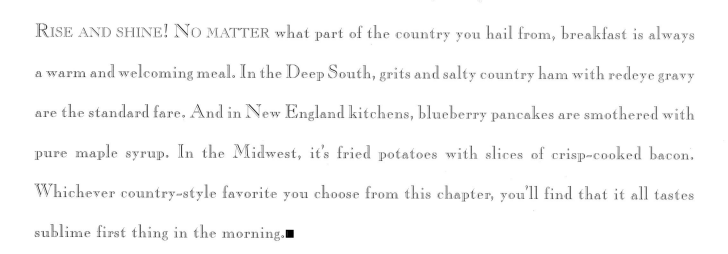

RISE AND SHINE! NO MATTER what part of the country you hail from, breakfast is always a warm and welcoming meal. In the Deep South, grits and salty country ham with redeye gravy are the standard fare. And in New England kitchens, blueberry pancakes are smothered with pure maple syrup. In the Midwest, it's fried potatoes with slices of crisp-cooked bacon. Whichever country-style favorite you choose from this chapter, you'll find that it all tastes sublime first thing in the morning.■

BLUEBERRY–BUTTERMILK HOTCAKES

The name pancake didn't become common until the late 1800s. Before that, these delicious cakes were called flapjacks, buckwheat cakes, griddle cakes, hotcakes, flannel cakes, hoecakes, or slapjacks.

Pictured on page 109.

1 cup all-purpose flour
2 tablespoons yellow cornmeal
1 tablespoon sugar
1 teaspoon baking powder
½ teaspoon baking soda
¼ teaspoon salt
¼ teaspoon ground cinnamon
1 beaten egg
1 cup buttermilk or *sour milk (see tip, page 188)*
2 tablespoons cooking oil
1 cup fresh or *frozen blueberries*
  Maple syrup, maple-flavored syrup, or *sifted powdered sugar (optional)*

FOR BATTER, IN A LARGE MIXING BOWL STIR together flour, cornmeal, sugar, baking powder, baking soda, salt, and cinnamon.

—■—

In a small mixing bowl stir together egg, buttermilk or sour milk, and cooking oil. Add to flour mixture all at once. Stir mixture just till combined but still slightly lumpy. Gently fold blueberries into batter.

—■—

For each pancake, pour about ¼ *cup* batter onto a hot, lightly greased griddle or heavy skillet. Cook over medium heat about 2 minutes on each side or till pancakes are golden brown, turning to second sides when pancakes have bubbly surfaces and edges are slightly dry.

—■—

Serve warm. If desired, serve with syrup or powdered sugar. Makes 8 to 10 pancakes.

GERMAN APPLE PANCAKE

2 tablespoons margarine or butter
3 eggs
½ cup milk
2 tablespoons cooking oil
¼ cup all-purpose flour
¼ cup whole wheat flour
½ teaspoon apple pie spice
¼ teaspoon salt
2 tablespoons brown sugar
2 teaspoons cornstarch
½ teaspoon apple pie spice
½ cup apple cider or apple juice
1 tablespoon lemon juice
2 medium cooking apples, cored and thinly sliced
½ of an 8-ounce package (5 links) brown-and-serve sausage links, thinly sliced
1 tablespoon margarine or butter
¼ cup broken walnuts, toasted (optional)

PLACE THE 2 TABLESPOONS MARGARINE OR BUTTER in a 10-inch ovenproof skillet. Place the skillet in a cold oven, then turn oven to 400°.

———■———

Meanwhile, for batter, in a medium mixing bowl combine eggs, milk, and cooking oil. Beat with a wire whisk or rotary beater till combined. Add all-purpose flour, whole wheat flour, ½ teaspoon apple pie spice, and salt. Beat till mixture is smooth.

———■———

Remove skillet from the oven and *immediately* pour batter into the skillet. Return skillet to the oven and bake for 15 minutes. Prick the pancake with tines of a fork and bake about 10 minutes more or till very firm.

———■———

Meanwhile, for sauce, in a medium saucepan combine brown sugar, cornstarch, and ½ teaspoon apple pie spice. Add apple cider or juice and lemon juice. Cook and stir till thickened and bubbly. Add apple slices. Cook and stir gently, uncovered, for 2 to 3 minutes or till apples are just tender. Stir in sliced sausage links and the 1 tablespoon margarine or butter. If desired, stir in nuts. Cook till heated through.

———■———

To serve, transfer pancake to a warm serving plate. Spoon apple-sausage sauce onto top center of pancake. Cut into wedges. Serve at once. Makes 4 servings.

This large puffy pancake is easy to cook—pop it into the oven and forget it until the timer rings. Then, top it with the spicy apple-sausage sauce or just sprinkle the pancake with powdered sugar.

HONEY–WHEAT WAFFLES

1 cup all-purpose flour
1 cup whole wheat flour
1 tablespoon baking powder
½ teaspoon ground cinnamon
¼ teaspoon salt
2 egg yolks
1½ cups milk
½ cup cooking oil
¼ cup honey
2 egg whites
Maple syrup or maple-flavored syrup (optional)

Electric waffle bakers weren't invented until the 1930s. However, waffles were made for centuries before that, using long-handled gridded irons. The irons were heated in coals and then placed on a wooden block. Waffles were cooked while the iron was on the board, not in the coals. Later, cast-iron waffle bakers were developed to cook waffles on top of the cookstove.

FOR BATTER, IN A LARGE MIXING BOWL COMBINE all-purpose flour, whole wheat flour, baking powder, cinnamon, and salt. In a medium bowl beat egg yolks slightly; stir in milk, oil, and honey. Add egg yolk mixture to dry ingredients all at once. Stir just till combined but still slightly lumpy.

———■———

In a small bowl beat egg whites till stiff peaks form (tips stand straight). Gently fold beaten egg whites into batter, leaving a few fluffs of egg white in the batter. *Do not overmix.*

———■———

Pour batter onto grids of a preheated, lightly greased waffle baker according to the manufacturer's directions. Close lid quickly; do not open during baking. Bake according to the manufacturer's directions. When done, use a fork to lift waffle off the grid.*

———■———

Repeat with remaining batter. If desired, serve waffles with syrup. Makes six 8-inch waffles.

———■———

*NOTE: To keep waffles warm, place them in a single layer on a wire rack. Set the rack on a baking sheet and place it in a 300° oven.

CHOCOLATE-PISTACHIO-STUFFED FRENCH TOAST

6 1½-inch-thick slices French bread
1 1- to 1.6-ounce milk chocolate bar
2 tablespoons chopped pistachio nuts
4 beaten eggs
1 cup milk
¼ cup coffee liqueur
½ teaspoon ground cinnamon
   Margarine, butter, or cooking oil
   Maple syrup, maple-flavored syrup,
     or sifted powdered sugar (optional)

CUT A POCKET IN EACH SLICE OF BREAD BY starting from the bottom crust and cutting horizontally to, but not through, the top crust. Break the candy bar into 6 pieces. Fill *each* bread pocket with *one* piece of candy and *1 teaspoon* of the chopped nuts. Set aside.

———■———

In a shallow bowl beat together eggs, milk, coffee liqueur, and cinnamon. Dip bread into egg mixture, letting bread remain in egg mixture about 15 seconds on each side.

———■———

In a hot skillet or on a hot griddle cook French bread in a small amount of margarine, butter, or oil over medium heat for 3 to 4 minutes on each side or till golden brown. Add additional margarine, butter, or oil as needed.

———■———

Serve warm. If desired, serve with syrup or sprinkle with powdered sugar. Makes 6 slices.

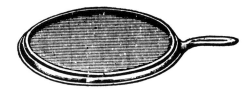

In Louisiana, French toast is known as pain perdu *or "lost bread." It got this name because French toast is usually made with day-old or stale bread—bread that would be "lost" if not converted into this breakfast classic.*

CAJUN-STYLE
EGGS BENEDICT

Although eggs Benedict was created in New York City, it fits the criteria for a great country breakfast: it's hearty and uses farm-fresh ingredients. In Cajun-Style Eggs Benedict, a flavor-packed tomato sauce is substituted for the hollandaise sauce used in the traditional recipe.

Cajun Sauce
2 *English muffins, split*
8 *slices Canadian-style bacon*
4 *eggs*
Lemon slices (optional)
Parsley sprigs (optional)

PREPARE CAJUN SAUCE; KEEP WARM. PLACE English muffin halves and Canadian-style bacon on a baking sheet in a single layer. Bake in a 350° oven for 10 to 15 minutes or till muffins are toasted and bacon is hot.

—■—

Meanwhile, to poach eggs, half-fill a 2-quart saucepan with water. Bring water to boiling. Reduce heat till water simmers (bubbles should begin to break the surface of the water).

—■—

Break *one* egg into a measuring cup. Carefully slide egg into simmering water, holding the lip of the cup as close to the water as possible. Repeat with remaining eggs, allowing each egg an equal amount of space. Simmer eggs, uncovered, for 5 minutes. Remove from water with a slotted spoon.

—■—

To serve, top *each* muffin half with *two* slices of bacon and an egg. Spoon Cajun Sauce over eggs. If desired, garnish with lemon slices and parsley. Makes 4 servings.

CAJUN SAUCE: In a heavy 2-quart saucepan stir together 2 tablespoons *all-purpose flour* and 2 tablespoons *cooking oil.* Cook and stir constantly over medium-high heat for 5 minutes. Reduce heat to medium. Cook and stir constantly about 5 minutes more or till mixture is reddish brown. Carefully add ½ cup chopped *onion,* ½ cup chopped *celery,* and ½ cup chopped *green or yellow sweet pepper.* Cook and stir for 5 minutes. Carefully stir in one 8-ounce can *undrained tomatoes,* cut up; ½ cup *water;* 2 tablespoons *tomato paste;* 1 *bay leaf;* and several dashes bottled *hot pepper sauce.* Bring to boiling; reduce heat. Simmer, uncovered, for 15 minutes. Stir in 2 tablespoons *dry white wine,* 1 tablespoon snipped *parsley,* and 1 teaspoon *lemon juice.* Discard bay leaf before serving. Makes about 2 cups.

Cajun-Style Eggs Benedict

Rustic Home-Fried Potatoes
(see recipe, page 117)

Redeye gravy gets its name from the crusty bits of ham and the meat drippings in the gravy that form tiny red circles or "eyes."

COUNTRY HAM WITH REDEYE GRAVY

2 8-ounce slices country-style ham, cut ¼ inch thick
2 tablespoons brown sugar
½ cup strong black coffee

IN THE REFRIGERATOR, SOAK HAM IN WATER FOR several hours or overnight. Drain; pat dry with paper towels.

Trim fat from ham slices. In a large skillet cook fat trimmings over medium-low heat for 6 to 8 minutes or till crisp. Discard trimmings; reserve *2 tablespoons* drippings in the skillet. Add ham slices to the skillet. Cook over medium heat for 9 to 12 minutes on each side or till brown. Remove ham slices from the skillet, reserving drippings in the skillet. Keep ham warm.

For gravy, stir brown sugar into drippings. Cook over medium heat till sugar dissolves, stirring constantly. Stir in coffee. Boil for 2 to 3 minutes or till gravy is slightly thickened and a rich, reddish brown color, scraping the skillet to loosen any crusty bits. Serve gravy over ham slices. Makes 4 servings.

A southern breakfast isn't complete unless there are grits on the plate. Grits can be served either as a side dish or as part of a main dish, such as Cheddar Grits and Sausage Bake.

CHEDDAR GRITS AND SAUSAGE BAKE

½ pound medium or *hot* bulk pork sausage
1¾ cups water
½ cup quick-cooking grits
1½ cups shredded cheddar or *American cheese (6 ounces)*
1 beaten egg
½ cup milk
3 tablespoons snipped parsley
⅛ teaspoon pepper

COOK SAUSAGE TILL NO LONGER PINK; DRAIN WELL. Meanwhile, in a large saucepan bring water to boiling. Slowly add grits, stirring constantly. Cook and stir till boiling; reduce heat. Cover and simmer about 5 minutes or till water is absorbed and mixture is thick, stirring occasionally. Add *1 cup* of the cheese, stirring till cheese melts. Remove pan from the heat.

In a small mixing bowl stir together egg and milk. Stir into grits. Stir in sausage, parsley, and pepper. Pour mixture into a greased 8x1½-inch round baking dish.

Bake in a 350° oven for 25 to 30 minutes or till a knife inserted near the center comes out clean. Sprinkle with the remaining cheese. Let stand 5 minutes before serving. Serves 4.

RUSTIC HOME-FRIED POTATOES

2 tablespoons margarine or butter
3 medium potatoes, thinly sliced (about 1 pound)
1 medium sweet onion, halved and thinly sliced
2 cloves garlic, minced
2 tablespoons snipped parsley
1 tablespoon snipped fresh rosemary or 1 teaspoon dried rosemary, crushed
¼ teaspoon salt
⅛ teaspoon ground red pepper
⅛ teaspoon black pepper

IN A LARGE SKILLET MELT MARGARINE OR BUTTER. (Add more margarine or butter as necessary during cooking.) Layer the sliced potatoes, onion, and garlic in the skillet. Sprinkle with parsley, rosemary, salt, ground red pepper, and black pepper.

Cook potato mixture, covered, over medium heat for 8 minutes.

Continue cooking, uncovered, for 8 to 10 minutes more or till potatoes are tender and brown, turning frequently. Makes 4 servings.

Because it's for a morning meal, a sweet onion is preferred in Rustic Home-Fried Potatoes. Sweet onion varieties include Vidalia, Walla Walla, Texas Sweet Spring, Maui, and Imperial Sweet.

Pictured on page 115.

CHAPTER SIX

OUR DAILY BREAD

WHETHER IT'S A HEARTY LOAF of yeast bread, a quick-to-mix coffee cake, of a soft, souffle- like spoon bread, nothing quite compares to the irresistible aroma of fresh-from-the-oven bread as it spills from a country kitchen. These tempting breads will be a hit whether you spread them with creamy butter, top them with chunky preserves, or use them to sop up gravy. ■

SWEET-POTATO–WHEAT TWIST

1¼ cups water
1 cup chopped peeled sweet potato (1 medium)
1 cup buttermilk or sour milk (see tip, page 188)
2 tablespoons shortening, margarine, or butter
2 tablespoons honey
2 teaspoons salt
4¾ to 5½ cups all-purpose flour
2 packages active dry yeast
1 egg
1½ cups whole wheat flour

IN A MEDIUM SAUCEPAN COMBINE WATER AND chopped sweet potato. Bring to boiling; reduce heat. Cover and simmer about 12 minutes or till very tender. *Do not drain.* Mash potato in the water. Measure potato-water mixture and, if necessary, add water to equal 1½ cups.

Return potato mixture to the saucepan. Add buttermilk, shortening, honey, and salt. Heat or cool, as necessary, and stir till warm (120° to 130°). In a large mixing bowl stir together *2 cups* of the all-purpose flour and the yeast. Add potato mixture and egg. Beat with an electric mixer on low speed for 30 seconds, scraping the sides of the bowl constantly. Beat on high speed for 3 minutes. Divide the batter in half.

To *half* of the batter, using a spoon, stir in the whole wheat flour and as much of the remaining all-purpose flour as you can (about ½ cup). Turn out onto a lightly floured surface. Knead in enough of the remaining flour (¼ to ½ cup) to make a moderately stiff dough that is smooth and elastic (6 to 8 minutes total). Shape into a ball. Place in a lightly greased bowl; turn once to grease surface. Cover and let rise in a warm place till double (about 45 minutes).

To the remaining batter, using a spoon, stir in as much of the remaining all-purpose flour as you can (about 2 cups). Turn out onto a lightly floured surface. Knead in enough of the remaining flour (¼ to ½ cup) to make a moderately stiff dough that is smooth and elastic (6 to 8 minutes total). Shape into a ball. Place in a lightly greased bowl; turn once to grease surface. Cover and let rise in a warm place till double (about 45 minutes).

Punch *each* ball of dough down and turn out onto a lightly floured surface. Divide *each* ball of dough in half. Cover and let rest for 10 minutes. Lightly grease two 9x5x3-inch loaf pans; set aside.

Roll each portion of dough into an evenly thick 10-inch-long rope. Loosely twist one plain and one whole wheat rope together; press ends together to seal. Place in one of the prepared loaf pans. Repeat with remaining two ropes. Cover and let rise in a warm place till nearly double (30 to 40 minutes).

Bake in a 375° oven about 40 minutes or till breads sound hollow when lightly tapped. If necessary, loosely cover bread with foil the last 10 minutes to prevent overbrowning. Remove from pans immediately. Cool on wire racks. Makes 2 loaves (32 servings).

ANADAMA BREAD

½ cup cornmeal
⅓ cup packed brown sugar
1 teaspoon salt
1 cup boiling water
⅓ cup cooking oil
4½ to 5 cups all-purpose flour
1 package active dry yeast
1 8¾-ounce can cream-style corn

IN A MEDIUM BOWL STIR TOGETHER THE cornmeal, brown sugar, and salt. Stir in the boiling water and oil. Cool mixture till warm (120° to 130°), stirring occasionally. (Allow mixture to cool 15 to 20 minutes.)

◼

In a large mixing bowl stir together *1 cup* of the flour and the yeast. Add cornmeal mixture and corn. Beat with an electric mixer on low speed for 30 seconds, scraping the sides of the bowl constantly. Beat on high speed for 3 minutes. Using a spoon, stir in as much of the remaining flour as you can. Turn out onto a lightly floured surface. Knead in enough of the remaining flour to make a moderately stiff dough that is smooth and elastic (6 to 8 minutes total).

◼

Shape dough into a ball. Place in a lightly greased bowl; turn once to grease surface. Cover and let rise in a warm place till double (about 1 hour).

◼

Punch dough down. Turn out onto a lightly floured surface. Divide dough in half. Cover and let rest for 10 minutes. Lightly grease two 1-quart casseroles or a large baking sheet.

◼

Shape each half of the dough into a round loaf. Place loaves in prepared casseroles or 3 inches apart on the baking sheet. Cover and let rise in a warm place till nearly double (about 40 minutes). Bake in a 375° oven about 40 minutes or till bread sounds hollow when lightly tapped. If necessary, loosely cover the bread with foil the last 20 minutes to prevent overbrowning. Remove from casseroles or baking sheet immediately. Cool on wire racks. Makes 2 loaves (32 servings).

COLONIAL THREE-GRAIN BREAD: Prepare Anadama Bread, *except* omit the cream-style corn, reduce the all-purpose flour to *1¾ to 2¼ cups*, and add ½ cup *whole wheat flour* and ½ cup *rye flour* with the stirred-in all-purpose flour. Reduce baking time to *30 minutes*. Makes 2 loaves (24 servings.)

Legend says Anadama bread was developed by a New England fisherman because his wife, Anna, was too lazy to bake bread. His bread supposedly got its name from his mumbling, "Anna, damn her."

DOUBLE-CHOCOLATE–PECAN
COFFEE CAKE

3 to 3½ cups all-purpose flour
1 package active dry yeast
⅔ cup milk
¼ cup sugar
¼ cup margarine or butter
½ teaspoon salt
2 eggs
½ cup semisweet chocolate pieces
2 tablespoons margarine or butter
1 cup chopped pecans
4 teaspoons margarine or butter

IN A LARGE MIXING BOWL STIR TOGETHER
1½ cups of the flour and the yeast. In a small saucepan heat and stir milk, sugar, the ¼ cup margarine or butter, and salt till warm (120° to 130°) and margarine almost melts. Add to flour mixture; add eggs. Beat with an electric mixer on low speed for 30 seconds, scraping the sides of the bowl constantly. Beat on high for 3 minutes. Using a spoon, stir in as much of the remain-ing flour as you can.

Turn out onto a lightly floured surface. Knead in enough of the remaining flour to make a moderately soft dough that is smooth and elastic (3 to 5 minutes total). Shape into a ball. Place in a lightly greased bowl; turn once to grease surface. Cover and let rise in a warm place till double (about 1¼ hours).

Punch dough down and turn out onto a lightly floured surface. Cover and let rest 10 minutes. Lightly grease a 10-inch fluted tube pan.

In a saucepan combine ¼ cup of the chocolate pieces and the 2 tablespoons margarine or butter. Cook over low heat till chocolate melts, stirring constantly. Set aside.

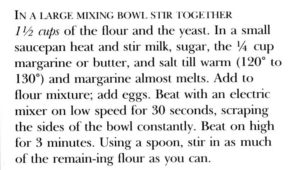

Roll dough into a 16x8-inch rectangle. Spread melted chocolate mixture over dough; sprinkle with nuts. Roll up from one of the long sides; moisten edge with water and pinch to seal seam well. Cut dough into 16 rolls. Stand 10 of the rolls in the prepared pan with cut edges toward outside of the pan. Stand remaining rolls around inside tube of pan. Cover and let rise in a warm place till nearly double (about 30 minutes).

Bake in a 375° oven for 30 to 35 minutes or till coffee cake sounds hollow when lightly tapped. If necessary, loosely cover coffee cake with foil the last 15 minutes of baking to prevent overbrowning. Invert the coffee cake onto a serving plate.

In a small saucepan combine the remaining chocolate pieces and the 4 teaspoons margarine or butter. Cook and stir over low heat till chocolate melts. Drizzle chocolate mixture over coffee cake. Serve warm. Makes 1 coffee cake (16 servings).

ORANGE–CINNAMON ROLLS

4 to 4½ cups all-purpose flour
1 package active dry yeast
½ cup milk
⅓ cup sugar
⅓ cup margarine or butter
2 eggs
2 teaspoons finely shredded orange peel
   (optional)
½ cup orange juice
⅔ cup packed brown sugar
½ cup chopped walnuts or raisins
1½ teaspoons ground cinnamon
3 tablespoons margarine or butter, melted
¾ cup whipping cream
   Orange Glaze

IN A LARGE MIXING BOWL STIR TOGETHER 2 cups of the flour and the yeast. In a small saucepan heat and stir milk, sugar, the ⅓ cup margarine, and ½ teaspoon salt till warm (120° to 130°) and margarine almost melts. Add to flour mixture; add eggs and orange juice. Beat with an electric mixer on low speed 30 seconds, scraping the sides of the bowl constantly. Beat on high speed for 3 minutes. If desired, add orange peel. Using a spoon, stir in as much of the remaining flour as you can.

Turn out onto a lightly floured surface. Knead in enough of the remaining flour to make a moderately soft dough that is smooth and elastic (3 to 5 minutes). Shape into a ball. Place in a lightly greased bowl; turn once to grease surface. Cover and let rise in a warm place till double (about 1 hour).

Punch dough down. Turn out onto a lightly floured surface. Divide in half. Cover and let rest 10 minutes. Combine brown sugar, nuts or raisins, and cinnamon; set aside. Lightly grease two 9x1½-inch round baking pans.

Roll half of the dough into a 12x8-inch rectangle. Brush with half of the melted margarine and sprinkle with half of the brown sugar mixture. Roll up from one of the long sides. Pinch to seal. Cut into 12 rolls. Repeat with remaining dough, melted margarine, and sugar mixture. Place rolls, cut side down, in prepared pans. Cover and let rise in a warm place till nearly double (about 30 minutes).

Drizzle whipping cream over rolls in both pans. Bake in a 375° oven for 20 to 25 minutes or till rolls sound hollow when lightly tapped. If necessary, loosely cover rolls with foil the last 5 minutes to prevent over-browning. Cool 5 minutes. Remove from the pans. Drizzle with Orange Glaze. Serve warm. Makes 24 rolls.

ORANGE GLAZE: In a small mixing bowl stir together 1½ cups sifted powdered sugar, ¼ teaspoon vanilla, and enough orange juice (4 to 5 teaspoons) to make a glaze of drizzling consistency.

You don't need to get up at the crack of dawn to serve these luscious breakfast rolls warm from the oven. Bake them at your convenience (do not glaze), wrap them in foil, and freeze. When you want to serve them, just place the frozen, foil-wrapped rolls in a 350° oven for 35 minutes or till heated through. Drizzle the rolls with the glaze and serve.

HONEY–WHEAT SPIRAL

*T*o shape this loaf, first arrange the ropes of dough spoke fashion on the baking sheet. Then, beginning at the 12 o'clock position, loop one rope of dough and tuck it under the rope next to it. Continue, clockwise, around the circle. Finally, place the small ball of dough in the center.

1¾ to 2¼ cups *all-purpose flour*
  1 package *active dry yeast*
  ¾ cup *milk*
  ¼ cup *honey*
  2 tablespoons *margarine* or *butter*
  1 teaspoon *salt*
  1 *egg*
  1 cup *whole wheat flour*
     Milk
     Honey Butter (optional)

IN A LARGE MIXING BOWL STIR TOGETHER *1 cup* of the all-purpose flour and the yeast. In a small saucepan heat and stir milk, honey, margarine or butter, and salt till warm (120° to 130°) and margarine or butter almost melts. Add to flour mixture; add egg. Beat with an electric mixer on low speed for 30 seconds, scraping the sides of the bowl constantly. Beat on high speed for 3 minutes.

—■—

Using a spoon, stir in whole wheat flour and as much of the remaining all-purpose flour as you can. Turn dough out onto a lightly floured surface. Knead in enough of the remaining flour to make a moderately stiff dough that is smooth and elastic (6 to 8 minutes total). Shape into a ball. Place in a lightly greased bowl; turn once to grease the surface. Cover and let rise in a warm place till double (1¼ to 1½ hours).

—■—

Punch dough down. Remove a walnut-size piece of dough; reserve for the center. Divide the remaining dough into 8 equal portions. Cover and let rest for 10 minutes. Lightly grease a baking sheet.

—■—

Roll *each* of the 8 portions of dough into an 8-inch-long rope. Arrange the ropes on the prepared baking sheet in spoke fashion with the ends touching in the center. Pinch the ropes together at the center. Loop a rope and tuck it securely underneath the next rope. Continue with the remaining ropes to make the spiral design.

—■—

Roll the reserved piece of dough into a small ball. Place in the center of the spiral. Cover and let rise in a warm place till nearly double (about 1 hour). Brush loaf with milk. Bake in a 350° oven about 25 minutes or till bread sounds hollow when lightly tapped. Cool. If desired, serve with Honey Butter. Makes 1 loaf (16 servings).

HONEY BUTTER: In a small mixing bowl stir together ½ cup softened *margarine or butter*, ¼ cup *honey*, and ½ teaspoon finely shredded *orange peel*. Makes ¾ cup.

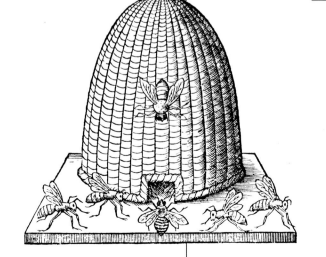

WILD RICE BREAD

In your great-grandmother's day, a round breadboard with a wheat design in the border was used for serving bread. Many of the boards had words such as "Staff of Life" or "Our Daily Bread" inscribed in the border. Sometimes these words, carved on the boards by immigrants, were in German, Norwegian, or other European languages.

⅓ cup wild rice
1 cup water
4 to 4½ cups all-purpose flour
2 packages active dry yeast
¾ cup milk
¼ cup margarine or butter
¼ cup honey
1 teaspoon salt
1 beaten egg
1 cup finely shredded carrot
1 beaten egg yolk
1 tablespoon water

PLACE RICE IN A STRAINER THAT HAS SMALL HOLES. Rinse under cold running water about 1 minute. In a small saucepan bring rice and the 1 cup water to boiling; reduce heat. Cover and simmer for 40 to 50 minutes or till rice is tender. Let cool.

■

In a large mixing bowl stir together 1½ cups of the flour and the yeast. In a small saucepan heat and stir milk, margarine or butter, honey, and salt just till warm (120° to 130°) and margarine almost melts. Add to flour mixture; add egg. Beat with an electric mixer on low-to-medium speed for 30 seconds, scraping the sides of the bowl constantly. Beat on high speed for 3 minutes. Using a spoon, stir in rice, carrot, and as much of the remaining flour as you can.

■

Turn dough out onto a lightly floured surface. Knead in enough of the remaining flour to make a moderately stiff dough that is smooth and elastic (6 to 8 minutes total). Shape into a ball. Place in a lightly greased bowl; turn once to grease surface. Cover and let rise in a warm place till double (about 1 hour).

■

Punch dough down. Turn out onto a long, lightly floured surface. Divide dough into 6 portions. Cover and let rest 10 minutes. Grease 2 large baking sheets. Form four 2-inch balls of foil; set aside.

■

Roll each portion of dough into a ball. Roll each dough ball into an evenly thick rope about 26 inches long. Line up 3 of the ropes, 1 inch apart, on a prepared baking sheet. Starting in the middle, loosely braid ropes by bringing left rope underneath center rope; lay it down. Then bring right rope under new center rope; lay it down. Repeat to the end. On the other end, loosely braid by bringing outside ropes alternately over center rope. Shape braid into a figure eight around 2 balls of foil; tuck ends of braid under. Use remaining 3 dough ropes to form another figure-eight loaf.

■

Cover and let rise in a warm place till nearly double (about 40 minutes). In a small bowl stir together egg yolk and the 1 tablespoon water. Brush loaves with egg yolk mixture.

■

Bake in a 375° oven about 25 minutes or till bread sounds hollow when lightly tapped. If necessary, loosely cover with foil the last 10 to 15 minutes to prevent overbrowning. Cool on wire racks. Makes 2 loaves (24 servings).

SALLY LUNN

4 cups all-purpose flour
1 package active dry yeast
1 cup milk
½ cup margarine or butter
⅓ cup sugar
1 teaspoon salt
3 eggs
1 teaspoon finely shredded lemon peel or 2 teaspoons finely shredded
    orange peel

IN A LARGE MIXING BOWL STIR TOGETHER
2 cups of the flour and the yeast. In a saucepan heat and stir milk, margarine or butter, sugar, and salt till warm (120° to 130°) and margarine almost melts. Add to flour mixture; add eggs. Beat with an electric mixer on low speed for 30 seconds, scraping the sides of the bowl constantly. Beat on high speed for 3 minutes. Using a spoon, stir in the remaining flour and lemon or orange peel.

———■———

Cover and let rise in a warm place till double (about 1 hour). Lightly grease a 10-inch tube pan or fluted tube pan.

———■———

Stir dough down. Transfer dough to the prepared pan. Cover and let rise in a warm place till nearly double (about 30 minutes).

———■———

Bake in a 350° oven about 40 minutes or till bread sounds hollow when lightly tapped. If necessary, loosely cover with foil the last 10 minutes to prevent overbrowning. Remove from the pan immediately. Serve warm or cool. Makes 1 loaf (20 servings).

FILLED SALLY LUNN: Prepare Sally Lunn, *except* while batter is rising the first time, place ¾ cup snipped *dried cherries or mixed dried fruit bits* in a small bowl. Pour enough boiling water over fruit to cover. Let stand for 5 minutes; drain well. Spoon *half* of the batter into the greased 10-inch tube pan; spread it to cover the bottom of the pan. Sprinkle with a mixture of ⅓ cup *sugar* and 1 teaspoon ground *cinnamon*. Spoon the drained cherries or mixed dried fruit bits into the center of the batter. Spoon remaining batter into the tube pan. Let rise and bake as directed.

*O*riginally made by Sally Lunn for her tea shop in England, this bread was popular among the American colonists. They baked the bread in a Turk's head mold (a tall, round, fluted pan). However, you don't have to invest in a special pan to make Sally Lunn. This recipe is adapted to bake in a regular or fluted tube pan.

Sourdough starters were a prized possession of chuck wagon cooks and Alaskan prospectors. On winter nights, they took the starter to bed with them so it wouldn't be damaged by exposure to the cold. If the starter were ruined, there would be no leavening for breads, biscuits, and flapjacks. Also, if a new starter were begun, it might not develop the same good flavor.

SOURDOUGH STARTER

1 medium potato (about 6 ounces), peeled and cut up
2 cups water
1 package active dry yeast*
1 cup all-purpose flour
1 tablespoon sugar
  All-purpose flour
  Warm water
  Sugar

IN A MEDIUM SAUCEPAN COOK POTATO IN THE 2 cups water, covered, for 20 to 25 minutes or till very tender. Cool 10 minutes. Press potato and liquid through a sieve or blend in an electric blender on low speed till nearly smooth. If necessary, add enough water to equal 2½ cups. Transfer mixture to a non-metal bowl. Cool to 110° to 115°.

━■━

Add yeast to potato mixture, stirring to dissolve. Add the 1 cup flour and 1 tablespoon sugar; mix well. Cover bowl with cheesecloth. Let stand at room temperature for 2 to 3 days or till mixture is bubbly and has a pleasant sour aroma, stirring each day. (Fermentation time depends on the room temperature; a warmer room hastens fermentation.)

━■━

To store, transfer starter to a wide-mouth jar. Cover jar with cheesecloth and refrigerate. *Do not cover jar tightly with a metal lid.*

━■━

To use starter, bring desired amount to room temperature. To replenish starter: For each cup used, add *¾ cup* all-purpose flour, *¾ cup* warm water, and *1 teaspoon* sugar. Cover with cheese-cloth. Let stand at room temperature over-night or till bubbly. Refrigerate for later use.

━■━

If starter isn't used within 10 days, stir in *1 teaspoon* sugar. Repeat every 10 days unless starter is used and replenished.

━■━

*NOTE: Do not use quick-rising yeast.

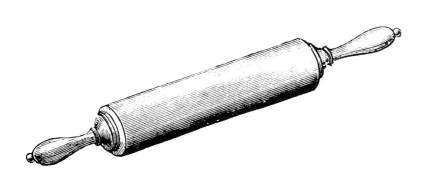

SOURDOUGH BREAD

1 cup Sourdough Starter (see recipe, opposite)
5¾ to 6¼ cups all-purpose flour
1 package active dry yeast
1½ cups buttermilk
3 tablespoons sugar
3 tablespoons cooking oil
1 teaspoon salt
1 egg
Cornmeal

BRING THE 1 CUP SOURDOUGH STARTER TO ROOM temperature. In a large mixing bowl combine 2½ cups of the flour and the yeast. In a medium saucepan heat and stir buttermilk, sugar, oil, and salt just till warm (120° to 130°). Add to flour mixture. Add Sourdough Starter and egg. Beat with an electric mixer on low-to-medium speed for 30 seconds, scraping the sides of the bowl constantly. Beat on high speed for 3 minutes. Using a spoon, stir in as much of the remaining flour as you can.

Turn dough out onto a lightly floured surface. Knead in enough of the remaining flour to make a moderately stiff dough that is smooth and elastic (6 to 8 minutes total). Shape dough into a ball. Place dough in a lightly greased bowl; turn once to grease surface. Cover and let rise in a warm place till double (45 to 60 minutes).

Punch dough down. Turn out onto a lightly floured surface. Divide dough in half. Cover and let rest for 10 minutes. Lightly grease 2 large baking sheets. Sprinkle baking sheets with cornmeal.

Shape *each* half of dough into a round loaf. Place loaves on the prepared baking sheets. Flatten each slightly to 6 inches in diameter. (*Or,* for long loaves, on a lightly floured surface roll each half of dough into a 15x10-inch rectangle. Roll up tightly, starting from a long side. Moisten edge with water and seal. Pinch and pull ends slightly to taper. Place loaves, seam side down, on the prepared baking sheets.)

With a sharp knife, make slashes about ¼ inch deep across the tops of the loaves. Cover and let rise in a warm place till nearly double (about 30 minutes).

Bake in a 375° oven for 30 to 35 minutes or till bread sounds hollow when lightly tapped. If necessary, loosely cover with foil the last 15 minutes to prevent overbrowning. Cool on wire racks. Makes 2 loaves (24 to 36 servings).

WHOLE WHEAT SOURDOUGH BREAD: Prepare Sourdough Bread, *except* reduce all-purpose flour to *4 to 4½ cups* and add 2 cups *whole wheat flour* with the stirred-in all-purpose flour. Continue as directed.

With a crunchy crust and slightly chewy center, these loaves of Sourdough Bread are similar to French bread, except they have a delicious sour tang.

LEMONY MORAVIAN SUGAR BREAD

The Moravians came to Pennsylvania, Georgia, and North Carolina in the 1700s to establish missions. Besides being devoted to their religion, they were outstanding cooks with a special talent for using spices. This yeast-raised coffee cake was a part of their heritage.

1 cup Sourdough Starter (see recipe, page 128)
3½ cups all-purpose flour
1 package active dry yeast
½ cup sugar
½ cup milk
¼ cup margarine or butter
½ teaspoon salt
2 slightly beaten eggs
2 teaspoons finely shredded lemon peel
2 tablespoons lemon juice
¾ cup packed brown sugar
⅓ cup margarine or butter
1 teaspoon ground cinnamon

BRING THE 1 CUP SOURDOUGH STARTER TO ROOM temperature. In a large mixing bowl stir together *1½ cups* of the flour and the yeast.

In a small saucepan heat and stir sugar, milk, the ¼ cup margarine, and salt till warm (120° to 130°) and margarine almost melts. Add to flour mixture. Add Sourdough Starter, eggs, and lemon juice. Beat with an electric mixer on low speed for 30 seconds, scraping the sides of the bowl constantly. Beat on high speed about 2 minutes. Using a spoon, stir in lemon peel and remaining flour.

Lightly grease a 13x9x2-inch baking pan. Transfer dough to the prepared baking pan and pat dough evenly into the pan with floured hands. Cover and let rise in a warm place till nearly double (about 1 hour).

In a small saucepan combine brown sugar, the ⅓ cup margarine, and cinnamon. Heat and stir till melted and smooth. Poke holes in dough with the handle of a wooden spoon. Pour brown sugar mixture over dough. Bake in a 375° oven for 20 to 25 minutes or till bread is done. Serve warm. Serves 12.

In early American colonies, inventive cooks made Boston Brown Bread using the plentiful New World ingredients molasses and cornmeal. With no oven for baking, the cooks steamed the bread in the kettle that hung over the fireplace.

BOSTON BROWN BREAD

½ cup cornmeal
½ cup whole wheat flour
½ cup rye flour
½ teaspoon baking powder
¼ teaspoon salt
¼ teaspoon baking soda
1 cup buttermilk or sour milk (see tip, page 188)
⅓ cup light molasses
2 tablespoons brown sugar
1 tablespoon cooking oil
¼ cup raisins or chopped walnuts
    Soft-style cream cheese or flavored soft-style cream cheese (optional)

IN A LARGE MIXING BOWL STIR TOGETHER cornmeal, whole wheat flour, rye flour, baking powder, salt, and baking soda.

—■—

In a mixing bowl combine buttermilk or sour milk, molasses, brown sugar, and oil. Gradually add milk mixture to flour mixture, stirring just till combined. Stir in raisins or chopped nuts. Pour into a well-greased 7½x3½x2-inch loaf pan. Grease a piece of foil. Place the foil, greased side down, over the loaf pan. Press foil around the edges to seal.

—■—

Place loaf pan on a rack in a 4- or 5-quart Dutch oven. Pour hot water into the Dutch oven around the loaf pan till water covers 1 inch of the loaf pan. Bring water to boiling; reduce heat. Cover and simmer for 2 to 2½ hours or till a toothpick inserted in the center comes out clean. Add additional *boiling* water as needed.

—■—

Remove loaf pan from the Dutch oven; let stand 10 minutes. Remove bread from the pan. Serve warm. If desired, serve with cream cheese. Makes 1 loaf (14 servings).

ORANGE-RHUBARB BREAD

1½ cups finely chopped rhubarb
1½ cups sugar
  3 cups all-purpose flour
  1 tablespoon baking powder
½ teaspoon salt
¼ teaspoon baking soda
  1 beaten egg
1¼ cups milk
¼ cup cooking oil
  2 teaspoons finely shredded orange peel
  1 cup chopped nuts
    Orange Drizzle

IN A MEDIUM MIXING BOWL STIR TOGETHER rhubarb and *1 cup* of the sugar. Set aside. Lightly grease one 9x5x3-inch loaf pan, three 7½x3½x2-inch loaf pans, or eight 4½x2½x1½-inch loaf pans. Set aside.

———■———

In a large mixing bowl stir together remaining sugar, flour, baking powder, salt, and baking soda. In another bowl combine beaten egg, milk, oil, and orange peel. Add egg mixture to flour mixture, stirring *just till combined*. Fold in rhubarb mixture and nuts.

———■———

Pour rhubarb batter into the prepared pans. Bake in a 350° oven about 1¼ hours for the 9x5x3-inch loaf, 40 to 45 minutes for the 7½x3½x2-inch loaves, 35 to 40 minutes for the 4½x2½x1½-inch loaves, or till a toothpick inserted near the center comes out clean. If necessary, cover large loaf loosely with foil the last 10 to 15 minutes of baking to prevent overbrowning.

———■———

Cool loaf or loaves in the pans on a rack for 10 minutes. Remove from pans; cool thoroughly on a wire rack. Wrap loaf or loaves in foil and store overnight before slicing. Top with Orange Drizzle. Makes 1 large loaf, 3 small loaves, or 8 miniloaves (24 servings).

ORANGE DRIZZLE: In a small mixing bowl stir together 1 cup sifted *powdered sugar*, ¼ teaspoon *vanilla*, and enough *orange juice* (1 to 2 tablespoons) to make a glaze of drizzling consistency. Makes ⅓ cup.

If you wish to bake miniature loaves but only have four tiny (4½x2½x1½ inches) loaf pans available, chill half the batter while the first batch bakes. When the first loaves are done, wash and refill the loaf pans. Allow the loaves made from the chilled batter a few more minutes to bake.

BRANDIED RAISIN–APPLESAUCE MUFFINS

In some parts of the country, muffins are called gems. This name comes from the early muffin pans, which were introduced around 1850. These pans were an arrangement of iron or tin "gem" cups fastened together.

½ cup raisins
2 tablespoons brandy or *apple juice*
1 ⅓ cups all-purpose flour
¾ teaspoon baking powder
¾ teaspoon apple pie spice
½ teaspoon baking soda
¼ teaspoon salt
2 beaten eggs
⅔ cup applesauce
⅓ cup margarine or *butter, melted*
¼ cup packed brown sugar

IN A SMALL BOWL COMBINE RAISINS AND BRANDY or apple juice. Let stand 10 to 15 minutes. Grease twelve 2½-inch muffin cups or line with paper bake cups; set aside.

—■—

In a large mixing bowl stir together flour, baking powder, apple pie spice, baking soda, and salt. Make a well in center of ingredients.

—■—

In another bowl combine eggs, applesauce, melted margarine or butter, brown sugar, and the raisin mixture. Add the egg mixture all at once to the well in the flour mixture. Stir *just till moistened* (batter should be lumpy).

—■—

Spoon batter into prepared muffin cups, filling each ⅔ full. Bake in a 400° oven for 20 to 25 minutes or till golden. Remove muffins from pans and cool slighty on a wire rack. Serve warm. Makes 12.

PEANUT BUTTER–STREUSEL
COFFEE CAKE

¼ cup all-purpose flour
¼ cup packed brown sugar
2 tablespoons peanut butter
1 tablespoon margarine or butter
¼ cup miniature semisweet chocolate pieces
¼ cup peanut butter
2 tablespoons margarine or butter
1 cup all-purpose flour
½ cup packed brown sugar
½ cup milk
1 egg
1 teaspoon baking powder
¼ teaspoon baking soda
¼ teaspoon salt
¼ cup miniature semisweet chocolate pieces

GREASE AN 8X8X2-INCH BAKING PAN; SET PAN ASIDE. For streusel topping, in a small mixing bowl combine the ¼ cup flour, the ¼ cup brown sugar, the 2 tablespoons peanut butter, and the 1 tablespoon margarine or butter. Stir together till crumbly. Stir in ¼ cup chocolate pieces. Set topping aside.

In a large mixing bowl beat the ¼ cup peanut butter and the 2 tablespoons margarine or butter with an electric mixer on medium-to-high speed about 30 seconds or till combined.

Add about *half* of the 1 cup flour, the ½ cup brown sugar, *half* of the milk, the egg, baking powder, baking soda, and salt. Beat till thoroughly combined, scraping the sides of the bowl.

Add remaining flour and remaining milk. Beat on low-to-medium speed *just till combined*. Stir in ¼ cup chocolate pieces. Pour batter into the prepared pan, spreading evenly. Sprinkle with streusel topping.

Bake in a 375° oven for 25 to 30 minutes or till a toothpick inserted near the center comes out clean. Cool on a wire rack for 15 minutes. Cut into squares. Serve warm. Serves 9.

This easy-to-fix coffee cake makes a tasty treat to tote to a meeting or the office or to serve for after-school snacks.

State fair visitors throughout the country look forward to the exhibits of garden produce and farm machinery, prizewinning livestock, and the great food sold from stands. One treat especially popular with fairgoers is the funnel cake, a Pennsylvania Dutch specialty.

FUNNEL CAKES

2 beaten eggs
1½ cups milk
¼ cup packed brown sugar
2 cups all-purpose flour
1½ teaspoons baking powder
¼ teaspoon salt
2 cups cooking oil
Powdered sugar or Caramel Sauce (optional)

FOR BATTER, IN A LARGE MIXING BOWL STIR together eggs, milk, and brown sugar. In another bowl combine flour, baking powder, and salt. Add flour mixture to egg mixture. Beat with a rotary beater till smooth.

In an 8-inch skillet heat cooking oil to 360°. Hold a funnel with a ½-inch spout (inside diameter), covering the bottom of the spout with your finger. Pour about ½ cup of the batter into the funnel. Remove your finger and carefully release the batter into the hot oil, starting at the center of the skillet and moving the funnel in a circular motion to form a spiral. (Or, if a funnel is not available, use a small glass measuring cup to carefully pour batter into the hot oil.)

Cook batter about 2½ minutes or till golden brown. Using 2 wide metal spatulas, carefully turn the funnel cake. Cook about 1 minute more or till golden. Remove the cake from the skillet and drain on paper towels. Repeat with the remaining batter.

If desired, sprinkle funnel cakes with powdered sugar or drizzle with Caramel Sauce. Serve warm. Makes 4 or 5 cakes.

CARAMEL SAUCE: In a heavy small saucepan stir together ¼ cup packed brown sugar and 1½ teaspoons cornstarch. Stir in ¼ cup milk, half-and-half, or light cream, 2 tablespoons water, and 1 tablespoon light corn syrup. Cook and stir till bubbly (mixture may appear curdled). Cook and stir 2 minutes more. Remove from the heat. Stir in 1 tablespoon margarine or butter and ½ teaspoon vanilla. Serve warm. Makes about ½ cup.

MARBLE DOUGHNUTS

2¼ cups all-purpose flour
2 teaspoons baking powder
¼ teaspoon salt
2 beaten eggs
1 cup sugar
1 teaspoon vanilla
⅔ cup milk
¼ cup margarine or butter, melted
½ cup all-purpose flour
⅔ cup all-purpose flour
2 squares (2 ounces) unsweetened chocolate,
   melted and cooled
Cooking oil or shortening for deep-fat frying
Chocolate Drizzle or sifted powdered sugar

IN A BOWL STIR TOGETHER THE 2¼ CUPS FLOUR, baking powder, and salt. Set aside.

———■———

In a large mixing bowl combine eggs, sugar, and vanilla. Beat with an electric mixer on medium-to-high speed about 4 minutes or till thick. In another bowl combine milk and melted margarine or butter. Add flour mixture and milk mixture alternately to egg mixture, beating just till combined after each addition.

———■———

Transfer *1 cup* of the dough to another bowl; stir in the ½ cup flour. To remaining dough, stir in the ⅔ cup flour and cooled chocolate. Cover each bowl of dough. Chill about 2 hours or till dough can be handled easily.

———■———

On a lightly floured surface roll chocolate dough into a 12x10-inch rectangle. Roll plain dough into a 12x5-inch rectangle. Place plain dough on half of the chocolate dough; fold remaining half of the chocolate dough over plain dough. Roll gently to ½-inch thickness. Cut doughnuts by pressing straight down with a floured 2½-inch doughnut cutter (do not twist the cutter). Reroll dough scraps, avoiding mixing the two doughs more than necessary, and continue cutting doughnuts.

———■———

In a heavy, deep, 3-quart saucepan or deep-fat fryer heat cooking oil or shortening to 375°. Using a slotted spoon, carefully add 2 or 3 doughnuts at a time to hot oil. Fry about 2 minutes or till golden, turning once. Drain on paper towels. Repeat with remaining doughnuts and doughnut holes.

———■———

Drizzle tops of warm doughnuts with Chocolate Drizzle, dip tops into glaze, or sprinkle with powdered sugar. Cool. Makes 15 to 18 doughnuts and doughnut holes.

CHOCOLATE DRIZZLE: In a small saucepan melt 1 square (1 ounce) *unsweetened chocolate* and 1 tablespoon *margarine or butter* over low heat, stirring constantly. Remove from the heat. Stir in 1 cup sifted *powdered sugar* and 1 teaspoon *vanilla*. Stir in enough *hot water* (1 to 2 tablespoons) to make a glaze of drizzling consistency. Makes about ⅓ cup.

APRICOT PRESERVE
BREAKFAST BISCUITS

    2 cups all-purpose flour
    1 tablespoon baking powder
   ¼ teaspoon salt
   ⅓ cup shortening
   ½ cup milk
   ⅓ cup apricot or pineapple preserves
    2 teaspoons sugar
   ⅛ teaspoon ground cinnamon
       Apricot, pineapple, or other desired preserves (optional)
       Margarine or butter (optional)

IN A MEDIUM MIXING BOWL STIR TOGETHER FLOUR, baking powder, and salt. Cut in shortening till the mixture resembles coarse crumbs. Make a well in the center of the dry ingredients. Combine milk and the ⅓ cup preserves; add all at once to well in flour mixture. Stir just till dough clings together.

Turn the dough out onto a lightly floured surface. Quickly knead dough by gently folding and pressing dough for 10 to 12 strokes. Lightly roll or pat dough to ½-inch thickness. Cut with a floured 2½-inch biscuit cutter, dipping the cutter into flour between cuts.

Transfer biscuits to an ungreased baking sheet. Stir together sugar and cinnamon; sprinkle over biscuits. Bake in a 450° oven for 7 to 10 minutes or till golden. Serve warm. If desired, pass additional preserves and margarine or butter. Makes 10.

APRICOT PRESERVE DROP BISCUITS: Prepare Apricot Preserve Breakfast Biscuits, *except* increase milk to ⅔ cup. *Do not knead, roll, or cut* dough. Drop dough portions from a tablespoon 1 inch apart on an ungreased baking sheet. Sprinkle with the sugar-cinnamon mixture. Bake and serve as directed. Makes 10 to 12.

Here's a different twist for biscuits: Stir your favorite homemade or purchased preserves into the dough for swirls of fruit flavor and color throughout the biscuits.

Old-time southern cooks beat biscuit dough with a mallet, iron rod, or hammer to make the biscuits crisp on the outside and soft on the inside. They often sang in an attempt to keep a steady rhythm with their strokes. You can use this same idea when making Beaten Biscuits—play music with a strong beat to make the pounding easier.

Pictured on page 7.

BEATEN BISCUITS

> 2 cups all-purpose flour
> 1 teaspoon sugar
> ½ teaspoon salt
> ⅛ teaspoon baking powder
> ¼ cup shortening or *lard*
> ⅓ cup ice water
> ⅓ cup cold milk

IN A MEDIUM MIXING BOWL STIR TOGETHER FLOUR, sugar, salt, and baking powder. Using a pastry blender or two knives, cut in shortening or lard till mixture resembles coarse crumbs. Make a well in the center of the dry ingredients. Add ice water and milk all at once. Using a fork, stir just till moistened. If necessary, stir in enough additional ice water to make dough cling together. (Dough will be very stiff.)

Turn dough out onto a lightly floured surface. Using the flat side of a wooden spoon or a metal meat mallet, beat dough vigorously for 15 minutes, folding dough over and giving it a quarter turn frequently. Dip spoon or mallet into flour as necessary to prevent sticking.

Lightly roll or pat dough to ⅜-inch thickness. Cut dough with a floured 2-inch biscuit cutter, dipping the cutter into flour between cuts. Place biscuits 1 inch apart on an ungreased baking sheet. Using the tines of a fork, prick biscuits several times.

Bake in a 400° oven about 20 minutes or till crisp and light brown. Remove biscuits from baking sheet. Serve warm. Makes 24.

CHEDDARY ASPARAGUS SPOON BREAD

10 ounces asparagus, cut into ½-inch pieces (2 cups), or one 10-ounce package
     frozen cut asparagus
1½ cups milk
½ cup cornmeal
2 cups shredded cheddar cheese (8 ounces)
1 tablespoon margarine or butter
1½ teaspoons baking powder
1 teaspoon sugar
¼ teaspoon salt
4 eggs

Puffy and airy, spoon bread is similar to a soufflé. Served warm with margarine or butter, it's a delicious substitute for potatoes or rice.

IN A SAUCEPAN COOK FRESH ASPARAGUS IN A small amount of boiling water for 5 to 6 minutes or till just tender. Drain well. (*Or,* cook frozen asparagus according to package directions. Drain and cut into ½-inch pieces.) Set aside.

———■———

In a large saucepan combine milk and cornmeal. Cook, stirring constantly, over medium-high heat till mixture is thickened and bubbly. Remove the saucepan from the heat.

———■———

Add cheese, margarine or butter, baking powder, sugar, and salt to cornmeal mixture. Beat with a wire whisk or wooden spoon till cheese melts.

———■———

Separate eggs. Add yolks, one at a time, to cornmeal mixture, stirring after each addition till combined. (Mixture will be thick).

———■———

In a large mixing bowl beat the 4 egg whites with an electric mixer on high till stiff peaks form (tips stand straight).

———■———

Gently fold beaten egg whites into cornmeal mixture till combined. Gently fold in asparagus. Transfer mixture to an ungreased 2-quart casserole or soufflé dish.

———■———

Bake in a 350° oven for 45 to 50 minutes or till a knife inserted near the center comes out clean. Serve immediately. Serves 6 to 8.

Buttermilk gives a pleasing, tangy flavor to this southern-style corn bread. If you like sweeter corn bread, use the upper range of the sugar called for in this recipe.

Corn Sticks are pictured on page 58.

BUTTERMILK CORN BREAD

1 cup all-purpose flour
1 cup yellow, white, or blue cornmeal
2 to 4 tablespoons sugar
1 tablespoon baking powder
¼ teaspoon salt
¼ teaspoon baking soda
2 eggs
1 cup buttermilk or sour milk (see tip, page 188)
¼ cup cooking oil

GREASE A 9X9X2-INCH BAKING PAN OR TWO 9X5X3-inch loaf pans. Set aside. In a large mixing bowl stir together flour, cornmeal, desired level of sugar, baking powder, salt, and baking soda. In another bowl beat together eggs, buttermilk or sour milk, and oil. Add buttermilk mixture to flour mixture and stir *just till moistened* (batter should be lumpy).

— ■ —

Pour batter into prepared pans. Bake in a 425° oven for 20 to 25 minutes or till golden brown.* Serve warm. Makes 8 or 9 servings.

— ■ —

*NOTE: If desired, cool, wrap, and freeze one of the baked loaves. Before serving, rewrap frozen loaf in foil and place in a 375° oven about 25 minutes or till heated through.

CORN STICKS OR CORN MUFFINS: Prepare Buttermilk Corn Bread, *except* spoon batter into greased corn stick pans or muffin cups, filling pans ⅔ full. Bake in a 425° oven for 12 to 15 minutes or till golden brown. Makes 24 to 26 corn sticks or 12 corn muffins.

SOUTHWESTERN CORN BREAD: Prepare Buttermilk Corn Bread, *except* add several dashes bottled *hot pepper sauce* with the oil. Gently stir one 12-ounce can *whole kernel corn with sweet peppers*, drained, and 1 cup shredded *Monterey Jack cheese with jalapeño peppers* into the batter.

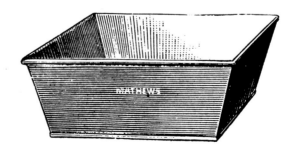

HUSH PUPPIES

       1 cup cornmeal
      ¼ cup all-purpose flour
       2 teaspoons sugar
      ¾ teaspoon baking powder
      ½ teaspoon garlic salt
      ¼ teaspoon ground red pepper
      ⅛ teaspoon onion powder
       1 beaten egg
      ½ cup milk
       3 slices bacon, crisp-cooked and finely crumbled
       2 tablespoons finely chopped green or sweet red pepper
          Cooking oil or shortening for deep-fat frying

IN A MEDIUM BOWL COMBINE CORNMEAL, FLOUR, sugar, baking powder, garlic salt, ground red pepper, and onion powder. Combine egg, milk, bacon, and chopped green pepper; add to dry ingredients. Stir *just till moistened.*

Drop batter by tablespoons into 2 inches deep hot fat (375°). Fry 4 or 5 at a time, for 3 minutes or till golden, turning once. Drain on paper towels. Repeat with remaining batter. Makes 14 to 18.

Hush Puppies were so named because as cooks fried fish coated in cornmeal batter, they threw fried nuggets of batter to the howling dogs to quiet them.

Pictured on page 53.

HAM AND CHEESE FRITTERS

      1½ cups all-purpose flour
       2 teaspoons baking powder
      ¾ cup milk
       1 beaten egg
      ¾ cup finely diced fully cooked ham (4 ounces)
      ½ cup finely shredded cheddar cheese (2 ounces)
          Cooking oil or shortening for deep-fat frying
          Pineapple Dipping Sauce

IN A MEDIUM MIXING BOWL STIR TOGETHER FLOUR and baking powder. Add milk and egg. Stir *just till moistened.* Fold in ham and cheese.

Drop batter by tablespoons into deep hot fat (375°). Fry 4 or 5 at a time, for 3 to 4 minutes or till golden brown, turning once. Drain on paper towels. Repeat. Serve warm with Pineapple Dipping Sauce. Makes about 20.

PINEAPPLE DIPPING SAUCE: In a small saucepan stir together one *undrained 8-ounce can crushed pineapple* (juice pack), ⅓ cup *water,* 2 tablespoons *brown sugar,* and 2 teaspoons *cornstarch.* Cook and stir till thickened and bubbly. Cook and stir 2 minutes more. Serve warm. Makes 1 cup.

CHAPTER SEVEN

GARDENER'S PRIDE

COUNTRY COOKS ARE MASTERS AT using flavorful, colorful vegetable dishes and salads to add variety and contrast to their menus. And with the recipes in this chapter and the cornucopia of produce that's available today, it's easy to dress up meals with tempting, country-style side dishes. From Beet and Apple Salad to Scalloped Corn, you'll love any and all of these delicious choices. ■

LAYERED GREEN BEAN
AND TOMATO SALAD

This fresh-tasting, colorful salad is a wonderful way to use that bumper crop of green beans, tomatoes, and peppers from your garden or local produce market.

Pictured on page 145.

3 tablespoons olive oil or salad oil
3 tablespoons red wine vinegar
2 tablespoons chopped onion or ¼ cup chopped shallots
1 tablespoon snipped fresh basil or 1 teaspoon dried basil, crushed
1 tablespoon snipped fresh chives
2 teaspoons Dijon-style mustard
1 teaspoon snipped fresh oregano or ¼ teaspoon dried oregano, crushed
1 teaspoon lemon juice
¼ teaspoon salt
¼ teaspoon pepper
1 pound green beans (about 4 cups), cut into 1½- to 2-inch pieces, or two 9-ounce packages frozen cut green beans
2 cups red and/or yellow cherry tomatoes, halved
2 large red and/or yellow sweet peppers, cut into bite-size pieces (about 2 cups)
Fresh chives (optional)
Nasturtium flowers (optional)

FOR DRESSING, IN A SCREW-TOP JAR COMBINE OLIVE oil or salad oil, vinegar, chopped onion or shallots, basil, chives, Dijon-style mustard, oregano, lemon juice, salt, and pepper. Cover and shake well. Set dressing aside.

Place a steamer basket in a saucepan; add water till it almost touches the bottom of the basket. Bring water to boiling. Add fresh green beans. Cover and steam for 18 to 22 minutes or till crisp-tender. (*Or*, cook frozen green beans according to package directions. Drain.) Rinse beans under cold running water; drain well.

Place green beans, tomatoes, and sweet pepper pieces in separate bowls. Shake dressing well and divide it among the 3 bowls containing the vegetables. Cover and chill vegetables for 4 to 24 hours, stirring often.

To serve, in a large salad bowl layer the pepper pieces, beans, and tomatoes. If desired, garnish with chives and nasturtium flowers. Makes 6 to 8 servings.

QUICK-MIX GREEN BEAN AND TOMATO SALAD: Prepare Layered Green Bean and Tomato Salad, *except* in a large salad bowl, toss together beans, tomatoes, and peppers. Shake dressing; pour over salad. Chill salad for 4 to 24 hours, stirring often. Toss salad just before serving.

PEACH AND WATERCRESS SALAD

¼ cup honey
½ teaspoon grated gingerroot or ⅛ teaspoon ground ginger
½ teaspoon finely shredded lemon peel
3 tablespoons lemon juice
½ cup salad oil
4 cups torn mixed greens
4 cups watercress (about 8 ounces)
1 cup sliced, peeled peaches (about 2 peaches)
1 cup strawberries, halved
½ cup coarsely chopped walnuts, toasted
2 tablespoons snipped fresh chives or sliced green onion (optional)

FOR DRESSING, IN A MEDIUM MIXING BOWL combine honey, gingerroot, lemon peel, and lemon juice. Beating with an electric mixer on medium speed, add oil in a thin, steady stream. Continue beating about 3 minutes or till mixture is thick. Set aside.

In a salad bowl combine torn greens, watercress, peach slices, and strawberries. Toss gently to mix. Sprinkle with walnuts. Drizzle with dressing. If desired, sprinkle with chives or green onion. Makes 6 servings.

Here's a variation on a favorite southern salad that usually features watercress and walnuts. In keeping with its southern lineage, this version uses peaches.

Pictured on page 83.

WILTED SUCCOTASH SALAD

3 cups torn red-tip leaf lettuce (about ½ head)
3 cups torn fresh spinach (about ¼ pound)
1 16-ounce can whole kernel corn, drained, or 2 cups cooked corn
1½ cups cherry tomatoes, halved
1 8-ounce can lima beans, drained, or 1 cup cooked lima beans
½ cup chopped red onion
¾ cup hot-style tomato juice
1 tablespoon lime juice
1 tablespoon salad oil

IN A LARGE SERVING BOWL COMBINE LETTUCE, spinach, corn, tomatoes, lima beans, and onion. Set aside. For dressing, in a small saucepan combine tomato juice, lime juice, and salad oil. Cook till heated through.

Immediately pour hot dressing over salad. Toss gently to coat salad with dressing. Season to taste with salt and freshly ground black pepper. Serve immediately. Makes 8 servings.

Succotash typically contains corn and lima beans. But here's a tasty variation that adds greens and a hot dressing.

MUSTARDY POTATO SALAD

If you love hot mustard, add even more zip to this salad by using extra-sharp Dijon-style mustard. Look for it in specialty stores and larger supermarkets.

4   medium potatoes (about 1¼ pounds)
¾   cup chopped red or yellow sweet pepper
½   cup thinly sliced celery (about 1 stalk)
⅓   cup chopped onion
¼   cup chopped dill pickles
½   cup mayonnaise or salad dressing
2   tablespoons Dijon-style mustard
2   tablespoons lemon juice
½   teaspoon cracked black pepper
¼   teaspoon salt
2   tablespoons mustard seed
1   tablespoon olive oil or cooking oil
    Watercress (optional)

IN A COVERED SAUCEPAN COOK POTATOES IN boiling water about 30 minutes or till just tender; drain well. Cool slightly. Peel and cube potatoes. In a large bowl combine the potatoes, chopped sweet pepper, celery, onion, and dill pickles.

—■—

For dressing, in a medium mixing bowl combine mayonnaise or salad dressing, Dijon-style mustard, lemon juice, cracked pepper, and salt. Pour the dressing over the potato mixture; toss gently to coat. Set aside.

—■—

In a small skillet combine the mustard seed and olive oil or cooking oil. Cook, covered, over medium heat about 3 minutes or till seeds begin to pop slightly, shaking the pan occasionally. Remove from heat. Continue shaking pan till seeds stop popping. Pour seeds and oil over the potato mixture. Stir gently to coat. Cover and chill for 4 to 24 hours.

—■—

To serve, transfer salad to a large serving bowl and, if desired, garnish with watercress. Makes 6 servings.

MIXED COUNTRY GREENS

For a tangy flavor contrast, country cooks love serving strong-flavored turnip, mustard, or collard greens with vinegar.

    5   slices bacon
    ½   cup chopped onion
    2   cloves garlic, minced
  1½   pounds turnip, mustard, and/or collard greens
    1   14½-ounce can chicken broth
    ½   cup finely chopped turnip
    2   teaspoons sugar
        Cider or herb-flavored vinegar (optional)

IN A 4-QUART DUTCH OVEN COOK BACON TILL crisp. Drain, reserving *2 tablespoons* drippings. Crumble bacon; set aside. Cook onion and garlic in reserved drippings till onion is tender but not brown. Stir in the greens of your choice, chicken broth, turnip, sugar, ¼ teaspoon *salt*, and ¼ teaspoon *pepper*.

Bring to boiling; reduce heat. Cover and simmer for 20 to 25 minutes or till greens are wilted and tender, stirring occasionally. Transfer greens to a serving bowl. Sprinkle with the crumbled bacon. Serve greens with a slotted spoon. If desired, pass cider or herb-flavored vinegar. Makes 6 to 8 servings.

AMISH FRUIT BOWL

Fresh fruit bowls with a citrus dressing originated with the Amish and Mennonites in Indiana.

    1   teaspoon finely shredded orange peel
    ¾   cup orange juice
    ⅔   cup sugar
    ¼   cup lemon juice
    ¼   teaspoon ground cinnamon
    2   small oranges
    1   cup chopped apple (about 1 apple)
    2   cups cubed cantaloupe
    1   15½-ounce can pineapple chunks (juice pack), drained
    1   cup blueberries

FOR DRESSING, IN A SMALL SAUCEPAN COMBINE orange peel, orange juice, sugar, lemon juice, and cinnamon. Bring mixture to boiling over medium-high heat. Cook and stir about 1 minute or till sugar dissolves. Remove from heat. Set aside to cool slightly.

Meanwhile, peel and section oranges over a bowl to catch juices. Place orange sections in juice. To assemble, layer apple, cantaloupe, pineapple, orange sections and juice, and blueberries in a glass bowl. Pour dressing over the top. Cover and chill for 3 hours. Toss before serving. Makes 6 to 8 servings.

*T*ry this delicious,
eye-catching salad
to see why beets
and apples make
such a wonderful
combination.

BEET AND APPLE SALAD

3 medium beets (about ¾ pound) or one 16-ounce can julienne beets,
    rinsed and drained
3 tablespoons salad oil
3 tablespoons white wine vinegar
1 teaspoon shredded orange peel
2 tablespoons orange juice
2 tablespoons sliced green onion
1 tablespoon snipped fresh mint or 1 teaspoon dried mint, crushed
1 teaspoon honey
2 cups torn romaine
1 coarsely chopped tart green apple (about 1 apple)
    Fresh mint (optional)

IN A MEDIUM SAUCEPAN COOK FRESH WHOLE beets, covered, in boiling water for 40 to 50 minutes or till tender; drain. Cool slightly; slip off skins and cut into julienne strips.

———■———

Meanwhile, for dressing, in a screw-top jar combine salad oil, white wine vinegar, orange peel, orange juice, green onion, mint, and honey. Cover and shake well.

———■———

In a mixing bowl combine beets and *half* of the dressing. Cover and refrigerate beet mixture and remaining dressing for 2 to 24 hours.

———■———

To serve, in a mixing bowl combine torn romaine and chopped apple. Toss apple mixture with the remaining half of the dressing. Divide the apple mixture among 4 salad plates. Using a slotted spoon, spoon beet mixture over apple mixture. If desired, garnish with fresh mint. Makes 4 servings.

Eating black-eyed peas on New Year's Day is believed by many people to bring a year of good luck, health, and happiness.

BLACK-EYED PEA SALAD

2 cups cooked black-eyed peas or *one 15-ounce can black-eyed peas, rinsed and drained*
1½ cups chopped, peeled tomatoes (about 2 tomatoes)
  1 cup cooked corn
  ¼ cup thinly sliced green onion
  1 medium jalapeño pepper, seeded and finely chopped
  ⅓ cup salad oil
  2 tablespoons red wine vinegar
  2 tablespoons lemon juice
  1 tablespoon snipped fresh thyme or *1 teaspoon dried thyme, crushed*
  1 tablespoon Dijon-style mustard
  ¼ teaspoon pepper

IN A LARGE MIXING BOWL STIR TOGETHER BLACK-eyed peas, chopped tomatoes, corn, green onion, and jalapeño pepper. Cover and chill for several hours.

———■———

For dressing, in a screw-top jar combine salad oil, red wine vinegar, lemon juice, thyme, mustard, and pepper. Cover and shake well. Chill dressing for several hours.

———■———

Just before serving, shake dressing well; pour dressing over the vegetable mixture. Toss gently to coat. Makes 6 servings.

SPICED APPLE WEDGES

4 small cooking apples (about 1 pound)
¾ cup sugar
2 tablespoons margarine or butter
½ teaspoon ground cinnamon
1½ cups water

IF DESIRED PEEL APPLES. CORE APPLES AND CUT into wedges. Set aside.

For syrup, in a large skillet combine the sugar, margarine or butter, and cinnamon. Add water. Cook and stir over medium heat till water boils and sugar dissolves.

Add apple wedges to syrup. Return to boiling; reduce heat. Simmer, uncovered, for 10 to 15 minutes or till just tender, spooning syrup over apples occasionally. Slightly cool apples in syrup. Serve warm with a small amount of syrup. Makes 6 servings.

Serve these spiced apples as either a side dish or a light dessert.

This version of old-fashioned baked beans gets extra flavor from molasses and rum.

MOLASSES AND RUM
BAKED BEANS

1 pound dry navy beans or dry great northern beans (2⅓ cups)
¼ pound bacon (6 slices) or salt pork, cut into ½-inch pieces
1 cup chopped onion
2 cloves garlic, minced
½ cup molasses or maple-flavored syrup
½ cup chili sauce or catsup
¼ cup dark rum
¼ cup packed brown sugar
2 teaspoons dry mustard
½ teaspoon salt
½ teaspoon ground ginger
¼ to ½ teaspoon pepper

RINSE BEANS. IN A 4½-QUART DUTCH OVEN combine beans and 8 cups *cold water.* Bring to boiling; reduce heat. Simmer for 2 minutes. Remove from heat. Cover and let stand for 1 hour. (*Or,* skip boiling the beans and soak the beans overnight in a covered pan.) Drain and rinse beans.

In the same pan mix beans and 8 cups *fresh cold water.* Bring to boiling; reduce heat. Cover and simmer about 1¼ hours or till tender. Drain beans, reserving hot liquid. Transfer beans to a 2½-quart casserole or bean pot.

In a medium saucepan or large skillet, cook bacon or salt pork till fat begins to accumulate. Add onion and garlic. Cook and stir over medium heat till onion is tender but not brown. Stir onion mixture into beans along with ½ *cup* of the reserved bean liquid, molasses or maple-flavored syrup, chili sauce or catsup, dark rum, brown sugar, dry mustard, salt, ground ginger, and pepper.

Bake, covered, in a 300° oven about 2½ hours or to desired consistency, stirring occasionally. If necessary, add additional reserved bean liquid. Makes 10 to 12 servings.

THREE-CHEESE MACARONI

  2 cups corkscrew macaroni
  ½ cup chopped onion
  1 clove garlic, minced
  2 tablespoons margarine or butter
  2 tablespoons all-purpose flour
  ¼ teaspoon cracked black pepper
    Dash ground red pepper
  2 cups milk
1½ cups shredded American cheese (6 ounces)
  1 3-ounce package cream cheese, cubed and softened
  2 teaspoons prepared mustard or Dijon-style mustard
  1 large tomato, peeled, seeded, and finely chopped (about 1 cup)
  ⅓ cup grated Parmesan cheese
  ¾ cup soft bread crumbs (1 slice)
  2 tablespoons margarine or butter, melted
  ¼ teaspoon paprika

The three cheeses—cream cheese, American, and Parmesan—in this version of macaroni and cheese make it especially rich.

COOK MACARONI ACCORDING TO PACKAGE directions; drain well. Meanwhile, for cheese sauce, in a saucepan cook onion and garlic in 2 tablespoons margarine or butter till tender but not brown. Stir in flour, black pepper, and ground red pepper. Add milk all at once. Cook and stir till slightly thickened and bubbly. Add shredded American cheese, cream cheese, and mustard; stir till cheese melts.

Stir tomato, Parmesan cheese, and cooked macaroni into cheese sauce. Transfer to a 1½-quart casserole. Combine the bread crumbs and 2 tablespoons melted margarine or butter. Sprinkle over macaroni mixture. Bake, uncovered, in a 350° oven for 25 to 30 minutes or till bubbly. Sprinkle with paprika. Let stand 10 minutes before serving. Makes 6 servings.

FARM-STAND RATATOUILLE

Ratatouille is a stewed vegetable combination. If you don't have a garden, look for the seasonal produce featured in this ratatouille at a roadside farm stand.

1 cup coarsely chopped onion
2 large cloves garlic, minced
2 tablespoons olive oil or cooking oil
1 medium eggplant (about 1 pound), peeled and cut into 1-inch pieces
    (about 4 cups)
2 medium zucchini, cut into ½-inch pieces (about 2½ cups)
3 medium tomatoes, seeded and cut into ¾-inch pieces (about 2½ cups)
3 small or 2 medium yellow summer squash, cut into ½-inch pieces
    (about 2½ cups)
1 large green pepper, coarsely chopped (about 1 cup)
2 tablespoons snipped fresh basil or 2 teaspoons dried basil, crushed
1 tablespoon snipped fresh oregano or 1 teaspoon dried oregano, crushed
½ teaspoon salt
¼ teaspoon pepper
1 cup shredded mozzarella cheese (4 ounces) (optional)

IN A 4- OR 5-QUART DUTCH OVEN COOK ONION AND garlic in hot olive oil or cooking oil for 3 to 4 minutes or till onion is tender but not brown. Stir in eggplant, zucchini, tomatoes, summer squash, green pepper, basil, oregano, salt, and pepper.

Cover and cook about 20 minutes or till vegetables are tender. Cook, uncovered, 5 to 10 minutes more or till liquid is slightly reduced. Remove from heat. Allow to cool slightly. If desired, stir in mozzarella cheese. Makes 8 to 10 servings.

COMPANY-SPECIAL
MASHED POTATOES

1½ pounds potatoes (about 5 medium), peeled and cut into 2-inch chunks
⅓ cup sliced leek (about 1 leek) or ⅓ cup sliced green onion
3 cloves garlic, minced
2 tablespoons margarine or butter
⅓ cup dairy sour cream
2 tablespoons half-and-half, light cream, or milk
½ teaspoon salt
⅛ teaspoon pepper
Dash ground red pepper (optional)
Half-and-half, light cream, or milk, heated (about ¼ cup) (optional)
1 tablespoon margarine or butter (optional)
1 tablespoon snipped parsley or finely chopped leek (optional)

IN A MEDIUM SAUCEPAN COMBINE THE POTATOES and enough boiling water to cover. Cover; bring to boiling. Reduce heat; simmer for 20 to 25 minutes or till potatoes are tender. Meanwhile, in a small skillet, cook the ½ cup chopped leek and garlic in the 2 tablespoons margarine or butter for 3 to 4 minutes or till leek is just tender.

Drain potatoes. Mash with a potato masher or beat with an electric mixer on low speed. Add the leek mixture, sour cream, half-and-half, salt, pepper, and, if desired, ground red pepper. (Beat in some of the additional half-and-half if a creamier consistency is desired.) Transfer potatoes to a large serving bowl. If desired, top with an additional tablespoon of margarine or butter and sprinkle with parsley or the 1 tablespoon chopped leek. Serve immediately. Makes 4 servings.

Leek and garlic dress up mashed potatoes for a company-special meal. Don't overbeat—a lump or two means they're the real thing.

SIDE DISHES

157

GERMAN-STYLE HOT POTATO SALAD

German immigrants, who adapted their old-world recipes to new-world ingredients, are responsible for this potluck or picnic favorite.

12 to 16 small red potatoes (about 2 pounds)
 6 slices bacon
¾ cup chopped red or green sweet pepper
¼ cup sliced green onion
 3 tablespoons pickled banana pepper slices
 2 tablespoons snipped parsley
⅓ cup vinegar
 4 teaspoons sugar
½ teaspoon caraway seed, crushed slightly
¼ teaspoon salt
¼ teaspoon pepper

IN A MEDIUM SAUCEPAN COMBINE POTATOES AND enough water to cover. Add *salt*, if desired. Cover; bring to boiling. Reduce heat; simmer for 15 to 20 minutes or till just tender; drain well. Cool slightly. Cut potatoes into ¼-inch-thick slices. Set potatoes aside.

━■━

In a large skillet cook bacon till crisp. Drain, reserving *2 tablespoons* of the drippings. Crumble bacon and set aside.

━■━

In a mixing bowl, combine potatoes, red or green pepper, green onion, pickled banana pepper slices, and parsley.

━■━

Stir vinegar, sugar, caraway seed, ¼ teaspoon salt, and pepper into reserved drippings in skillet. Cook and stir over medium heat for 2 to 3 minutes or till mixture is heated through. Add potato mixture. Heat through, stirring gently to coat. Transfer to a serving bowl. Sprinkle with bacon. Makes 6 servings.

GLAZED SWEET POTATOES

4 tablespoons margarine or butter
6 medium sweet potatoes (about 2 pounds)
⅓ cup coarsely chopped walnuts or pecans, toasted
3 tablespoons brown sugar
2 teaspoons finely shredded orange peel
2 tablespoons orange juice

GREASE A 12X7½X2-INCH BAKING DISH OR OVAL AU gratin dish with *1 tablespoon* of the margarine or butter. Set dish aside. Peel potatoes, cutting off woody portions and ends. Place potatoes in enough boiling salted water to cover. Cover; reduce heat. Simmer for 20 minutes. Drain; cool slightly. Cut into ¼-inch-thick slices.

Arrange slices in prepared baking dish. Dot potatoes with remaining margarine or butter, covering as many as possible. Sprinkle nuts, brown sugar, and orange peel evenly over sweet potatoes. Drizzle with orange juice. Bake, covered, in a 350° oven about 20 minutes or till potatoes are tender and lightly glazed. Serve immediately. Makes 6 servings.

HERBS FOR COOKING

COUNTRY COOKS HAVE LONG KNOWN THE delights of cooking with fresh herbs. Not only do herbs add flavor, but they make food smell and look appealing. You can have the wonderful fragrance and flavor of fresh herbs at your fingertips if you grow them at home or purchase them at your supermarket.

To grow them at home, just save a spot in your garden or on your windowsill. Herbs thrive in most well-drained soils in the garden or in pots and demand little more than sun and water. The easiest and most popular kitchen herbs to grow are basil, chives, dill, mint, oregano, parsley, rosemary, sage, tarragon, and thyme.

To use your fresh herbs, snip their leaves or sprigs as needed. Harvest garden herbs on a clear day as soon as the dew is dry, but before the heat of the day. The heat dries out the oils that give herbs their scent and flavor. Pick herbs that flower, such as chives, before they flower. That's when their flavor and aroma are best.

To get the fullest aroma from fresh herbs, run the leaves between your hands, then mince them with a sharp knife or snip them with kitchen shears. To substitute fresh herbs for dried, just triple the amount of dried leaf herb called for in a recipe. For example, if a recipe uses 1 teaspoon dried herb, add 1 tablespoon fresh.

BRANDY-GLAZED CARROTS

    1   pound baby carrots or medium carrots cut into 1-inch pieces
    1   large shallot, finely chopped, or 2 tablespoons finely chopped onion
    2   tablespoons margarine or butter
    ½   teaspoon finely shredded orange peel
    ¼   cup orange juice
    2   tablespoons honey
    2   tablespoons cognac or brandy
    ½   teaspoon cornstarch
    ¼   teaspoon ground cinnamon
    2   teaspoons snipped fresh mint or snipped parsley

IN A MEDIUM SAUCEPAN PLACE CARROTS IN A small amount of boiling water. Cook, covered, for 15 to 20 minutes or till crisp-tender. Drain; set aside.

In the same pan cook shallot or onion in margarine or butter till tender but not brown. Stir in orange peel, orange juice, honey,

cognac or brandy, cornstarch, and ground cinnamon. Cook and stir till thickened and bubbly. Add carrots. Cook and stir till carrots are coated and heated through. Season to taste with *salt* and *pepper*. Sprinkle with snipped fresh mint or parsley. Makes 4 servings.

After you taste Brandy-Glazed Carrots, you'll never view garden-fresh carrots in the same way. You'll find it hard to believe that carrots that taste so good are so easy to prepare.

BEANS WITH BLUE CHEESE

    1   pound green beans (about 4 cups) or two 9-ounce packages frozen
            French-style green beans
    3   slices bacon
    ½   cup chopped onion
    2   teaspoons lemon juice
    ½   cup crumbled blue cheese or Gorgonzola cheese (2 ounces)
    ½   cup walnut halves, toasted

PLACE A STEAMER BASKET IN A SAUCEPAN; ADD water till it almost touches the bottom of the basket. Bring water to boiling. Add fresh beans. Cover and steam for 18 to 22 minutes or till crisp-tender; drain. (Or, cook frozen beans according to package directions. Drain.)

Meanwhile, in a large skillet cook bacon till crisp. Drain, reserving drippings in skillet.

Crumble bacon; set bacon aside. Cook onion over medium heat in reserved drippings till tender but not brown. Stir in lemon juice. Add green beans; toss to coat. Heat through. Add crumbled blue cheese or Gorgonzola cheese and crumbled bacon. Heat and stir 1 minute more or till cheese begins to melt. Sprinkle with walnuts. Transfer to a serving bowl. Makes 4 to 6 servings.

Midwesterners claim blue cheese as one of their regional specialties. Three midwestern states— Illinois, Iowa, and Wisconsin—produce this zesty cheese.

SOUTH

This old-time dish was invented by pioneers as a way to use unripe tomatoes when frost threatened the last of the crop.

FRIED GREEN TOMATOES

1 pound green tomatoes (about 4 tomatoes)
½ cup white cornmeal
¼ cup all-purpose flour
2 tablespoons sesame seed
¼ teaspoon onion salt
⅛ teaspoon pepper
1 beaten egg
2 tablespoons milk
  Cooking oil for frying

SLICE TOMATOES INTO ¼-INCH-THICK SLICES. IN A pie plate or baking dish combine cornmeal, flour, sesame seed, onion salt, and pepper. In a small mixing bowl combine egg and milk. Dip tomato slices into egg mixture, then coat both sides of tomato slices with the cornmeal mixture.

In a heavy large skillet, heat about ¼ inch of cooking oil over medium heat. Fry tomato slices in a single layer about 2 minutes on each side or till golden brown. Drain on paper towels. Keep slices warm in a 300° oven while frying remaining tomatoes. Serve immediately. Makes 4 to 6 servings.

EAST

The robust flavor of onion mellows when cooked with naturally sweet apple cider.

CIDER-BRAISED ONIONS

1 pound boiling onions (about 16 onions)
2 tablespoons margarine or butter
¾ cup apple cider or apple juice
1 tablespoon cider vinegar
2 teaspoons soy sauce
3 inches stick cinnamon
¼ teaspoon whole cloves
1 tablespoon snipped fresh chives

PEEL ONIONS, TRIMMING OFF ROOT ENDS AND about ⅛ inch of the top. Using a sharp knife, score a shallow cross in each root end. In a heavy large skillet, melt the margarine or butter over medium heat. Add onions, stirring to coat well. Stir in apple cider or juice, vinegar, soy sauce, cinnamon, and whole cloves. Increase heat to high and bring mixture just to boiling; reduce heat.

Cover tightly and simmer about 10 minutes or till onions are tender when pierced with a fork. Uncover; increase heat and return to boiling. Boil hard for 3 to 5 minutes or till cider mixture is reduced to a light glaze. Remove cinnamon and cloves. Transfer onions to a serving dish. Sprinkle with chives. Makes 4 to 6 servings.

SCALLOPED CORN

½ cup chopped red or green sweet pepper
½ cup chopped onion
⅓ cup shredded carrot
¼ cup water
 1 17-ounce can cream-style corn
 1 8¾-ounce can whole kernel corn, drained
 1 cup milk
 1 cup coarsely crushed saltine crackers (about 20 crackers)
¾ cup shredded cheddar cheese (3 ounces)
 2 slightly beaten eggs
¼ cup shredded cheddar cheese (1 ounce)

IN A SMALL SAUCEPAN COMBINE RED OR GREEN sweet pepper, onion, shredded carrot, and water. Bring to boiling; reduce heat. Simmer, covered, for 5 to 7 minutes or till vegetables are crisp-tender. Drain well, pressing out excess liquid.

—■—

Meanwhile, in a large mixing bowl stir together the cream-style corn, whole kernel corn, milk, crushed crackers, the ¾ cup shredded cheddar cheese, and eggs. Stir in cooked vegetables. Transfer to a greased 8x1½-inch round baking dish.

—■—

Bake, uncovered, in a 325° oven for 50 to 55 minutes or till center is set. Sprinkle with the ¼ cup shredded cheddar cheese. Let stand 10 minutes before serving. Makes 8 servings.

Scalloped Corn is a homey favorite that has been served since colonial times. Although today the dish usually is reserved for holiday and Sunday dinners, it was considered everyday fare in early times.

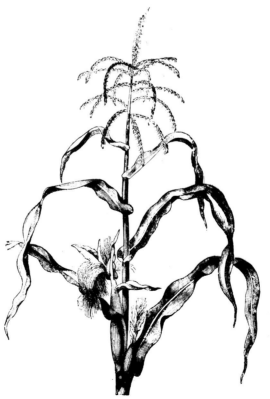

FAMILY REUNIONS

COUSINS HUG, GRANDPARENTS reminisce, and everyone

settles on the lawn to hear the latest family news—that's the heart of

any family reunion. But no reunion is complete

without a table heaped with yummy food. So next time you're taking

food to a family gathering, consider one of these home-style side

dishes. Designed to serve 6 or 12, they can be made ahead

and toted out to the backyard or 50 miles down the road.■

COMPANY SCALLOPED
POTATOES

SERVES 6

½ cup chopped onion
2 cloves garlic, minced
2 tablespoons margarine or butter
2 tablespoons all-purpose flour
4 teaspoons snipped fresh marjoram or
    basil, or 1½ teaspoons dried
    marjoram or basil, crushed
1¾ cups milk
4 cups sliced, unpeeled potatoes
¼ teaspoon salt
¼ teaspoon pepper
¼ cup grated Parmesan cheese

SERVES 12

1 cup chopped onion
4 cloves garlic, minced
¼ cup margarine or butter
¼ cup all-purpose flour
3 tablespoons snipped fresh marjoram
    or basil, or 1 tablespoon dried
    marjoram or basil, crushed
3½ cups milk
8 cups sliced, unpeeled potatoes
½ teaspoon salt
½ teaspoon pepper
½ cup grated Parmesan cheese

FOR SAUCE, IN A MEDIUM SAUCEPAN COOK ONION and garlic in margarine or butter till tender but not brown. (For 12 servings, use a large saucepan.) Stir in flour and marjoram or basil. Add milk all at once. Cook and stir till thickened and bubbly. Remove from heat.

———■———

Layer *half* of the potatoes in a greased 1½-quart casserole. (For 12 servings, use a 3-quart casserole.) Sprinkle with the salt and pepper. Cover with *half* of the sauce. Sprinkle with *half* of the Parmesan cheese. Repeat layers of potatoes and sauce.

———■———

Bake, covered, in a 350° oven for 1¼ hours. (For 12 servings, bake for 1½ hours.) Uncover and sprinkle with the remaining Parmesan cheese. Bake about 30 minutes more or till potatoes are tender. Let stand 5 minutes before serving.

TO TRANSPORT: Prepare Company Scalloped Potatoes. Cover the hot dish with foil, then wrap in a towel. Place in an insulated container to keep warm. Serve within 2 hours.

Pictured on page 165.

CHEESY CAULIFLOWER BAKE

SERVES 6

4 slices bacon
½ cup chopped onion
2 cloves garlic, minced
5 cups cauliflower flowerets (1 pound)
1 cup thinly sliced carrots (2 medium)
2 tablespoons all-purpose flour
¼ teaspoon pepper
⅛ teaspoon salt
⅛ teaspoon ground nutmeg
1⅓ cups milk
½ cup shredded Swiss cheese (2 ounces)
½ cup crushed rich round crackers

SERVES 12

8 slices bacon
1 cup chopped onion
4 cloves garlic, minced
10 cups cauliflower flowerets
2 cups thinly sliced carrots
¼ cup all-purpose flour
½ teaspoon pepper
¼ teaspoon salt
¼ teaspoon ground nutmeg
2⅔ cups milk
1 cup shredded Swiss cheese (4 ounces)
1 cup crushed rich round crackers

IN A LARGE SAUCEPAN COOK BACON TILL CRISP. Drain bacon, reserving *3 tablespoons* drippings. (For 12 servings, reserve ¼ cup drippings.) Crumble bacon; set aside. Cook onion and garlic in reserved drippings over medium heat 2 minutes; add cauliflower and carrots. Cover and cook 5 minutes or till just crisp-tender.

———■———

Stir in flour, pepper, salt, and nutmeg. Add milk all at once. Cook and stir till thickened and bubbly. Add bacon and cheese, stirring till cheese melts.

———■———

Transfer cauliflower mixture to a 1½-quart casserole or a 10x6x2-inch baking dish. (For 12 servings, transfer to a 3-quart casserole or a 13x9x2-inch baking dish.)*

———■———

Sprinkle crushed crackers over cauliflower mixture. Bake in a 350° oven for 12 to 15 minutes or till heated through.

*TO MAKE AHEAD: Prepare Cheesy Cauliflower Bake, *except* do not top with crumbs or bake. Cover and chill up to 24 hours. Bake casserole, covered, in a 350° oven for 25 to 30 minutes or till heated through, stirring after 15 minutes. (For 12 servings, bake about 40 minutes, stirring after 20 minutes.) Uncover and sprinkle with crushed crackers; bake 5 minutes more.

TO TRANSPORT: Prepare Cheesy Cauli-flower Bake. Cover the hot dish with foil, then wrap in a towel. Place in an insulated container to keep warm. Serve within 2 hours.

SWEET POTATO AND
FRUIT SALAD

SERVES 6

3 medium sweet potatoes
1 teaspoon finely shredded orange peel
2 oranges
½ cup seedless grapes, halved
⅓ cup raisins
¼ cup thinly sliced celery
1 3-ounce package cream cheese,
   softened
1 tablespoon honey
   Orange juice
½ cup broken walnuts (optional)

SERVES 12

6 medium sweet potatoes
2 teaspoons finely shredded orange peel
4 oranges
1 cup seedless grapes, halved
⅔ cup raisins
½ cup thinly sliced celery
2 3-ounce packages cream cheese,
   softened
2 tablespoons honey
   Orange juice
1 cup broken walnuts (optional)

SCRUB SWEET POTATOES. IN A LARGE SAUCEPAN or Dutch oven cook potatoes in boiling water for 15 to 20 minutes or till just tender. Cool. Peel and cut potatoes into ¾-inch cubes.

—■—

Peel and section oranges over a bowl, reserving juices. In a large bowl combine potato cubes, orange sections, grapes, raisins, and celery.

—■—

For dressing, in a small bowl stir together orange peel, cream cheese, and honey. Stir in *1 tablespoon* of the reserved orange juice. (For 12 servings, use *2 tablespoons* of the reserved orange juice.) Pour over potato mixture; gently toss. Cover and chill for 4 to 24 hours.*

—■—

Before serving, stir in *1 to 2 tablespoons* orange juice, if necessary, to make of desired consistency. (For 12 servings, stir in *2 to 4 tablespoons* juice.) If desired, stir in nuts.

*TO TRANSPORT: Prepare Sweet Potato and Fruit Salad, *except* after chilling, place salad, *2 tablespoons* orange juice (¼ *cup* orange juice for 12 servings), and, if desired, nuts in separate containers. Pack salad and the containers in an insulated cooler with ice. Serve within 4 hours. Before serving, stir enough of the orange juice into the salad to make of desired consistency. If desired, stir in the nuts.

Pictured on page 165.

BLACK BEAN AND
CORN SALAD

SERVES 6

1   15-ounce can black beans
1   8¾-ounce can whole kernel corn,
    drained
½   cup chopped green or red sweet
    pepper
½   cup sliced celery
¼   cup chopped onion
¾   cup salsa
1   tablespoon lemon juice
½   teaspoon ground cumin
    Dash garlic powder
1   cup cubed Monterey Jack cheese
    (4 ounces)
    Lettuce leaves (optional)

SERVES 12

2   15-ounce cans black beans
1   17-ounce can whole kernel corn,
    drained
1   cup chopped green or red sweet
    pepper
1   cup sliced celery
½   cup chopped onion
1½ cups salsa
2   tablespoons lemon juice
1   teaspoon ground cumin
⅛   teaspoon garlic powder
2   cups cubed Monterey Jack cheese
    (8 ounces)
    Lettuce leaves (optional)

RINSE AND DRAIN BLACK BEANS. IN A LARGE BOWL combine black beans, drained corn, chopped green or red sweet pepper, celery, and onion.

——■——

In a small bowl stir together salsa, lemon juice, cumin, and garlic powder. Pour over black bean mixture; toss gently. Cover and chill for 2 to 24 hours.*

——■——

Just before serving, stir cheese into salad. If desired, serve in a lettuce-lined bowl.

*TO TRANSPORT: Prepare Black Bean and Corn Salad, *except* chill salad at least 4 hours and do not stir in cheese. Place cheese and, if desired, lettuce in separate containers. Pack salad and the containers in an insulated cooler with ice. Serve within 4 hours. Just before serving, stir cubed cheese into salad. If desired, serve in a lettuce-lined bowl.

Pictured on page 165.

ZUCCHINI–BARLEY SALAD

SERVES 6

1 1/4 cups water
 1 cup quick-cooking barley
 1 medium cucumber
 1 medium zucchini or yellow summer
   squash
 1/2 cup shredded carrot
 1/2 cup mayonnaise or salad dressing
 3 tablespoons vinegar
1 1/2 teaspoons snipped fresh basil or 1/2
   teaspoon dried basil, crushed
 1/4 teaspoon salt
 1/8 teaspoon pepper
 1/3 cup slivered almonds, toasted

IN A SAUCEPAN COMBINE WATER AND BARLEY.
Bring to boiling; reduce heat. Cover and
simmer for 10 to 12 minutes or till liquid is
absorbed.

—■—

Meanwhile, quarter cucumber lengthwise;
thinly slice cucumber quarters. Coarsely chop
zucchini or squash. In a large bowl combine
the cooked barley, cucumber, zucchini or
squash, and carrot.

—■—

For dressing, in a small bowl stir together
mayonnaise or salad dressing, vinegar, basil,
salt, and pepper. Pour dressing over barley
mixture. Toss till coated. Cover and chill for 2
to 24 hours.* Just before serving, stir almonds
into salad.

SERVES 12

2 1/2 cups water
 2 cups quick-cooking barley
 2 medium cucumbers
 2 medium zucchini or yellow summer
   squash
 1 cup shredded carrot
 1 cup mayonnaise or salad dressing
 6 tablespoons vinegar
 1 tablespoon snipped fresh basil or 1
   teaspoon dried basil, crushed
 1/2 teaspoon salt
 1/4 teaspoon pepper
 2/3 cup slivered almonds, toasted

*TO TRANSPORT: Prepare Zucchini-Barley
Salad, except do not stir in almonds.
Wrap almonds separately. Pack covered
salad and almonds in an insulated cooler
with ice. Serve within 4 hours. Just
before serving, stir almonds into salad.

VEGETABLE SALAD
WITH PARMESAN DRESSING

SERVES 6

⅓ cup mayonnaise or salad dressing
3 tablespoons grated Parmesan cheese
2 tablespoons buttermilk
1 tablespoon snipped fresh dill or
    1 teaspoon dried dillweed
¼ teaspoon garlic powder
¼ teaspoon onion powder
⅛ teaspoon pepper
2 cups cauliflower flowerets
1 cup sliced radishes
1 cup chopped green, red, or
    yellow sweet pepper
1 cup sliced celery
1 cup frozen peas

SERVES 12

⅔ cup mayonnaise or salad dressing
⅓ cup grated Parmesan cheese
¼ cup buttermilk
2 tablespoons snipped fresh dill or
    2 teaspoons dried dillweed
½ teaspoon garlic powder
½ teaspoon onion powder
¼ teaspoon pepper
4 cups cauliflower flowerets
2 cups sliced radishes
2 cups chopped green, red, or
    yellow sweet pepper
2 cups sliced celery
2 cups frozen peas

FOR DRESSING, IN A SMALL BOWL STIR TOGETHER mayonnaise or salad dressing, Parmesan cheese, buttermilk, dill, garlic powder, onion powder, and pepper.

———■———

In a large salad bowl combine cauliflower, radishes, chopped pepper, celery, and peas.* Pour dressing over vegetable mixture. Gently toss till vegetables are well coated.

*TO TRANSPORT: Prepare Vegetable Salad with Parmesan Dressing, *except* do not pour dressing over vegetable mixture. Place dressing and vegetable mixture in separate containers. Cover and chill for 2 to 24 hours. Pack the two containers in an insulated cooler with ice. Serve within 4 hours. Just before serving, pour dressing over vegetable mixture. Gently toss till vegetables are well coated.

Pictured on page 165.

CHAPTER EIGHT

THE FRUIT CELLAR

PRESERVING THE ABUNDANCE OF FRESH fruits and vegetables from the garden—either to enjoy during the winter months or to give as gifts to friends — has long been a country tradition and a labor of love. Grandma called it "putting summer in a jar," and there's hardly a country cook anywhere whose pantry shelf isn't lined with jars of colorful jams, jellies, and pickles. After all, there are few pleasures greater than bringing a taste of summer to the table long after the harvest is over.■

GINGER-APPLE BUTTER

Freeze this subtly flavored spread if you don't have time for canning. Whether it's canned or frozen, use the spread within one year for the best flavor and quality.

Pictured on page 173.

6 pounds tart cooking apples, cored and quartered (about 18 cups)
6 cups apple cider or apple juice
3 cups sugar
2 tablespoons finely chopped crystallized ginger

IN AN 8-QUART KETTLE OR DUTCH OVEN COMBINE apples and cider. Bring to boiling; reduce heat. Cover and simmer for 30 minutes, stirring often. *Do not drain.* Press through a food mill or sieve. (You should have about 12 cups.)

Return pulp to the kettle or Dutch oven. Stir in sugar and ginger. Bring to boiling; reduce heat. Simmer, uncovered, about 2 hours or till mixture is very thick, stirring often. Ladle hot apple butter at once into hot, *sterilized* half-pint jars, leaving a ¼-inch headspace.

Wipe rims and adjust lids. Process in a boiling-water canner for 5 minutes. (Begin timing when water boils.) Makes about 6 half-pints (96 one-tablespoon servings).

FREEZING DIRECTIONS: Prepare Ginger-Apple Butter, *except* after simmering 2 hours, place kettle of apple butter in a sink of *ice* water till cool; stir often. Ladle into wide-top freezing or canning jars, leaving ¾-inch headspace. Wipe rims, seal, and label. Freeze up to 12 months.

CANNING BASICS

Processing times given in this book are for altitudes less than 1,000 feet above sea level. If you live at a higher altitude, call your county extension agent for timing adjustments.

FOR PANTRY STORAGE, ALL JAMS, PRESERVES, pickles, and relishes must be processed in a boiling-water canner to prevent spoilage. For the most recent canning directions, call your county extension agent. General steps for canning follow.

Use a boiling-water canner or a large kettle with a rack and a lid. The kettle must be deep enough to hold 1 inch of water above the tops of the jars. Fill the canner or kettle half full of water. Cover and heat till the water is hot.

Sterilize the canning jars by immersing them in boiling water for 10 minutes.

Ladle the hot mixture into the hot jars, leaving the specified headspace. Wipe the jar rims to remove all food. Cover the jars with flat metal canning lids and screw bands. Place the jars in the canner or kettle on the rack. Jars should not touch.

When all of the jars are in the canner, add boiling water till it is 1 inch above the tops of the jars. Cover and heat to a rolling boil. Boil for the time given in the recipe.

Remove the jars and place them on a board or a towel. When the jars are completely cool, remove the screw bands and check each seal. Refrigerate any unsealed jars and use the contents immediately.

APRICOT–ORANGE MARMALADE

2 medium oranges
1 medium lemon
1 cup water
⅛ teaspoon baking soda
2 pounds apricots
6½ cups sugar
½ of a 6-ounce package (1 foil pouch) liquid fruit pectin

USING A VEGETABLE PEELER, PEEL ORANGES AND lemon. (Peel should have no white membrane attached.) Cut peels into very thin strips.

— ■ —

In a medium saucepan combine peels, water, and baking soda. Bring to boiling; reduce heat. Cover and simmer 20 minutes. *Do not drain.*

— ■ —

Meanwhile, remove white membranes from oranges and lemon. Section oranges and lemon over a bowl, reserving juices. Discard seeds. Add orange sections, lemon sections, and juices to peel mixture. Return to boiling; reduce heat. Cover and simmer for 10 minutes. Measure *1½ cups.*

— ■ —

Pit apricots; *do not peel.* Finely chop apricots. Measure *3 cups.*

— ■ —

In an 8- or 10-quart kettle or Dutch oven combine the 1½ cups orange mixture, apricots, and sugar. Bring to a full rolling boil, stirring constantly. Quickly stir in pectin. Return to a full rolling boil and boil hard for 1 minute, stirring constantly. Remove from the heat. Quickly skim off foam with a large metal spoon.

— ■ —

Ladle at once into hot, *sterilized* half-pint jars, leaving a ¼-inch headspace. Wipe rims and adjust lids. Process in a boiling-water canner for 15 minutes. (Begin timing when water boils.) Makes about 8 half-pints (128 one-tablespoon servings).

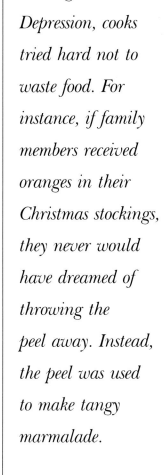

During the Great Depression, cooks tried hard not to waste food. For instance, if family members received oranges in their Christmas stockings, they never would have dreamed of throwing the peel away. Instead, the peel was used to make tangy marmalade.

NECTARINE–RASPBERRY CONSERVE

A jam by any other name tastes just as sweet. But here's a rundown of what those other names mean. Jelly is a translucent mixture made of fruit juice and sugar. Jam is made with crushed fruit and sugar, and contains small pieces of fruit. A preserve is similar to jam, except the fruit pieces are larger. A conserve is a jam made with two or three kinds of fruit and may include raisins or nuts.

> 3 cups finely chopped, peeled nectarines or peaches (about 2 pounds) or
>   6 cups frozen unsweetened peach slices, thawed and finely chopped
>   (1½ sixteen-ounce packages)
> 2 cups red raspberries, crushed, or 2 cups frozen unsweetened red raspberries,
>   thawed and crushed
> 2 tablespoons lemon juice
> 1 1¾-ounce package powdered fruit pectin
> ½ teaspoon margarine or butter
> 5½ cups sugar
> 1 cup chopped walnuts, toasted

IN AN 8- OR 10-QUART KETTLE COMBINE THE chopped nectarines or peaches, raspberries, and lemon juice. Stir in fruit pectin and margarine or butter. Bring to a full rolling boil, stirring constantly. Stir in sugar.

— ■ —

Return mixture to a full rolling boil. Boil hard for 1 minute, stirring constantly. Stir in nuts. Remove from the heat. Quickly skim off foam with a large metal spoon.

— ■ —

Ladle at once into hot, *sterilized* half-pint jars, leaving a ¼-inch headspace. Wipe rims and adjust lids. Process in a boiling-water canner for 5 minutes. (Begin timing when water boils.) Makes 6 to 7 half-pints (96 one-tablespoon servings).

Ginger–Apple Butter
(see recipe, page 174)

Nectarine–Raspberry Conserve

SPICED PEACH FREEZER JAM

    2   pounds peaches
    6   cups sugar
    1   6-ounce package (2 foil pouches) liquid fruit pectin
    ⅓   cup lemon juice
    1   teaspoon ground cinnamon
    ½   teaspoon ground nutmeg

PEEL, PIT, AND FINELY CHOP PEACHES. MEASURE 2¾ *cups.* In a large bowl stir together peaches and sugar. Let stand for 10 minutes.

In a small bowl stir together pectin, lemon juice, cinnamon, and nutmeg. Stir pectin mixture into peach mixture. Stir for 3 minutes.

Ladle jam at once into wide-top, half-pint freezing or canning jars, leaving a ½-inch headspace. Wipe rims of jars, seal, and label. Let stand at room temperature for 24 hours. Store up to 3 weeks in the refrigerator or 12 months in the freezer. Makes 6 to 7 half-pints (96 one-tablespoon servings).

THREE-FRUIT CONSERVE

    3   cups strawberries or red raspberries
    3   cups fresh or frozen unsweetened, pitted, tart red cherries
    1   15¼-ounce can crushed pineapple (juice pack), drained
    1   teaspoon finely shredded lemon peel
    1   tablespoon lemon juice
    1   1¾-ounce package powdered fruit pectin
    ½   teaspoon margarine or butter
    7   cups sugar

CRUSH STRAWBERRIES OR RASPBERRIES AND cherries. Measure 3½ *cups.* In an 8- or 10-quart kettle or Dutch oven combine berry-cherry mixture, drained pineapple, lemon peel, and lemon juice. Stir in fruit pectin and margarine or butter. Bring to a full rolling boil, stirring constantly. Stir in the sugar.

Return fruit mixture to a full rolling boil. Boil hard for 1 minute, stirring constantly. Remove from the heat. Quickly skim off foam with a large metal spoon.

Ladle at once into hot, *sterilized* half-pint jars, leaving a ¼-inch headspace. Wipe rims and adjust lids. Process in a boiling-water canner for 5 minutes. (Begin timing when water boils.) Makes about 8 half-pints (128 one-tablespoon servings).

Homemade jams and preserves that capture the flavors of summer fruits are welcome gifts at holiday time. Just a few simple touches make these flavor-packed jars extra special. Cover the top of each jar with a circle of cloth and tie a ribbon around the neck. Then, slip a spoon for serving the jam under the ribbon. On the gift tag, mention any serving ideas or special instructions, such as keeping the jam refrigerated.

PICCALILLI

2 pounds green tomatoes, cored and chopped (about 6 cups)
2 cups chopped cucumber
1 cup chopped onion
1 cup chopped green pepper (about 1 medium)
½ cup chopped radishes
¼ cup pickling salt
12 whole allspice
1 teaspoon whole cloves
6 inches stick cinnamon, broken
2 cups sugar
2 cups white vinegar

IN A VERY LARGE BOWL COMBINE TOMATOES, cucumbers, onion, green pepper, and radishes. Sprinkle with pickling salt. Let stand, loosely covered, overnight. Rinse well and drain.

———■———

For a spice bag, cut a double thickness of 100 percent cotton cheesecloth into a 6- or 8-inch square. Place allspice, cloves, and cinnamon in the center of the cheesecloth. Bring up the corners of the cheesecloth and tie them together with a clean string. Set aside.

———■———

In an 8- or 10-quart kettle or Dutch oven combine vegetable mixture, sugar, and vinegar. Add the spice bag. Bring to boiling; reduce heat. Simmer, uncovered, for 30 minutes.

———■———

Remove and discard the spice bag. Ladle vegetable mixture at once into hot, *sterilized* half-pint jars, leaving a ½-inch headspace. Wipe rims and adjust lids. Process in a boiling-water canner for 15 minutes. (Begin timing when water boils.) Makes 7 half-pints (112 one-tablespoon servings).

*T*his spicy, sweet, and tart Piccalilli makes a delicious relish for hamburgers and hot dogs, or a fine accompaniment for lamb and poultry.

Pictured on page 173.

THE FRUIT CELLAR

PEPPY GREEN TOMATO CHUTNEY

Chutneys are relishes made with vegetables or fruit. They can be mild or hot. Jalapeño peppers give this chutney a snappy flavor.

Pictured on page 173.

      1   pound green tomatoes, cored and coarsely chopped (about 3 cups)
      2½ cups coarsely chopped cooking apples (about 2 medium)
      1   cup chopped onion
      ¼   cup chopped red sweet pepper
      2   jalapeño peppers, seeded and finely chopped
      2   cups sugar
      1¾ cups vinegar
      1   tablespoon mustard seed
      1   teaspoon celery seed

IN A 4-QUART DUTCH OVEN COMBINE TOMATOES, apples, onion, red sweet pepper, and jalapeño peppers. Stir in sugar, vinegar, mustard seed, celery seed, and ½ teaspoon *salt*. Bring to boiling, stirring often. Reduce heat. Boil gently, uncovered, about 35 minutes or till slightly thickened, stirring occasionally. Cool.

Ladle into freezer containers, leaving a ½-inch headspace. Seal and label. Store up to 4 weeks in the refrigerator or 3 months in the freezer. Makes 3½ cups (56 one-tablespoon servings).

The wonderful sweet–tart flavor of Cherry–Apple Chutney complements turkey, chicken, or ham.

CHERRY–APPLE CHUTNEY

      4   cups fresh or frozen unsweetened pitted tart red cherries (about 1 pound)
      3   cups coarsely chopped, peeled, tart cooking apples (about 3 medium)
      2   cups sugar
      1   cup raisins
      1   cup chopped onion
      1   cup chopped celery
      1   cup vinegar
      ⅓   cup lemon juice
      ½   teaspoon salt
      ½   teaspoon ground allspice

IN A 4-QUART DUTCH OVEN COMBINE ALL OF THE ingredients. (Measure depth of mixture with a clean wooden ruler at start and finish.) Bring to boiling, stirring often. Reduce heat. Simmer, uncovered, 40 minutes or till mixture is reduced by about one-third, stirring often.

Ladle at once into hot, *sterilized* half-pint jars, leaving a ½-inch headspace. Wipe rims of jars and adjust lids. Process in a boiling-water canner for 10 minutes. (Begin timing when water boils.) Makes 6 half-pints (96 one-tablespoon servings).

BRANDIED PEACHES

2 cups sugar
⅔ cup vinegar
⅔ cup honey
6 inches stick cinnamon, broken
32 whole allspice
1½ teaspoons whole cloves
5 pounds small peaches, peeled, halved, and pitted
⅓ cup brandy or peach brandy

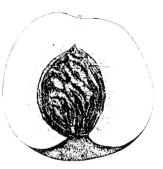

IN A 6-QUART DUTCH OVEN COMBINE THE SUGAR, vinegar, honey, cinnamon, allspice, cloves, and 1⅓ cups *water*. Bring to boiling, stirring often. Add peach halves. Return to boiling; reduce heat. Simmer, uncovered, for 5 minutes. Stir in brandy. Return to boiling; cook 1 minute.

Spoon peach halves at once into hot, *sterilized* pint jars, leaving a ½-inch headspace. Pour syrup into the jars maintaining the ½-inch headspace. Wipe rims and adjust lids. Process in a boiling-water canner for 20 minutes. (Begin timing when water boils.) Makes 5 pints (20 servings).

Chill Brandied Peaches before serving to bring out their full spicy flavor.

Pictured on page 7.

ORANGE MINCEMEAT

2 teaspoons finely shredded orange peel
3 medium oranges
Orange juice
5 pounds cooking apples
1 15-ounce box (2½ cups) raisins
2 cups packed brown sugar
1 8-ounce package pitted whole dates, snipped
1 teaspoon ground cinnamon
¼ teaspoon ground ginger
¼ teaspoon ground nutmeg
⅛ teaspoon ground cloves

PEEL AND SECTION ORANGES OVER A BOWL, reserving juices. Add enough orange juice to reserved juices to equal 1½ cups. Peel, core, and finely chop apples. Measure 9 cups.

In a 6- or 8-quart kettle or Dutch oven combine orange peel, orange sections, juice, apples, raisins, sugar, dates, cinnamon, ginger, nutmeg, and cloves. Bring to boiling; reduce

heat. Cover and simmer 30 to 40 minutes or till thickened, stirring often to prevent sticking.

Cool mixture. Divide into three 3⅓-cup portions. Ladle into three 1-quart freezer containers. Wipe rims of containers. Seal and label. Freeze up to 12 months. To use the mincemeat, thaw in the refrigerator overnight. Makes about 10 cups.

Use this fruity mincemeat in Cranberry–Pear Mince Pie (see recipe, page 93) or substitute it for purchased mincemeat in pie, cookie, and tart recipes.

CORN RELISH

Pictured on page 173.

12 to 16 fresh ears of corn
3 cups chopped cabbage
2 cups chopped green and/or *red sweet pepper (about 2 medium)*
1 cup chopped onion
2½ cups white vinegar
2 cups sugar
1 tablespoon celery seed
⅓ cup all-purpose flour
2 tablespoons dry mustard
1 teaspoon ground turmeric

CUT CORN FROM COBS (DO NOT SCRAPE COBS). Measure *8 cups.* In an 8- or 10-quart kettle or Dutch oven combine corn and 2 cups *water.* Bring to boiling; reduce heat. Cover; simmer about 12 minutes or till nearly tender. *Do not drain.* Add cabbage, chopped pepper, and onion. Stir in *2 cups* of the vinegar, the sugar, and celery seed. Return to boiling. Boil, uncovered, 5 minutes, stirring occasionally.

Stir together the remaining vinegar, flour, mustard, and turmeric; stir into corn mixture. Cook and stir till bubbly; cook 1 minute more.

Ladle at once into hot, *sterilized* pint jars, leaving a ½-inch headspace. Wipe rims and adjust lids. Process in a boiling-water canner for 15 minutes. (Begin timing when water boils.) Makes about 7 pints (224 one-table-spoon servings).

DILL-PICKLED OKRA

You'll discover why Southerners love the asparaguslike flavor of okra when you taste crisp Dill Pickled Okra.

Pictured on page 173.

2½ pounds small whole okra
3 cups cider vinegar
2 tablespoons pickling salt
6 cloves garlic
1 tablespoon mustard seed
12 heads fresh dill or 3 tablespoons dillseed
1½ teaspoons crushed red pepper

WASH OKRA. TRIM STEM ENDS. SET ASIDE. IN A saucepan mix vinegar, salt, and 2 cups *water.* Bring to boiling. Keep warm over low heat. In *each* of *six* hot, *sterilized* pint jars, place *1 clove* garlic, *½ teaspoon* mustard seed, *2 heads* fresh dill or *1½ teaspoons* dillseed, and *¼ teaspoon* crushed red pepper.

Immediately pack okra loosely into the jars, standing okra upright and leaving a ½-inch headspace. Pour *hot* vinegar mixture over okra maintaining the ½-inch headspace. Wipe rims and adjust lids. Process in a boiling-water canner for 10 minutes. (Begin timing when water boils.) Let stand 1 week before opening. Makes 6 pints (36 servings).

QUICK SWEET-SOUR PICKLES

4 quarts sliced medium unwaxed cucumbers
⅓ cup pickling salt
   Cracked ice
5 cups sugar
4 cups cider vinegar
2 tablespoons mustard seed
2 teaspoons coriander seed
1½ teaspoons ground turmeric
½ teaspoon whole cloves
3 bay leaves

IN A VERY LARGE BOWL COMBINE CUCUMBERS AND salt. Stir in a large amount of ice (about 1½ quarts). Let stand 3 hours. Drain well. (*Do not rinse.*) In an 8- or 10-quart kettle or Dutch oven combine sugar, vinegar, mustard seed, coriander seed, turmeric, and cloves. Add cucumbers; bring to boiling. Pack cucumbers and liquid into hot, *sterilized* quart jars, leaving a ½-inch headspace. Add a bay leaf to each jar. Wipe rims; adjust lids. Process in a boiling-water canner 10 minutes. (Begin timing when water boils.) Makes 3 quarts (60 servings).

SWEET PICKLED BEETS

2 pounds beets
2 medium onions, thinly sliced
1⅓ cups vinegar
1 cup sugar
4 whole cloves
3 inches stick cinnamon, broken
1 teaspoon mustard seed
2 sprigs celery leaves
¼ teaspoon whole black peppercorns

COOK FRESH WHOLE BEETS, COVERED, IN BOILING water for 40 to 50 minutes or till tender. Drain. Slip off skins. Slice ¼ inch thick.

—■—

In a 4-quart Dutch oven combine onions, vinegar, sugar, and ⅔ cup *water.* Tie cloves, cinnamon, mustard seed, celery leaves, and peppercorns in a 100 percent cotton cheesecloth bag. Add to vinegar mixture.

Bring to boiling; reduce heat. Cover and simmer 15 minutes. Discard bag.

—■—

Pack beets into hot, *sterilized* half-pint jars. Pour onions and vinegar mixture over beets, leaving a ½-inch headspace. Wipe rims and adjust lids. Process in a boiling-water canner for 30 minutes. (Begin timing when water boils.) Makes 5 half-pints (20 servings).

Before the days of commercially canned and frozen foods, virtually any vegetable or fruit was pickled to preserve it. Favorites included pickled asparagus, beans, cauliflower, mushrooms, cabbage, beets, and cucumbers. Peaches and apricots were two popular fruits to pickle because they held their shape. In the South, cooks also pickled such delicacies as sassafras blossoms and nasturtium buds. Both recipes pictured on page 173.

CAJUN-STYLE CATSUP

Made with three kinds of pepper, spicy Cajun-Style Catsup lives up to its name.

Pictured on page 173.

8 pounds tomatoes (about 24 medium)
½ cup chopped onion
½ cup chopped green pepper (about 1 small)
4 cloves garlic, minced
¾ teaspoon black pepper
½ teaspoon ground red pepper
½ cup sugar
½ cup packed brown sugar
1 cup vinegar
1 teaspoon whole cloves
1 teaspoon celery seed
1 tablespoon salt
¼ teaspoon bottled hot pepper sauce

WASH, CORE, AND QUARTER TOMATOES. DRAIN IN a colander; discard liquid. Place tomatoes in an 8- or 10-quart kettle or Dutch oven. Add onion, green pepper, garlic, black pepper, and red pepper. Bring to boiling; reduce heat. Simmer, uncovered, for 30 minutes, stirring often. Cool slightly.

Put mixture through a food mill or sieve; discard seeds and skins. Return puree to kettle. Stir in sugar and brown sugar. (Measure depth of mixture with a clean wooden ruler now and at the end of 1½ to 2 hours cooking.)

Bring tomato mixture to boiling; reduce heat. Simmer, uncovered, for 1½ to 2 hours or till reduced by half, stirring occasionally to prevent sticking.

Meanwhile, in a stainless steel or enamel saucepan combine vinegar, cloves, and celery seed. Bring to boiling. Remove from the heat. Using a colander lined with 100 percent cotton cheesecloth or a bowl-shaped coffee filter, strain vinegar mixture into tomato mixture. Discard solids. Stir in salt and pepper sauce.

Return to boiling; reduce heat. Simmer, uncovered, about 30 minutes or until catsup is of desired consistency, stirring frequently.

Ladle hot catsup at once into hot, *sterilized* pint or half-pint jars, leaving a ½-inch headspace. Wipe rims and adjust lids. Process in a boiling-water canner for 15 minutes for pint jars or 10 minutes for half-pint jars. (Begin timing when water boils.) Makes 2 pints or 4 half-pints (64 one-tablespoon servings).

REFRIGERATION AND FREEZING DIRECTIONS: Prepare Cajun-Style Catsup, *except* after simmering to desired consistency, place kettle or Dutch oven of catsup in a sink of *ice water* till cool; stir occasionally. Ladle catsup into wide-top canning jars or freezer containers, leaving a ½-inch headspace. Wipe rims, seal, and label. Refrigerate for up to 1 month or freeze for up to 10 months.

HERB VINEGAR

½ cup tightly packed fresh tarragon, thyme, mint, rosemary, or basil leaves
2 cups white wine vinegar
   Tarragon, thyme, mint, rosemary, or basil sprigs (optional)

WASH DESIRED HERBS; PAT DRY WITH PAPER towels. In a small stainless steel or enamel saucepan combine herbs and vinegar. Bring *almost* to boiling. Remove from heat and cover loosely with cheesecloth; cool. Pour mixture into a clean 1-quart jar. Cover jar tightly with a nonmetallic lid (*or* cover with plastic wrap and then tightly seal with a metal lid). Let stand in a cool, dark place for 2 weeks.

———■———

Line a colander with several layers of 100 percent cotton cheesecloth. Pour vinegar mixture through the colander and let it drain into a bowl. Discard herbs. Transfer strained vinegar to a clean 1½-pint jar or bottle. If desired, add an additional sprig of fresh herb to the jar or bottle.

———■———

Cover the jar or bottle with a nonmetallic lid (*or* cover with plastic wrap and tightly seal with a metal lid). Store in a cool, dark place for up to 6 months. Makes about 2 cups (32 one-tablespoon servings).

GARLIC VINEGAR: Prepare Herb Vinegar as directed, *except* omit herbs. Peel and quarter 10 cloves *garlic*. Heat garlic with the vinegar. Continue as directed.

FRUIT-FLAVORED VINEGAR

1 cup fresh or frozen unsweetened tart red cherries, blueberries, or raspberries
2 cups white wine vinegar
   Tart red cherries, blueberries, or raspberries (optional)

THAW FRUIT, IF FROZEN. IN A SMALL STAINLESS steel or enamel saucepan combine the 1 cup fruit and the vinegar. Bring to boiling; reduce heat. Boil gently, uncovered, for 3 minutes. Cover loosely with cheesecloth. Cool.

———■———

Pour mixture into a 1-quart jar. Cover tightly with a nonmetallic lid (*or* cover with plastic wrap, then seal tightly with a metal lid). Let stand in a cool, dark place for 2 weeks.

———■———

Line a colander with several layers of 100 percent cotton cheesecloth. Strain vinegar mixture through colander; let drain into a bowl. Discard fruit. Transfer strained vinegar to a clean 1-pint jar or bottle. If desired, add a few additional pieces of fresh fruit to jar. Cover tightly with a nonmetallic lid (*or* cover with plastic wrap, then seal tightly with a metal lid). Store in a cool, dark place for up to 6 months. Makes about 1½ cups (24 one-tablespoon servings).

THE FRUIT CELLAR

In the days when store-bought vinegar wasn't available, Americans made their own in the spring and summer. They mixed molasses, water, and yeast in a barrel and set it by the fireplace for 24 hours. Then they moved the barrel into the sunshine for three months so it could ferment. If the weather was hot and the barrel was shaken daily, the vinegar might be ready in one month. You'll find these vinegars much easier to make.

CHAPTER NINE

COUNTRY ENDINGS

NOTHING SAYS HOME-SWEET-HOME cooking like lofty layer cakes, bubbling fresh fruit tucked beneath mounds of fluffy dumplings, and warm-from-the-oven bread pudding. Ever satisfying and always tasty, these old-fashioned desserts are truly the epitome of country goodness. Serve any of these praise worthy desserts with confidence that they are fitting ends to a country meal.■

CHOCOLATE CAKE
WITH TRUFFLE FILLING

*N*o buttermilk on hand? A handy substitute is sour milk, which is easy to make. Add 1 tablespoon lemon juice or vinegar to a glass measuring cup. Then pour in enough milk to make 1 cup. Let stand 5 minutes before using.

2 cups all-purpose flour
2 cups sugar
1 teaspoon baking powder
¾ teaspoon baking soda
1¼ cups buttermilk or *sour milk (see tip, left)*
½ cup shortening
½ cup *margarine or butter,* softened
4 squares (4 ounces) *unsweetened chocolate,* melted and cooled
2 teaspoons vanilla
4 eggs
Truffle Filling
Creamy Chocolate Glaze

IN A LARGE BOWL COMBINE FLOUR, SUGAR, BAKING powder, and baking soda. Add buttermilk, shortening, margarine, melted chocolate, and vanilla. Beat with an electric mixer on low-to-medium speed for 30 seconds or till combined. Beat on medium-to-high speed for 2 minutes. Add eggs; beat 2 minutes more. Pour batter into 3 greased and floured 8x1½- or 9x1½-inch round baking pans.

Bake in a 350° oven 25 to 30 minutes or till a toothpick comes out clean. Cool on racks 10 minutes. Remove from pans. Cool completely. Spread Truffle Filling between layers. Spoon Creamy Chocolate Glaze over top of cake, allowing excess to drip down sides. Store in the refrigerator. Makes 16 servings.

CREAMY CHOCOLATE GLAZE: Melt 1 square (1 ounce) *unsweetened chocolate* and 2 tablespoons *margarine or butter.* Stir in 1 cup sifted *powdered sugar* and 1 teaspoon *vanilla.* Stir in 1 tablespoon *boiling water,* then an additional 1 cup sifted *powdered sugar.* Gradually add 2 to 3 tablespoons *boiling water* till glaze is smooth and of drizzling consistency.

TRUFFLE FILLING: In a heavy saucepan combine 6 squares (6 ounces) *semisweet chocolate,* coarsely chopped; ¼ cup *margarine or butter;* and 3 tablespoons *whipping cream.* Cook over low heat till chocolate melts, stirring constantly. Gradually stir about *half* of the hot mixture into 1 beaten *egg yolk;* return this mixture to the saucepan. Cook and stir over medium-low heat for 2 minutes. Remove from heat. Transfer to a small mixing bowl; chill about 1 hour or till mixture is completely cool, stirring occasionally. Beat the cooled mixture with an electric mixer on medium speed till smooth and slightly fluffy, scraping the sides of the bowl.

CURRANT

POUND CAKE

1 cup butter (do not use margarine)
4 eggs
1 cup buttermilk or sour milk (see tip, opposite)
3 cups all-purpose flour
1 teaspoon baking powder
½ teaspoon baking soda
¼ teaspoon ground nutmeg or ground mace
2 cups sugar
1 teaspoon finely shredded lemon peel
1 tablespoon lemon juice
½ cup dried currants or finely chopped toasted nuts
  Lemon Drizzle Icing

Butter is what makes pound cake rich, flavorful, and smooth.

BRING BUTTER, EGGS, AND BUTTERMILK OR SOUR milk to room temperature (do not allow eggs to sit at room temperature longer than 30 minutes). In a bowl stir together flour, baking powder, baking soda, and nutmeg or mace; set aside.

In a large mixing bowl beat butter with an electric mixer on medium-to-high speed about 30 seconds or till softened. Gradually add sugar, *2 tablespoons* at a time, beating on medium-to-high speed about 8 minutes total or till very light and fluffy.

Add lemon peel and lemon juice. Add eggs, one at a time, beating on low to medium speed for 1 minute after adding each egg, and scraping the bowl often. Alternately add flour mixture and buttermilk or sour milk, beating on low speed *just till combined.* Stir in currants or nuts.

Spread batter in a greased and lightly floured 10-inch tube pan. Bake in a 325° oven for 1 to 1¼ hours or till a toothpick inserted near the center comes out clean. Cool cake in pan on a wire rack for 10 minutes. Remove cake from pan and cool completely. Drizzle Lemon Drizzle Icing over cooled cake. Makes 16 to 20 servings.

LEMON DRIZZLE ICING: Combine 1½ cups sifted *powdered sugar,* 1 tablespoon *lemon juice,* and enough *water* (3 to 4 teaspoons) to make icing of drizzling consistency.

JAM CAKE WITH
CARAMEL FROSTING

This cake is a tasty way to show off your homemade jam. But if you don't have any homemade jam, store-bought will work just as well.

2 cups all-purpose flour
1⅓ cups sugar
2 teaspoons baking powder
1 teaspoon ground cinnamon
½ teaspoon baking soda
¼ teaspoon ground nutmeg
⅛ teaspoon ground allspice
1 cup buttermilk or sour milk (see tip, page 188)
⅔ cup margarine or butter
1 teaspoon vanilla
3 eggs
¾ cup seedless blackberry or raspberry jam
Caramel Frosting

IN A BOWL COMBINE FLOUR, SUGAR, BAKING powder, cinnamon, baking soda, nutmeg, and allspice. Add buttermilk or sour milk, margarine or butter, and vanilla. Beat with an electric mixer on low-to-medium speed till combined. Beat on high speed for 2 minutes. Add eggs and beat 2 minutes more.

— ■ —

Pour into 2 greased and floured 8x1½- or 9x1½-inch round baking pans. Bake in a 350° oven for 30 to 35 minutes or till a toothpick inserted near the centers comes out clean. Cool on wire racks for 10 minutes. Remove cakes from pans. Cool completely on racks.

— ■ —

Split cake layers horizontally. Place 1 cake layer on a serving plate. Spread with about *one-third* of the jam. Top with a second cake layer and spread with another *one-third* of the jam. Top with a third cake layer and spread with the remaining jam. Finally, top with remaining cake layer. Frost top and sides of cake with Caramel Frosting. Makes 12 servings.

CARAMEL FROSTING: In a medium saucepan combine ¾ cup packed *brown sugar* and ½ cup *whipping cream.* Cook and stir over medium heat till mixture comes to a boil. Cook 2 minutes more, stirring constantly. Transfer to a medium mixing bowl. Cool to room temperature (about 1 hour). With an electric mixer on medium speed, gradually beat in about 2 cups sifted *powdered sugar* to make frosting of spreading consistency. *Immediately* frost cake. Makes about 1⅓ cups.

SPICY BLACK-WALNUT CAKE

2¾ cups all-purpose flour
1¾ cups sugar
1 tablespoon baking powder
½ teaspoon ground cinnamon
¼ teaspoon ground nutmeg
⅛ teaspoon salt
1 cup milk
1 cup margarine or butter, softened
2 teaspoons vanilla
4 eggs
1½ cups chopped black walnuts
Browned Butter Frosting

IN A LARGE MIXING BOWL STIR TOGETHER FLOUR, sugar, baking powder, cinnamon, nutmeg, and salt. Add milk, softened margarine or butter, and vanilla. Beat with an electric mixer on low-to-medium speed about 30 seconds or till combined. Beat on medium-to-high speed for 2 minutes, scraping the sides of the bowl occasionally. Add eggs and beat for 2 minutes more. Fold in 1¼ cups of the black walnuts; reserve remaining nuts.

Pour batter into a greased and floured 10-inch fluted tube pan. Bake in a 350° oven about 50 minutes or till a toothpick inserted near the center comes out clean. Cool in pan on a wire rack for 10 minutes. Remove cake from pan. Cool completely on the wire rack. Pour Browned Butter Frosting over the top of the cake, allowing excess to drip down sides. Sprinkle with reserved nuts. Makes 16 servings.

BROWNED BUTTER FROSTING: In a small saucepan melt ¼ cup butter (do not use margarine). Heat and stir till golden (do not overbrown). Gradually stir in 2½ cups sifted powdered sugar and ½ teaspoon vanilla (mixture will be crumbly). Add enough half-and-half, light cream, or milk (3 to 4 tablespoons) to make frosting of drizzling consistency.

Black walnuts have a stronger, more pungent walnut flavor than their lighter-skinned counterparts, commonly known as English walnuts.

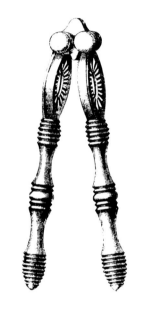

LEMON-FILLED CAKE

Here's a smaller version of a New Orleans Doberge Cake, which typically has six layers and a luscious lemon filling. This cake has just four layers, but it is just as flavorful and elegant.

Lemon Filling
2 *cups all-purpose flour*
2 *teaspoons baking powder*
4 *eggs*
2 *cups sugar*
1 *cup milk*
¼ *cup margarine or butter*
1 *teaspoon finely shredded lemon peel (optional)*
Seven-Minute Frosting

PREPARE AND CHILL LEMON FILLING (SEE RECIPE, at right). Combine flour and baking powder. In a bowl beat eggs with an electric mixer on high speed about 4 minutes or till thick. Gradually add sugar; beat at medium speed for 4 to 5 minutes or till fluffy. Add flour mixture; beat at low-to-medium speed just till combined. In a saucepan heat and stir milk and margarine till margarine melts; add to batter, beating till combined. If desired, add lemon peel. Pour batter into 4 greased and floured 9x1½-inch round pans.

Bake in a 350° oven 18 to 20 minutes or till done. Cool on wire rack 10 minutes; remove from pans and cool thoroughly. Spread *one* of the cooled cake layers with a *third* of the Lemon Filling. Repeat with two more of the cake layers and remaining Lemon Filling. Stack the three layers. Top this stack with the remaining layer. (If filling has gotten soft and the layers are sliding apart, let the cake stand, covered, in the refrigerator at least 2 hours before frosting.) Frost with Seven-Minute Frosting (see recipe, at right). If desired, garnish with twisted *lemon slices* and *mint sprigs.* Store, covered, in refrigerator. Serves 16.

*NOTE: If necessary, you can bake the cake layers two at a time. While the first two layers are baking, refrigerate remaining batter. Simply remove the cooled cake layers as directed; then wash, grease, and flour the pans as directed before using them a second time.

LEMON FILLING: Finely shred 1 tablespoon lemon peel; set aside. In a 2-quart saucepan stir together 2 cups *sugar*, ¼ cup *all-purpose flour*, and 2 tablespoons *cornstarch.* Slowly stir in 2 beaten *eggs* and 1 cup *cold water*, stirring till all lumps are dissolved. Stir in 1 cup *lemon juice.* Cook and stir mixture over medium heat till thickened and bubbly. Cook and stir 2 minutes more. Stir 2 tablespoons *margarine or butter* and the lemon peel into the mixture; cool. Cover and chill thoroughly in the refrigerator.

SEVEN-MINUTE FROSTING: In the top of a double boiler stir together 2 *egg whites*, 1½ cups *sugar*, ⅓ cup *cold water*, 2 teaspoons *light corn syrup or* ¼ teaspoon *cream of tartar*, and dash *salt.* Beat with an electric mixer on low speed for 30 seconds. Place the top of the double boiler over boiling water (the upper pan should not touch the water in the bottom of the double boiler). Cook while beating constantly with an electric mixer on high speed about 7 minutes or till the icing forms stiff peaks. Remove from the heat; add 1 teaspoon *vanilla.* Beat on high speed for 2 to 3 minutes more or till the icing reaches spreading consistency.

OLD-FASHIONED
CORNMEAL GINGERBREAD

Cornmeal first was added to gingerbread about 200 years ago when wheat flour was in short supply. Today, some cooks still like to add cornmeal to gingerbread recipes because it gives the molasses-flavored cakes a pleasantly coarse texture.

½ cup light molasses
¼ cup margarine or butter
1 cup sour milk (see tip, page 188)
½ cup yellow cornmeal
½ cup all-purpose flour
½ cup whole wheat flour
¾ teaspoon ground ginger
½ teaspoon baking powder
½ teaspoon baking soda
½ teaspoon ground cinnamon
1 beaten egg
Lemon Curd

IN A MEDIUM SAUCEPAN COMBINE MOLASSES AND margarine or butter. Heat and stir till margarine or butter melts. Remove from heat. Stir in sour milk and cornmeal.

— ■ —

In a small mixing bowl combine all-purpose flour, whole wheat flour, ginger, baking powder, baking soda, and cinnamon; add to molasses mixture along with the egg. Stir till smooth.

— ■ —

Pour batter into a greased and floured 8x8x2-inch baking pan. Bake in a 350° oven for 25 to 30 minutes or till a toothpick inserted near the center comes out clean. Cool on a wire rack for 10 minutes. Remove from pan. Serve warm with Lemon Curd. Makes 9 servings.

LEMON CURD: In a small saucepan combine ½ cup *sugar*, 2 teaspoons *cornstarch*, and 1 teaspoon finely shredded *lemon peel*. Add ¾ cup *water*. Cook and stir till thickened and bubbly. Gradually stir about *1 cup* of the hot mixture into 2 beaten *egg yolks*; return all of the egg mixture to the saucepan. Cook and stir over medium heat till the mixture boils. Cook and stir 2 minutes more. Remove from heat. Stir in ¼ cup *lemon juice* and 2 tablespoons *margarine or butter*, stirring till margarine or butter melts. Serve warm. Makes about 1⅓ cups.

UPSIDE-DOWN PINEAPPLE
AND CARROT CAKE

  1 13½-ounce can pineapple tidbits
  ¼ cup margarine or butter
  ¾ cup coarsely chopped walnuts
  ½ cup packed brown sugar
  1 cup all-purpose flour
  ⅓ cup packed brown sugar
  ½ teaspoon baking powder
  ½ teaspoon baking soda
  ½ teaspoon ground cinnamon
1½ cups finely shredded carrot
  2 eggs
  ¼ cup cooking oil
      Whipped cream (optional)
      Finely shredded carrot (optional)

DRAIN PINEAPPLE, RESERVING PINEAPPLE SYRUP.
Set syrup aside. Melt margarine or butter in a
9x1½-inch round baking pan. Stir in pineapple
tidbits, walnuts, the ½ cup brown sugar, and
1 tablespoon of the reserved pineapple syrup;
spread evenly in the pan. Set pan aside.

For batter, in a medium mixing bowl stir
together flour, the ⅓ cup brown sugar, baking
powder, baking soda, and cinnamon. Stir in
the 1½ cups shredded carrot, eggs, oil, and
2 tablespoons of the reserved pineapple syrup.
Stir till combined.

Gently spoon batter evenly into the pan over
the pineapple mixture. Bake in a 350° oven
about 35 minutes or till a wooden toothpick
inserted near the center comes out clean. Cool
on a wire rack for 5 minutes. Loosen sides of
the cake from pan and invert cake onto a
serving plate. Serve warm. If desired, top with
whipped cream and garnish with finely
shredded carrot. Makes 8 servings.

This recipe combines two favorites— pineapple upside-down cake and carrot cake—into one dessert.

LEMON CHESS PIE

Pastry for 9-Inch Single-Crust Pie
4 eggs
1½ cups sugar
¼ cup margarine or butter, melted
2 teaspoons finely shredded lemon peel
2 tablespoons lemon juice
1 tablespoon cornmeal
1½ teaspoons vanilla
½ cup light raisins

There are many versions of the classic chess pie, but one thing that all versions typically have in common is the thin top "crust" that rises to the surface of the lemony-butter mixture.

LINE THE BOTTOM OF A PASTRY-LINED 9-INCH PIE plate with a double thickness of foil. Bake in a 450° oven for 5 minutes. Remove foil. Bake for 5 minutes more.

———■———

For filling, in a large mixing bowl beat the eggs lightly till combined. Stir in the sugar, margarine or butter, lemon peel, lemon juice, cornmeal, and vanilla. Mix well. Stir in raisins. Place the prepared pastry shell on the oven rack. Pour filling into the pastry shell.

———■———

To prevent overbrowning, cover the edge of the pie with foil. Reduce oven temperature to 350° and bake for 20 minutes. Remove foil. Bake for 20 to 25 minutes more or till a knife inserted near the center comes out clean. Cool pie on a wire rack. Cover and chill to store. Makes 8 servings.

PASTRY FOR 9-INCH SINGLE-CRUST PIE: In a mixing bowl stir together 1¼ cups *all-purpose flour* and ¼ teaspoon *salt*. Cut in ⅓ cup *shortening or lard* till pieces are the size of small peas.

Using a total of 3 to 4 tablespoons *cold water*, sprinkle *1 tablespoon* over part of the mixture; gently toss with a fork. Push to side of bowl. Repeat till all is moistened. Form dough into a ball.

On a lightly floured surface, flatten dough with your hands. Roll dough from center to edges, forming a circle about 12 inches in diameter. Wrap pastry around the rolling pin. Unroll onto a 9-inch pie plate. Ease pastry into the pie plate, being careful not to stretch pastry.

Trim to ½ inch beyond edge of pie plate; fold under extra pastry. Make a fluted, rope-shaped, or scalloped edge. *Do not prick pastry.* Bake as directed.

PUMPKIN–HAZELNUT
CRUNCH PIE

1   16-ounce can pumpkin
¾   cup sugar
1   teaspoon ground cinnamon
½   teaspoon ground ginger
½   teaspoon ground nutmeg
3   eggs
1   8-ounce carton dairy sour cream
¼   cup milk
½   cup packed brown sugar
3   tablespoons margarine or butter, melted
1   cup chopped hazelnuts (filberts) or pecans
    Pastry for 9-Inch Single-Crust Pie (see recipe, opposite)

FOR FILLING, IN A LARGE MIXING BOWL COMBINE pumpkin, sugar, cinnamon, ginger, and nutmeg. Add eggs. Beat lightly with a rotary beater or fork. Stir in the sour cream and milk. Mix well.

For nut topping, in a medium bowl combine brown sugar and melted margarine or butter. Stir in chopped hazelnuts or pecans.

Place a pastry-lined 9-inch pie plate on the oven rack. Pour the filling into the prepared pastry shell. Sprinkle evenly with nut topping.

To prevent overbrowning, cover the edge of the pie with foil. Bake in a 375° oven for 25 minutes. Remove foil. Bake about 20 minutes more or till center appears nearly set when shaken (see tip, page 213). Cool on a wire rack. Cover and chill to store. Serves 8.

Pumpkin pie has been a holiday favorite ever since the Pilgrims served it at their second Thanksgiving in 1623. This pumpkin pie has an added treat—a sweet and crunchy hazelnut topping.

BROWNIE-WALNUT PIE

When you want to serve a quick but decadent dessert, try this two-in-one treat that combines the taste of fudgy brownies with pie. To make preparation even faster, substitute a frozen pastry shell (thawed) or refrigerated ready-to-use piecrust for the from-scratch crust.

½ cup margarine or butter
3 squares (3 ounces) unsweetened chocolate, cut up
3 beaten eggs
1½ cups sugar
½ cup all-purpose flour
1 teaspoon vanilla
1 cup chopped walnuts
  Pastry for 9-Inch Single-Crust Pie (see recipe, page 196)
  Chocolate Sauce
  Vanilla or coffee ice cream (optional)

FOR FILLING, IN A SMALL HEAVY SAUCEPAN MELT margarine or butter and chocolate over low heat, stirring frequently. Cool for 20 minutes. In a large mixing bowl stir together eggs, sugar, flour, and vanilla. Stir in the cooled chocolate and walnuts. Pour filling into a pastry-lined 9-inch pie plate.

———■———

Bake in a 350° oven for 50 to 55 minutes or till a knife inserted near the center comes out clean. Cool on a wire rack. Serve warm with Chocolate Sauce. If desired, top with ice cream. Makes 8 servings.

CHOCOLATE SAUCE: In a heavy small saucepan melt ½ cup margarine or butter and 2 squares (2 ounces) unsweetened chocolate over low heat, stirring frequently. Stir in 2 cups sifted powdered sugar and one 5-ounce can (⅔ cup) evaporated milk. Bring to boiling; reduce heat. Simmer, uncovered, for 8 to 10 minutes, stirring frequently. Remove from heat. Stir in 1 teaspoon vanilla. Serve warm. Makes about 1⅔ cups.

Molasses Hermits
(see recipe, page 215)

Brownie–Walnut Pie

PECAN PIE WITH SPICY CRUST

It is reported that Thomas Jefferson so loved pecans that he planted hundreds of pecan trees in eastern Virginia, and even gave the nuts as gifts to friends like George Washington. Today, pecan trees are a common sight in the East—from Virginia to Georgia.

3 eggs
1 cup corn syrup
⅔ cup packed brown sugar
⅓ cup margarine or butter, melted
1 tablespoon bourbon or 2 teaspoons vanilla
1½ cups pecan halves
   Spicy Crust
   Whipped Cream Topping

FOR FILLING, IN A LARGE MIXING BOWL BEAT EGGS lightly with a rotary beater or a fork till combined. Stir in corn syrup, brown sugar, melted margarine or butter, and bourbon or vanilla. Stir well. Stir in pecan halves.

———◼———

Place a 9-inch pie plate lined with Spicy Crust on the oven rack. Pour the filling into the prepared pastry shell.

———◼———

To prevent over-browning, cover the edge of pie with foil. Bake in a 350° oven for 25 minutes. Remove foil. Bake for 20 to 25 minutes more or till a knife inserted near the center comes out clean. Cool pie on a wire rack. Cover and chill to store. Serve with Whipped Cream Topping. Makes 8 servings.

WHIPPED CREAM TOPPING: In a chilled bowl combine 1 cup *whipping cream* and 2 tablespoons *brown sugar*. Beat with chilled beaters of an electric mixer on medium speed till soft peaks form. Makes 2 cups.

SPICY CRUST: In a mixing bowl stir together 1¼ cups *all-purpose flour*, ½ to 1 teaspoon *ground cinnamon*, ¼ teaspoon *salt*, and ¼ teaspoon *ground nutmeg*. Cut in ⅓ cup *shortening or lard* till pieces are the size of small peas.

Using a total of 3 to 4 tablespoons *cold water*, sprinkle *1 tablespoon* over part of the mixture; gently toss with a fork. Push to side of bowl. Repeat till all is moistened. Form dough into a ball.

On a lightly floured surface, flatten dough with your hands. Roll dough from center to edges, forming a circle about 12 inches in diameter. Wrap pastry around the rolling pin. Unroll onto a 9-inch pie plate. Ease pastry into the pie plate, being careful not to stretch pastry.

Trim to ½ inch beyond edge of pie plate; fold under extra pastry. Make a fluted, rope-shaped, or scalloped edge. *Do not prick pastry.* Bake as directed.

SOUR CREAM RAISIN PIE
WITH NUT PASTRY

¼ cup all-purpose flour
¼ cup packed brown sugar
¼ teaspoon ground cinnamon
2 tablespoons margarine or butter
¼ cup finely chopped almonds, pecans, hazelnuts (filberts), or walnuts
1 cup raisins
3 beaten eggs
1 cup sugar
¾ teaspoon ground cinnamon
¼ teaspoon ground cloves
1½ cups dairy sour cream
Nut Pastry

FOR CRUMB TOPPING, IN A MIXING BOWL COMBINE flour, brown sugar, and the ¼ teaspoon cinnamon. Cut in margarine or butter till crumbly. Stir in finely chopped nuts. Set aside.

For filling, pour *boiling water* over raisins in a bowl. Let stand for 5 minutes; drain. Meanwhile, in a large mixing bowl stir together eggs, sugar, the ¾ teaspoon cinnamon, and cloves. Add drained raisins and sour cream. Stir till combined. Place a 9-inch pie plate lined with Nut Pastry on the oven rack. Pour filling into prepared pastry shell.

To prevent over-browning, cover the edge of the pie with foil. Sprinkle crumb topping evenly over the top. Bake in a 375° oven for 20 minutes. Remove foil. Bake for 20 to 25 minutes more or till center appears set when pie is gently shaken (see tip, page 213). Cool pie on a wire rack. Cover and chill to store. Makes 8 servings.

NUT PASTRY: In a mixing bowl stir together 1 cup *all-purpose flour;* ¼ cup ground *almonds, pecans, hazelnuts (filberts), or walnuts;* and ¼ teaspoon *salt.* Cut in ⅓ cup *shortening or lard* till pieces are the size of small peas.

Using a total of 3 to 4 tablespoons *cold water,* sprinkle 1 *tablespoon* over part of the mixture; gently toss with a fork. Push to side of bowl. Repeat till all is moistened. Form dough into a ball.

On a lightly floured surface, flatten dough with your hands. Roll dough from center to edges, forming a circle about 12 inches in diameter. Wrap pastry around the rolling pin. Unroll onto a 9-inch pie plate. Ease pastry into the pie plate, being careful not to stretch pastry.

Trim to ½ inch beyond edge of pie plate; fold under extra pastry. Make fluted, rope-shaped, or scalloped edge. *Do not prick pastry.* Bake as directed.

PEACH COBBLER WITH
CINNAMON-SWIRL BISCUITS

A cobbler is typically a deep-dish pie with a plain, biscuitlike topping. But we made this topping special, with swirls of cinnamon.

Pictured on page 187.

1 cup all-purpose flour
1 tablespoon brown sugar
1½ teaspoons baking powder
⅛ teaspoon baking soda
¼ cup margarine or butter
⅓ cup milk
½ cup finely chopped walnuts
3 tablespoons brown sugar
¼ teaspoon ground cinnamon
1 tablespoon margarine or butter, melted
⅔ cup packed brown sugar
4 teaspoons cornstarch
½ teaspoon finely shredded lemon peel
6 cups sliced, peeled peaches or 6 cups frozen unsweetened peach slices
Sour Cream Topping or ice cream

FOR BISCUIT TOPPING, IN A MEDIUM MIXING BOWL stir together flour, the 1 tablespoon brown sugar, baking powder, baking soda, and ¼ teaspoon *salt*. Cut in the ¼ cup margarine till the mixture is crumbly. Make a well in the center. Add milk all at once. Using a fork, stir just till dough clings together.

—■—

On a lightly floured surface, knead dough gently for 10 to 12 strokes. Roll or pat dough into a 12x8-inch rectangle. Combine walnuts, the 3 tablespoons brown sugar, and cinnamon; brush dough with the 1 tablespoon melted margarine and sprinkle with nut mixture. Roll up jelly-roll style, starting from one of the short sides. Seal edge. With a sharp knife, cut into eight 1-inch-thick slices. Set aside.

—■—

For filling, in a large saucepan stir together the ⅔ cup brown sugar, cornstarch, and lemon peel. Add peaches and ⅔ cup *water*. Cook and stir till bubbly. Transfer to a 12x7½x2-inch baking dish. Arrange biscuit slices, cut side down, on *hot* filling. Bake, in a 400° oven

about 25 minutes or till biscuit slices are golden. Serve warm with Sour Cream Topping or ice cream. Makes 8 servings.

SOUR CREAM TOPPING: Combine ½ cup *dairy sour cream*, 1 tablespoon *brown sugar*, and ⅛ teaspoon *ground cinnamon*. Makes ½ cup.

APPLE COBBLER: Substitute 6 cups sliced, peeled *cooking apples* for the peaches and add 1 teaspoon *apple pie spice* to the filling.

RHUBARB COBBLER: Substitute 6 cups sliced *rhubarb* for the peaches and use 1¼ *cups* brown sugar in the filling.

SAUCY APPLE DUMPLINGS

½ cup dairy sour cream
1 beaten egg
2 tablespoons milk
2¼ cups all-purpose flour
¼ cup sugar
2 teaspoons baking powder
¼ teaspoon baking soda
¼ teaspoon salt
⅓ cup margarine or butter
3 cups chopped, peeled cooking apples or ripe pears
¼ cup packed brown sugar
½ teaspoon ground cinnamon
¼ teaspoon ground nutmeg
1 cup sugar
1 cup packed brown sugar
¼ cup all-purpose flour
1½ cups water
2 tablespoons lemon juice
2 tablespoons margarine or butter
Ice cream (optional)

We've taken some of the work out of making apple dumplings. Rather than making several individual bundles of pastry and apples, you make one large bundle, cut it into slices, and then bake the slices.

FOR DOUGH, IN A LARGE MIXING BOWL COMBINE sour cream, egg, and milk. In a medium mixing bowl stir together the 2¼ cups flour, the ¼ cup sugar, baking powder, baking soda, and salt; cut in the ⅓ cup margarine or butter till mixture is crumbly. Add to sour cream mixture. Stir till combined.

On lightly floured surface, knead dough gently for 10 to 12 strokes. Roll dough into a 12-inch square. Spread the chopped apples or pears evenly over the dough.

In a small bowl combine the ¼ cup brown sugar, cinnamon, and nutmeg; sprinkle over the apples or pears. Carefully roll up dough jelly-roll style, starting from one of the short sides. Seal edge. With a sharp knife, cut dough into twelve 1-inch-thick slices.

Place slices, cut side down, in a greased 13x9x2-inch baking pan. Stir together the 1 cup sugar, the 1 cup brown sugar, and the ¼ cup flour. Stir in the water and lemon juice; pour over slices in pan. Dot slices with the 2 tablespoons margarine or butter.

Bake in a 350° oven for 35 to 40 minutes or till golden. Serve warm. If desired, top with ice cream. Makes 12 servings.

CHILLED BERRY TART

Use almost any berry in this summertime dessert. You can substitute blueberries, red or black raspberries, or blackberries for the strawberries.

1 cup finely crushed graham crackers (about 14 squares)
¾ cup finely crushed vanilla wafers (18 to 20 cookies)
¼ cup finely chopped walnuts
⅓ cup margarine or butter, melted
1 envelope unflavored gelatin
1¾ cups unsweetened white grape juice
1 8-ounce package cream cheese, softened
¼ cup sugar
1 teaspoon vanilla
2 cups blueberries
1½ cups sliced strawberries
Slivered lime peel (optional)

FOR CRUST, IN A MEDIUM MIXING BOWL COMBINE crushed graham crackers, crushed vanilla wafers, and walnuts. Add melted margarine or butter; toss to mix well. Press crumb mixture onto bottom and 1½ inches up the sides of a 9-inch springform pan to form a firm, even crust. Bake in a 375° oven for 5 minutes. Cool on a wire rack.

——■——

In a medium saucepan soften gelatin in the grape juice for 5 minutes. Cook and stir over low heat till gelatin dissolves. Transfer gelatin mixture to a bowl. Chill about 1 hour or till partially set (consistency of unbeaten egg whites), stirring occasionally. (Start watching mixture closely after 40 minutes.)

——■——

Meanwhile, in a small mixing bowl combine the cream cheese, sugar, and vanilla. Beat with an electric mixer on medium speed till smooth. Spread mixture over bottom of cooled crust. Spoon *half* of the gelatin mixture over cream cheese layer. Top with *half* of the blueberries, all of the sliced strawberries, and then the remaining blueberries. Spoon the remaining gelatin mixture over the berries.

——■——

Chill tart for 4 to 6 hours or till set. To serve, loosen crust from sides of pan with a narrow spatula; remove the sides of the springform pan. If desired, garnish with slivers of lime peel. Makes 12 to 16 servings.

CHERRY–PEAR CRISP

Serve ice cream or frozen yogurt with this warm-from-the-oven crisp.

3 cups fresh or frozen unsweetened pitted tart red cherries or raspberries
3 cups sliced, peeled pears or apples
½ cup sugar
2 tablespoons amaretto or 2 tablespoons orange juice plus a few drops almond extract
1 tablespoon all-purpose flour
½ cup packed brown sugar
½ cup rolled oats
¼ cup all-purpose flour
¼ cup margarine or butter
¼ cup chopped walnuts, pecans, or almonds

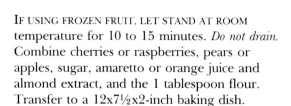

IF USING FROZEN FRUIT, LET STAND AT ROOM temperature for 10 to 15 minutes. *Do not drain.* Combine cherries or raspberries, pears or apples, sugar, amaretto or orange juice and almond extract, and the 1 tablespoon flour. Transfer to a 12x7½x2-inch baking dish.

Combine brown sugar, oats, and the ¼ cup flour. Cut in margarine till crumbly; stir in nuts. Sprinkle over fruit mixture. Bake in a 375° oven for 30 to 35 minutes (50 minutes for frozen fruit) or till center is bubbly. If desired, serve with ice cream. Serves 6 to 8.

BERRY CRUNCH ICE CREAM

Here's a peachy variation you'll love: omit the strawberries and use 4 cups sliced, peeled peaches instead.

1 cup coarsely chopped blanched almonds
½ cup sugar
2 tablespoons margarine or butter
4 cups fresh strawberries or frozen unsweetened strawberries, thawed
3 cups half-and-half or light cream
1¾ cups sugar
2 teaspoons vanilla
¼ teaspoon almond extract
4 cups whipping cream

IN A HEAVY SKILLET COMBINE ALMONDS, THE ½ cup sugar, and margarine or butter. Cook and stir over medium heat for 8 to 10 minutes or till sugar melts and turns a rich brown color. Remove from heat and spread nut mixture in a thin layer on a buttered baking sheet or foil. Cool. Break nut mixture into small chunks.

In a blender container, blend strawberries till nearly smooth. In a very large mixing bowl combine the blended strawberries, half-and-half or light cream, the 1¾ cups sugar, vanilla, and almond extract; stir till sugar dissolves. Stir in almond chunks and whipping cream. Freeze in a 4- or 5-quart ice-cream freezer according to manufacturer's directions. Makes 3 quarts (24 servings).

DESSERTS
206

BERRY SLUMP

 3 cups fresh or *frozen blueberries, thawed*
 2 cups sliced strawberries or *frozen unsweetened*
  whole strawberries, thawed
 ½ cup sugar
 2 tablespoons finely chopped crystallized ginger
 1 teaspoon finely shredded lemon peel
 1 tablespoon lemon juice
 ¾ cup all-purpose flour
 ¼ cup sugar
 1 teaspoon baking powder
 ⅛ teaspoon salt
 ⅛ teaspoon ground ginger
 ¼ cup margarine or *butter*
 ¼ cup milk
 1 tablespoon sugar
  Ice cream (optional)

In a medium saucepan combine blueberries, strawberries, the ½ cup sugar, crystallized ginger, lemon peel, and lemon juice. Cook over medium heat, stirring occasionally, till bubbly.

———■———

Meanwhile, for dumplings, in a mixing bowl combine flour, the ¼ cup sugar, baking powder, salt, and ground ginger. Cut margarine or butter into flour mixture till mixture resembles coarse crumbs. Add milk, stirring just till mixture is moistened.

———■———

Drop the dumpling mixture into 6 mounds atop the bubbling berry mixture in the saucepan. Sprinkle dumplings with the 1 tablespoon sugar.

———■———

Cover and simmer over medium heat for 12 to 15 minutes or till a toothpick inserted in a dumpling comes out clean. (*Do not lift cover except to test for doneness.*) Serve warm. If desired, top with ice cream. Makes 6 servings.

A slump is a New England dessert that is similar to a cobbler, except that it's steamed rather than baked. On Cape Cod, a slump also may be called a "grunt." However, in other parts of New England, a grunt usually is a steamed pudding rather than a cobbler.

APPLE–CHERRY PANDOWDY

Pandowdy is a molasses- or maple-flavored, deep-dish apple dessert. The name comes from the fact that the dish is usually "dowdied" before serving—that is, the crust is broken up and then stirred into the filling. In this version, tart red cherries accent the natural sweetness of apples.

    4 cups sliced, peeled cooking apples
 1½ cups fresh or frozen unsweetened pitted tart red cherries, thawed
 ¾ cup sugar
    3 tablespoons all-purpose flour
 ¼ teaspoon ground nutmeg
    Dash ground cloves
    1 cup all-purpose flour
 ¼ teaspoon salt
 ¼ cup margarine or butter
    1 egg yolk
    2 tablespoons cold water
    Whipped cream or ice cream (optional)

FOR THE FILLING, IN A MIXING BOWL COMBINE apples, cherries, sugar, the 3 tablespoons flour, nutmeg, and cloves. Transfer fruit filling to a 10x6x2-inch baking dish.

—■—

For crust, in another mixing bowl combine the 1 cup flour and the salt. Cut in the margarine or butter till mixture resembles coarse crumbs. Make a well in the center of the dry ingredients. Beat together egg yolk and cold water. Add to flour mixture. Using a fork, stir till dough forms a ball.

—■—

On a lightly floured surface, roll dough into a 12x8-inch rectangle; place atop fruit filling in baking dish. Fold under edge of crust to fit dish; crimp to sides of dish. Cut a 3-inch slit in crust to allow steam to escape.

—■—

Place baking dish on a baking sheet (to catch any filling that bubbles over). Bake in a 350° oven for 40 to 45 minutes or till golden. To "dowdy" the crust, use a sharp knife to cut a lattice pattern in the crust. Cool on a wire rack for 30 minutes. If desired, serve with whipped cream or ice cream. Makes 6 servings.

APPLE–DATE BAKE

4 cups sliced, peeled cooking apples
¼ cup water
1 cup all-purpose flour
¼ cup sugar
2 teaspoons baking powder
¼ teaspoon salt
¼ teaspoon ground nutmeg
    Dash ground cloves
¼ cup margarine or butter
½ cup milk
⅓ cup chopped pitted dates
¼ cup chopped pecans or walnuts
1 cup packed brown sugar
1 tablespoon all-purpose flour
1 cup boiling water
    Ice cream (optional)

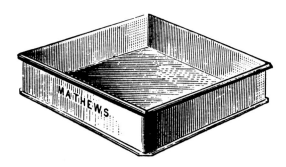

IN A MEDIUM SAUCEPAN COMBINE APPLES AND THE ¼ cup water. Bring to boiling; reduce heat. Cover and simmer for 4 to 5 minutes or till apples are slightly tender. Drain; set aside.

For topping, in a medium mixing bowl stir together the 1 cup flour, sugar, baking powder, salt, nutmeg, and cloves. Cut in margarine or butter till mixture resembles coarse crumbs. Stir in milk just till combined. Stir in dates and pecans or walnuts. Place apples in a greased 8x8x2-inch baking dish. Drop topping in mounds over the apples. Spread to cover.

In a small mixing bowl combine brown sugar and the 1 tablespoon flour. Sprinkle over topping. Carefully pour the 1 cup boiling water over all ingredients.

Bake in a 350° oven for 30 to 35 minutes or till golden and topping springs back when touched. Serve warm. If desired, top with ice cream. Makes 8 servings.

Is it a pudding cake or a cobbler? You be the judge. This yummy dessert has the biscuitlike topping of a cobbler, but makes its own sauce as it bakes, like a pudding cake.

WHISKEY-SAUCED
BREAD PUDDING

For the best bread pudding, be sure to use dry bread. To air-dry bread, spread the slices in a single layer and cover them with a towel. Let the slices stand at room temperature for 8 to 12 hours or till they are dry. To dry soft bread quickly, place the bread slices on a rack in a 300° oven. Bake the bread about 15 minutes or till it's dry but not brown.

4   slices dry cinnamon-raisin bread
⅓   cup soft-style cream cheese
1¾ cups milk
4   beaten eggs
⅓   cup sugar
2   tablespoons bourbon
1   teaspoon finely shredded lemon peel
      Whiskey Sauce or *whipped cream*

GENEROUSLY SPREAD 2 SLICES OF THE DRY BREAD with cream cheese. Top with remaining bread slices. Cut bread "sandwiches" into cubes and place in an 8x1½-inch round baking dish.

■

In a mixing bowl beat together milk, eggs, sugar, bourbon, and lemon peel. Pour over bread cubes in dish.

■

Bake in a 325° oven for 35 to 40 minutes or till a knife inserted near the center comes out clean. Cool slightly. Serve warm with Whiskey Sauce or whipped cream. Makes 6 to 8 servings.

WHISKEY SAUCE: In a small saucepan melt ¼ cup *margarine or butter*. Stir in ½ cup *sugar*, 1 beaten *egg yolk*, and 2 tablespoons *water*. Cook and stir constantly over medium-low heat for 5 to 6 minutes or till sugar dissolves and mixture boils. Remove from heat. Stir in 2 tablespoons *bourbon* and 1 tablespoon *lemon juice*. Serve warm. Makes about ¾ cup.

LEMON–GINGERBREAD
SOUFFLÉ

In Lemon–Ginger-bread Soufflé, we've combined the flavors of lemon and molasses in a delicate dessert.

Margarine or butter
Sugar
3 tablespoons margarine or butter
3 tablespoons all-purpose flour
¾ cup milk
4 beaten egg yolks
1 teaspoon finely shredded lemon peel
1 tablespoon lemon juice
½ cup packed brown sugar
1 teaspoon ground ginger
½ teaspoon ground cinnamon
¼ teaspoon ground nutmeg
⅛ teaspoon ground cloves
4 egg whites
¼ teaspoon cream of tartar
Whipped cream (optional)

BUTTER THE SIDES OF A 2-QUART SOUFFLÉ DISH. Coat sides with sugar. Set dish aside.

——◼——

In a small saucepan melt the 3 tablespoons margarine or butter. Stir in flour. Add milk all at once. Cook and stir till thickened and bubbly. (Mixture will be very thick.) Gradually stir the thickened milk mixture into beaten egg yolks. Stir in lemon peel and lemon juice. Gradually add ¼ cup of the brown sugar, the ginger, cinnamon, nutmeg, and cloves, stirring till smooth. Set aside.

——◼——

In a large mixing bowl combine egg whites and cream of tartar. Beat till soft peaks form (tips curl over). Gradually add remaining brown sugar, beating till stiff peaks form (tips stand straight). Fold about ½ cup beaten egg white mixture into egg yolk mixture to lighten. Then fold the yolk mixture into the remaining egg white mixture. Transfer to the prepared soufflé dish.

——◼——

Bake in a 350° oven for 40 to 45 minutes or till a knife inserted near the center comes out clean. Serve *immediately*. If desired, top with whipped cream. Makes 6 servings.

DUTCH APPLE–BRANDY
CHEESECAKE

1½ cups finely crushed graham crackers
⅓ cup walnuts or pecans, ground
⅓ cup margarine or butter, melted
½ teaspoon ground cinnamon
4 8-ounce packages cream cheese, softened
1 cup sugar
1 teaspoon ground cinnamon
½ teaspoon vanilla
⅛ teaspoon ground nutmeg
4 eggs
1 cup chunk-style applesauce
¼ cup milk
3 tablespoons apple brandy or apple juice
  Streusel Topping
1 medium apple, cored and thinly sliced (optional)

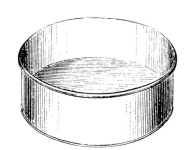

FOR CRUST, IN A MEDIUM MIXING BOWL COMBINE crushed graham crackers, ground walnuts or pecans, melted margarine or butter, and the ½ teaspoon cinnamon. Press mixture onto bottom and 1½ inches up sides of a 10-inch springform pan. Bake in a 375° oven for 9 minutes. Cool on a wire rack.

In a large mixing bowl beat cream cheese and sugar with an electric mixer on low speed till smooth. Add the 1 teaspoon cinnamon, vanilla, and nutmeg. Beat on low speed till well combined. Add eggs all at once, beating on low speed *just till combined.* (Do not overbeat.) Stir in applesauce, milk, and brandy or apple juice. Pour mixture into the crust-lined pan.

Place springform pan in a shallow baking pan in oven. Bake in a 375° oven for 55 to 60 minutes or till center is nearly set when shaken (see tip at right). Cool 5 minutes on a wire rack. Loosen crust from sides of pan with a narrow spatula. Cool 30 minutes more. Remove sides of springform pan. Cool completely. Sprinkle Streusel Topping around outside edge of cheesecake. Chill at least 4 hours. If desired, garnish with apple slices. Makes 16 servings.

STREUSEL TOPPING: Stir together ½ cup chopped *walnuts or pecans;* ¼ cup packed *brown sugar;* 2 tablespoons *all-purpose flour;* 1 tablespoon *margarine or butter,* softened; and ¼ teaspoon *ground cinnamon.* Place in a pie plate. Bake in a 375° oven for 10 to 12 minutes or till nuts are toasted and topping is crispy, stirring once. Cool.

One secret to perfect cheesecake is proper baking. To test the doneness of your cheesecake, gently shake the pan. The center should appear nearly set. A 1-inch area in the center will jiggle slightly when the cheesecake is done, but will firm after cooling.

SHORTENIN' ROUNDS

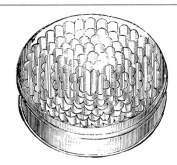

In the South, shortbread often is called shortenin' bread. The name comes from its most important ingredient— shortening.

1 cup all-purpose flour
¼ cup sugar
¼ cup ground toasted almonds
½ cup butter
⅓ cup semisweet chocolate pieces
1 teaspoon shortening
½ cup toasted sliced almonds

IN A MIXING BOWL COMBINE FLOUR, SUGAR, AND almonds. Cut in butter till mixture resembles fine crumbs and starts to cling. Shape into a ball and knead till smooth. On a lightly floured surface, pat or roll dough to ½-inch thickness. Cut into rounds with a 1½-inch round cookie cutter. Place rounds 1 inch apart on an ungreased cookie sheet. Bake at 325° for 20 to 25 minutes or till bottoms just start to brown. Cool on a wire rack.

Melt chocolate pieces and shortening together over low heat, stirring occasionally. Spread sliced almonds in an even layer on waxed paper. Using a pastry brush, brush bottom sides of cookies with melted chocolate mixture. Press cookies, chocolate side down, into sliced almonds. Place cookies, chocolate side up, on a wire rack till set. Makes about 18.

NUTTY COCONUT MACAROONS

These deliciously chewy cookies are extra special because they're crunchy, too.

3 egg whites
½ teaspoon vanilla
1 cup sugar
1 3½-ounce can (1⅓ cups) flaked coconut
½ cup ground almonds, hazelnuts (filberts), or pecans

IN A LARGE MIXING BOWL BEAT EGG WHITES AND vanilla with an electric mixer on medium speed till soft peaks form (tips curl over). Gradually add sugar, 1 tablespoon at a time, beating on high speed about 8 minutes or till very stiff peaks form (tips stand straight) and sugar is almost dissolved. Fold in coconut and nuts.

Drop coconut mixture from rounded teaspoons 2 inches apart onto lightly greased cookie sheets. Bake in a 325° oven for 18 to 20 minutes or till edges are lightly browned. Remove cookies from cookie sheets and cool on a wire rack. Makes about 45.

MOLASSES HERMITS

½ cup margarine or butter
2 cups all-purpose flour
¾ cup packed brown sugar
¼ cup molasses
2 eggs
1 teaspoon vanilla
½ teaspoon baking soda
½ teaspoon ground cinnamon
¼ teaspoon ground nutmeg
⅛ teaspoon ground cloves
1 cup raisins, dried currants, or *snipped pitted whole dates*
½ cup chopped nuts

If you like soft raisins or currants in baked goods, plump them by soaking them briefly in warm water or fruit juice.

Pictured on page 199.

BEAT MARGARINE WITH AN ELECTRIC MIXER ON medium to high speed for 30 seconds. Add about *half* of the flour, the brown sugar, molasses, eggs, vanilla, baking soda, cinnamon, nutmeg, and cloves. Beat till thoroughly combined. Beat in remaining flour. Stir in raisins and nuts. Drop by rounded teaspoons 2 inches apart onto a greased cookie sheet. Bake in a 375° oven 6 to 8 minutes or till edges are light brown. Cool on rack. Makes about 40.

TAKE ME TO THE FAIR

FAIRS ARE KNOWN for corn dogs and cotton candy, midway lights, and fierce culinary competitions. City and country cooks vie for blue-ribbon glory with their best creations. In this chapter, you'll find recipes for fair favorites, such as mile-high cakes, picture-perfect pies, and cookie-jar classics. You be the judge and give our selection of unbeatable treats a try in your own kitchen. ■

WHOOPIE PIES

½ cup shortening
2 cups all-purpose flour
1¼ cups buttermilk or sour milk (see tip, page 188)
1 cup sugar
⅔ cup unsweetened cocoa powder
1 egg
1 teaspoon baking soda
1 teaspoon vanilla
¾ cup milk
¼ cup all-purpose flour
¾ cup margarine or butter
2 cups sifted powdered sugar
1 teaspoon vanilla
Chocolate Butter Frosting

FOR COOKIES, BEAT SHORTENING WITH AN electric mixer on medium-to-high speed 30 seconds. Add about *1 cup* of flour, *half* the buttermilk, the sugar, cocoa, egg, baking soda, vanilla, and ⅛ teaspoon *salt*. Beat till thoroughly combined. Beat in 1 cup flour and remaining buttermilk. Drop by rounded tablespoons 2 inches apart onto ungreased cookie sheets. Bake in a 350° oven 8 to 10 minutes or till edges are firm. Cool.

For filling, combine milk and the ¼ cup flour. Cook and stir till thickened and bubbly. Cook and stir 2 minutes more. Remove from heat; cool thoroughly. Beat margarine with an electric mixer on medium-to-high speed for 30 seconds. Add powdered sugar; beat till fluffy. Add vanilla. Beat cooled milk mixture, 1 large spoonful at a time, into margarine mixture. Beat on high for 1 minute or till smooth and fluffy.

Spread about *2 tablespoons* of the filling on each flat side of *half* of the cooled cookies. Top with remaining cookies, flat side down. Frost with Chocolate Butter Frosting. Store in the refrigerator. Makes 14 filled cookies.

CHOCOLATE BUTTER FROSTING: Beat together ¼ cup *unsweetened cocoa powder* and 3 tablespoons *butter or margarine*. Gradually beat in 1 cup sifted *powdered sugar*. Slowly beat in 2 tablespoons *milk* and ½ teaspoon *vanilla*. Gradually beat in another 1 cup sifted *powdered sugar*. Beat in additional *milk*, if needed, to make a frosting of spreading consistency.

Pictured on page 217.

MARBLE CHIFFON CAKE

2¼ cups sifted cake flour or 2 cups sifted all-purpose flour
1½ cups sugar
1 tablespoon baking powder
½ cup cooking oil
7 egg yolks
1 teaspoon vanilla
7 egg whites
½ teaspoon cream of tartar
2 squares (2 ounces) unsweetened chocolate, melted
2 tablespoons sugar
Chocolate Glaze

IN A LARGE BOWL COMBINE FLOUR, THE 1½ CUPS sugar, baking powder, and ¼ teaspoon *salt*. Add oil, egg yolks, vanilla, and ¾ cup *water*. Beat with an electric mixer on low speed till combined. Beat on high speed 5 minutes or till satin smooth. Transfer to another bowl.

———■———

Thoroughly wash and dry bowl and beaters. In the same large bowl combine egg whites and cream of tartar. Beat till stiff peaks form (tips stand straight). Pour egg yolk mixture in a thin stream over beaten egg white mixture; fold in gently. Reserve about *one-third* of this batter in a separate bowl.

———■———

In a small bowl combine melted chocolate, the 2 tablespoons sugar, and ¼ cup *boiling water*; stir till well combined. Fold chocolate into the reserved portion of batter. Spoon *half* of the light batter into an *ungreased* 10-inch tube pan; top with *half* of the chocolate batter.

Repeat layers. Swirl a narrow spatula gently through batters to marble.

———■———

Bake in a 325° oven for 60 to 70 minutes or till top springs back when lightly touched. *Immediately* invert cake (leave in pan). Cool. Remove from pan. Top with Chocolate Glaze. Makes 12 servings.

CHOCOLATE GLAZE: In a small saucepan combine 3 squares (3 ounces) *semisweet chocolate,* cut up; 3 tablespoons *milk;* 2 tablespoons *margarine or butter;* and 1 tablespoon *light corn syrup.* Heat and stir over low heat till chocolate is melted. Remove from heat; stir in 1 cup sifted *powdered sugar* and ½ teaspoon *vanilla.* If necessary, add a little *hot water* to make of drizzling consistency. Spoon over cake, allowing excess to drip down sides.

Pictured on page 217.

CHOCOLATE–OATMEAL
COOKIES

1 cup margarine or butter
1½ cups all-purpose flour
1½ cups sugar
3 squares (3 ounces) unsweetened chocolate, melted and cooled
1 egg
1 teaspoon baking powder
1 teaspoon vanilla
½ teaspoon baking soda
2 cups quick-cooking rolled oats
1 6-ounce package (1 cup) semisweet chocolate pieces

IN A LARGE MIXING BOWL BEAT MARGARINE OR butter with an electric mixer on medium-to-high speed for 30 seconds. Add about *half* of the flour, the sugar, melted chocolate, egg, baking powder, vanilla, and baking soda. Beat till thoroughly combined. Beat in remaining flour. Stir in the rolled oats and semisweet chocolate pieces.

Drop dough by level tablespoons about 3 inches apart onto an ungreased cookie sheet. Bake in a 375° oven for 10 to 12 minutes or till edges are firm. Cool cookies on a wire rack. Makes about 48 cookies.

DUTCH APPLE PIE

¾ cup sugar
2 tablespoons all-purpose flour
½ teaspoon finely shredded lemon peel
½ teaspoon ground cinnamon
⅛ teaspoon ground nutmeg
8 medium cooking apples, peeled,
     cored, and cut into 1-inch chunks
     (about 8 cups)
⅓ cup raisins
   Pastry for 10-Inch Double-Crust Pie
¼ cup whipping cream
   Milk
1½ teaspoons sugar

IN A LARGE MIXING BOWL STIR TOGETHER THE ¾ cup sugar, flour, lemon peel, cinnamon, and nutmeg. Add apple chunks and raisins. Toss till apples and raisins are coated. Spoon apple mixture into a pastry-lined 10-inch pie plate.

—■—

Pour whipping cream over apples. Add top crust. Trim, seal, and flute edge. Brush top crust with milk and sprinkle with the 1½ teaspoons sugar.

—■—

To prevent over-browning, cover the edge of the pie with foil. Bake in a 375° oven for 30 minutes. Remove foil. Bake about 30 minutes more or till the top is golden and apples are tender. Cool on a wire rack. Serve warm. Store in the refrigerator. Makes 8 servings.

PASTRY FOR 10-INCH DOUBLE-CRUST PIE: Combine 2½ cups *all-purpose flour* and ½ teaspoon *salt*. Cut in ¾ cup *shortening or lard* till pieces are the size of small peas. Using a total of 8 to 9 tablespoons *water*, sprinkle *1 tablespoon* over part of the mixture; gently toss with a fork. Push to one side of bowl. Repeat till all is moistened. Divide dough in half. Form each half into a ball.

On a lightly floured surface, flatten a ball of dough with your hands. Roll dough from center to edges, forming a circle about 15 inches in diameter. Wrap pastry around rolling pin. Unroll into a 10-inch pie plate. Ease pastry into pie plate, being careful not to stretch pastry. Trim pastry even with rim of pie plate.

For top crust, roll out remaining dough. Cut slits in crust to allow steam to escape. Fill pastry in pie plate with desired filling. Place top crust on filling. Trim top crust ½ inch beyond edge of plate. Fold edge of top crust under bottom crust; flute edge. Bake as directed.

A
SOUTHERN
TEA TABLE

THROUGHOUT THE SOUTH in the early 1900s, elaborate

teas offered a respite from the bustle of daily life.

Today, some country cooks carry on this tradition

with their own afternoon get-togethers. What to serve?

A tea wouldn't be complete without finger sandwiches, scones,

and dainty sweets. So pull out your best china and give our

delicious assortment of teatime delights a try. ∎

TEATIME PETITS FOURS

1¼ cups all-purpose flour
1 cup sugar
½ teaspoon baking powder
¼ teaspoon baking soda
¾ cup buttermilk or sour milk (see tip, page 188)
¼ cup shortening
½ teaspoon vanilla
¼ teaspoon almond extract
2 egg whites
¼ cup apricot jam or currant jelly
　Petits Fours Icing
　Piping Icing
　Candied Flowers (see recipe, opposite)

COMBINE FLOUR, SUGAR, BAKING POWDER, BAKING soda, and a dash *salt*. Add buttermilk, shortening, vanilla, and almond extract. Beat with an electric mixer on low speed 30 seconds. Beat on medium-to-high speed 2 minutes. Add egg whites; beat 2 minutes. Pour into a greased and floured 9x9x2-inch baking pan. Bake in a 350° oven 30 minutes or till done. Cool on rack 10 minutes. Remove from pan. Cool. Makes 36.

———■———

Trim sides of cake to make smooth, straight edges. Cut cake into 1½-inch squares, diamonds, or circles. Heat jam till melted. Cut *each* cake piece in half horizontally; spread top of bottom half with a little melted jam. Restack cake halves. Brush off crumbs. Insert a long-handled fork into the side of a cake stack. Holding cake over saucepan of Petits Fours Icing, spoon on enough icing to cover sides and top. Place frosted petit fours on a rack over waxed paper, making sure petits fours do not touch. Repeat with remaining cake stacks. Let cakes dry 15 minutes.

———■———

Pictured on page 223.

Coat with a second layer of icing, except set each petit four *on top* of the prongs of the fork (do not spear it). If desired, coat with a third layer of icing. If necessary, reuse the icing that has dripped onto the waxed paper beneath the wire rack, reheating and straining to remove crumbs. Decorate as desired with Piping Icing and/or Candied Flowers.

PETITS FOURS ICING: Combine 4 cups sifted *powdered sugar*, ⅓ cup *water*, and 2 tablespoons *light corn syrup*. Cook and stir over low heat until icing reaches pouring consistency (about 100° to 110°). If desired, tint with paste food coloring. Use at once; reheat as necessary.

PIPING ICING: Beat 2 tablespoons *margarine or butter* 30 seconds. Gradually beat in ¾ cup sifted *powdered sugar*. Beat in 1 tablespoon *milk* and ½ teaspoon *vanilla*. Beat in ½ to ¾ cup additional sifted *powdered sugar* till icing is of piping consistency.

CANDIED FLOWERS

Edible flowers (rose, viola, pansy, marigold, or violet)
2 *tablespoons water*
1 *tablespoon frozen egg product, thawed*
   Superfine sugar

WASH FLOWERS GENTLY IN WATER; LET AIR-DRY on paper towels or blot dry. If flowers are large or tight petaled, remove petals from stem. Combine water and egg product. Brush water mixture on both sides of petals in a thin, even layer with a small, clean paintbrush.

Sprinkle flowers evenly with sugar; shake off excess (coating should not be thick). Lay flowers on waxed paper for 2 to 4 hours or till dry. Store or freeze flowers in an airtight container between layers of waxed paper. Use to decorate desserts, candies, and cakes. (Nutritive content and calories of Candied Flowers are negligible.)

CHICKEN CANAPÉS

1 *3-ounce package cream cheese, softened*
2 *tablespoons Italian salad dressing*
2 *tablespoons mayonnaise or salad dressing*
1 *tablespoon milk*
¼ *teaspoon dry mustard*
1 *cup ground cooked chicken*
¼ *cup finely chopped pecans or walnuts*
¼ *cup finely chopped celery*
24 *slices bread or party bread*
   Assorted toppings (slices of hard-cooked egg, olives, or cherry tomatoes; pimiento strips; pecan, walnut, or grape halves; watercress or parsley; or sweet pepper pieces)

COMBINE CREAM CHEESE, ITALIAN SALAD dressing, mayonnaise, milk, and dry mustard; mix well. Stir in chicken, nuts, and celery.

If desired, use a cookie cutter to cut bread into different shapes. Spread bread slices with about *1 tablespoon* of the cream cheese mixture. Garnish with desired toppings. Chill up to 1 hour. Makes 24 canapés.

Recipes pictured on page 223.

SOUR CREAM
COUNTRY SCONES

¾ *cup dried currants* or *mixed dried fruit bits*
2 *cups all-purpose flour*
3 *tablespoons sugar*
2 *teaspoons baking powder*
¾ *teaspoon salt*
½ *teaspoon baking soda*
⅓ *cup margarine* or *butter*
1 *8-ounce carton dairy sour cream*
1 *egg yolk*
1 *slightly beaten egg white*
2 *teaspoons sugar*
¼ *teaspoon ground cinnamon*

PLACE CURRANTS OR FRUIT BITS IN A SMALL mixing bowl. Pour enough *hot water* over the currants or fruit bits to cover; let stand 5 minutes. Drain well; set aside.

———■———

In a large mixing bowl combine flour, the 3 tablespoons sugar, baking powder, salt, and baking soda. Using a pastry blender, cut in margarine or butter till mixture resembles coarse crumbs. Stir in currants or fruit bits.

———■———

In a small bowl combine sour cream and egg yolk. Add all at once to dry mixture, stirring *just till dough clings together.*

———■———

On a lightly floured surface, knead the dough gently for 10 to 12 strokes. Divide dough into 5 portions. Pat or lightly roll *each* portion of dough into a 4-inch circle about ½-inch thick. Place each circle on an ungreased baking sheet. Using a sharp knife, cut each circle completely through into quarters, but *do not separate.* Brush tops of scones with beaten egg white. Combine the 2 teaspoons sugar and the cinnamon; sprinkle atop scones.

———■———

Bake in a 400° oven about 12 minutes or till lightly browned. Cool on a wire rack for 5 minutes. Break apart. Serve warm. Makes 20.

Pictured on page 223.

MAID-OF-HONOR TARTS

1 cup all-purpose flour
1 tablespoon sugar
¼ teaspoon salt
¼ cup margarine or *butter*
¼ cup milk
¾ cup sugar
2 tablespoons margarine or *butter, softened*
1 tablespoon all-purpose flour
¼ teaspoon ground nutmeg
2 beaten eggs
2 tablespoons cream sherry
¾ cup ground almonds
2 tablespoons strawberry, raspberry, or *plum jam*

IN A MEDIUM MIXING BOWL STIR TOGETHER THE 1 cup flour, the 1 tablespoon sugar, and salt. Cut in the ¼ cup margarine or butter till mixture resembles small peas. Sprinkle *1 tablespoon* milk over part of the mixture. Toss with a fork; push to side of bowl. Repeat till all is moistened.

———■———

Form dough into a ball. On a lightly floured surface, roll dough ⅛ inch thick. Cut dough into twenty-four 2½-inch circles, rerolling if necessary. Press dough onto the bottom and sides of ungreased 1¾-inch muffin cups. Set aside.

———■———

For filling, in a small mixing bowl beat together the ¾ cup sugar, the 2 tablespoons softened margarine or butter, the 1 tablespoon flour, and nutmeg. Beat in eggs and sherry; stir in ground almonds.

———■———

Fill *each* dough-lined muffin cup with about ¼ *teaspoon* jam. Top *each* with about *1 tablespoon* filling. Bake in a 375° oven for 15 to 20 minutes or till a toothpick inserted near the center comes out clean. Remove tarts from cups. Cool on a wire rack. Makes 24.

Pictured on page 223.

NUTRITION ANALYSIS

We've analyzed the nutrition content of each recipe serving for you. When a recipe gives an ingredient substitution, we used the first choice in the analysis. And if it makes a range of servings, we used the smallest number. Ingredients listed as optional weren't included in the calculations.

RECIPE	Servings	Calories	Protein (g)	Carbohydrates (g)	Fat (g)	Saturated Fat (g)	Cholesterol (mg)	Sodium (g)
Amish Fruit Bowl, p. 149	6	206	2	53	1	0	0	8
Anadama Bread, p. 121	32	106	2	19	2	0	0	89
Apple–Cherry Pandowdy, p. 208	6	326	4	59	9	2	36	181
Apple Cobbler, p. 202	8	359	4	54	15	4	7	177
Apple–Date Bake, p. 209	8	325	3	61	9	2	1	227
Apricot–Honey-Glazed Duckling, p. 82	4	498	23	29	32	11	95	752
Apricot–Orange Marmalade, p. 175	128	43	0	11	0	0	0	1
Apricot Preserve Breakfast Biscuits, p. 139	10	190	3	28	7	2	1	148
Apricot Preserve Drop Biscuits, p. 139	10	192	3	28	7	2	1	150
Artichoke–Squash Chicken Potpie, p. 76	4	499	29	42	24	5	59	847
Baked Chicken Country Captain, p. 79	4	552	35	59	19	5	94	544
Baked Country Ham, p. 8	25	321	24	14	18	7	67	1,296
Baked Scallops Newburg, p. 64	4	486	27	22	32	11	178	639
Banana Pudding, p. 43	6	462	9	82	12	4	136	234
Barbecued Chicken (Maple Barbecue Sauce), p. 71	4	358	31	17	18	5	97	767
Barbecued Chicken (Peach Barbecue Sauce), p. 71	4	375	30	30	15	4	97	154
Batter-Fried Shrimp, p. 62	4	488	24	24	33	5	219	206
Beans with Blue Cheese, p. 161	4	264	9	13	21	7	28	351
Beaten Biscuits, p. 140	24	59	1	8	2	1	0	48
Beef and Wild Rice Soup, p. 97	4	267	27	19	10	3	65	755
Beef Tenderloin with Peppercorns, p. 26	2	420	32	5	30	10	105	379
Beet and Apple Salad, p. 150	4	153	2	15	11	1	0	49
Berry Crunch Ice Cream, p. 206	24	302	3	25	22	12	66	40
Berry Slump, p. 207	6	303	3	56	8	2	1	193
Bierocks, p. 17	6	428	22	60	11	4	53	657
Black Bean and Corn Salad, p. 169	6	168	10	19	6	4	17	440
Black-Eyed Pea Salad, p. 152	6	212	6	21	13	2	0	170
Blueberry–Buttermilk Hotcakes, p. 110	8	134	4	19	5	1	28	195
Boston Brown Bread, p. 132	14	94	2	19	1	0	1	84
Bourbon-and-Mustard-Glazed Pork Chops, p. 12	4	368	47	12	16	6	113	603
Braised Chicken with Sawmill Gravy, p. 72	6	428	26	36	19	5	74	563
Brandied Peaches, p. 181	20	161	1	41	0	0	0	2
Brandied Raisin–Applesauce Muffins, p. 134	12	163	3	25	6	1	36	169
Brandy-Glazed Carrots, p. 161	4	161	2	26	6	1	0	140
Brownie–Walnut Pie, p. 198	8	858	11	93	53	15	85	380
Buttermilk Corn Bread, p. 142	8	225	6	30	9	1	54	249
Cajun-Style Catsup, p. 184	64	26	1	6	0	0	0	106
Cajun-Style Eggs Benedict, p. 114	4	342	22	25	17	4	240	1,082
Caramel Sauce, p. 136	8	51	0	9	2	0	1	25
Cheddar Grits and Sausage Bake, p. 116	4	383	21	18	25	13	124	662
Cheddary Asparagus Spoon Bread, p. 141	6	305	18	15	19	10	187	490

RECIPE	Servings	Calories	Protein (g)	Carbohydrates (g)	Fat (g)	Saturated Fat (g)	Cholesterol (mg)	Sodium (g)
Cheesy Bierocks, p. 17	6	514	27	61	18	8	75	789
Cheesy Cauliflower Bake, p. 167	6	221	9	16	14	6	31	301
Cheesy Chicken Shortcake, p. 74	4	562	39	45	25	10	151	1,118
Cheesy Vegetable Chowder, p. 102	6	236	15	18	13	8	41	511
Cherry–Apple Chutney, p. 180	96	28	0	7	0	0	0	13
Cherry–Pear Crisp, p. 206	6	386	4	68	12	2	0	100
Chicken and Dumplings, p. 78	6	372	27	31	15	4	70	594
Chicken and Ham Gumbo, p. 107	4	633	43	50	29	6	97	1,485
Chicken Canapés, p. 225	24	133	5	17	5	2	10	203
Chicken-Fried Steak with Gravy, p. 25	4	355	30	22	16	4	121	545
Chicken–Rice Patties, p. 80	4	594	29	30	40	14	106	928
Chilled Berry Tart, p. 205	12	256	4	27	15	6	24	204
Chocolate Cake with Truffle Filling, p. 188	16	486	6	59	28	10	71	2,022
Chocolate–Oatmeal Cookies, p. 220	48	114	1	14	6	2	4	61
Chocolate–Pistachio-Stuffed French Toast, p. 113	6	274	10	30	10	3	147	307
Christmas Fruit Slaw, p. 90	8	195	3	34	7	1	1	32
Cider-Braised Onions, p. 162	4	118	1	16	6	1	0	250
Cioppino, p. 103	4	200	25	11	5	1	109	515
Colonial Three-Grain Bread, p. 121	24	99	2	16	3	0	0	91
Company Scalloped Potatoes, p. 166	6	243	8	40	6	2	9	243
Company-Special Mashed Potatoes, p. 157	4	114	1	4	11	4	11	350
Cornish Game Hens with Corn Bread Stuffing, p. 81	4	528	47	20	30	4	129	640
Cornmeal Dinner Rolls, p. 92	20	136	3	21	4	1	22	100
Corn Muffins, p. 142	12	150	4	20	6	1	36	166
Corn on the Cob (Cilantro–Lime Butter), p. 50	8	150	3	19	9	5	21	77
Corn on the Cob (Pepper Butter), p. 50	8	150	3	20	9	5	21	77
Corn Relish, p. 182	224	14	0	3	0	0	0	1
Corn Sticks, p. 142	24	75	2	10	3	0	18	83
Country Ham with Redeye Gravy, p. 116	4	244	25	7	13	4	68	1,391
Country Ribs with Gingery Barbecue Sauce, p. 10	4	353	41	19	14	4	102	705
Crab Cakes, p. 62	4	216	19	13	10	2	117	453
Cranberry-Glazed Ham, p. 9	18	162	21	9	2	2	45	1,111
Cranberry–Orange Streusel Muffins, p. 42	12	171	3	27	6	1	18	115
Cranberry–Pear Mince Pie, p. 93	8	562	5	85	24	5	0	397
Crawfish Étouffée, p. 65	4	391	23	56	9	1	75	350
Crispy Batter-Fried Chicken, p. 69	6	612	25	17	48	8	102	256
Currant Pound Cake, p. 189	16	358	5	57	13	8	85	174
Deviled Swiss Steak, p. 24	4	222	25	11	9	2	59	669
Dill-Pickled Okra, p. 182	36	15	1	4	0	0	0	358
Double-Chocolate–Pecan Coffee Cake, p. 122	16	236	5	26	13	3	28	142
Dutch Apple–Brandy Cheesecake, p. 213	16	430	8	33	31	14	115	310

PER SERVING

RECIPE	Servings	Calories	Protein (g)	Carbohydrates (g)	Fat (g)	Saturated Fat (g)	Cholesterol (mg)	Sodium (g)
				PER SERVING				
Dutch Apple Pie, p. 221	8	506	5	72	23	7	10	139
Farm-Stand Ratatouille, p. 156	8	79	2	11	4	1	0	143
Filled Sally Lunn, p. 127	20	192	4	31	6	1	33	176
Fish 'n' Chips, p. 59	4	728	32	82	31	5	104	306
Fried Green Tomatoes, p. 162	4	347	6	26	25	4	54	132
Fruit-Flavored Vinegar, p. 185	24	6	0	1	0	0	0	7
Funnel Cakes, p. 136	4	725	13	66	46	7	115	326
Garlic-Marinated Grilled Lamb, p. 34	12	320	21	3	21	8	83	519
Garlic–Mustard Green Beans, p. 91	8	42	2	7	1	0	1	145
German Apple Pancake, p. 111	4	458	12	36	31	8	182	529
German-Style Hot Potato Salad, p. 158	6	256	6	42	8	3	14	294
Ginger–Apple Butter, p. 174	96	44	0	11	0	0	0	1
Glazed Ham Balls, p. 38	6	347	31	32	11	4	138	1,507
Glazed Sweet Potatoes, p. 160	6	299	3	46	12	2	0	113
Green Chili and Corn Chowder, p. 101	4	267	13	22	15	7	36	870
Ham and Bean Soup, p. 106	4	287	20	50	2	1	12	532
Ham and Cheese Fritters, p. 143	20	108	4	11	5	1	18	130
Hamburger Pie with Lattice Cheese Crust, p. 19	4	528	28	44	27	10	141	890
Herb and Pecan Oven-Fried Chicken, p. 70	4	324	33	11	16	3	138	242
Herbed Garlic Chops, p. 12	4	239	32	4	11	4	79	211
Herb Vinegar, p. 185	32	2	0	1	0	0	0	5
Honey Butter, p. 124	16	67	0	4	6	1	0	67
Honey–Wheat Spiral, p. 124	16	116	3	21	2	1	14	161
Honey–Wheat Waffles, p. 112	6	406	9	46	22	4	77	287
Hush Puppies, p. 143	14	134	2	11	9	1	17	107
Jam Cake with Caramel Frosting, p. 190	12	485	5	84	16	5	68	252
Kentucky Burgoo, p. 96	5	414	36	45	11	3	89	613
Lamb Chops with Blue Cheese Sauce, p. 30	4	247	22	4	15	5	69	205
Layered Green Bean and Tomato Salad, p. 146	6	106	2	11	7	1	0	151
Leg of Lamb with Peppercorns and Mustard, p. 35	12	258	29	3	14	4	91	187
Lemon Chess Pie, p. 196	8	415	6	62	17	4	107	167
Lemon-Filled Cake, p. 192	16	414	5	86	7	2	81	138
Lemon–Gingerbread Soufflé, p. 212	6	202	6	23	10	3	145	140
Lemony Moravian Sugar Bread, p. 130	12	327	6	53	10	2	36	215
Lentil, Barley, and Ham Soup, p. 104	4	336	25	41	10	2	31	1,271
Lime-Seasoned Salmon, p. 57	4	337	24	8	23	3	74	66
Maid-of-Honor Tarts, p. 227	24	110	2	13	6	1	18	63
Make-Ahead Twice-Baked Sweet Potatoes, p. 88	8	268	3	48	8	1	0	122
Maple-Glazed Pot Roast, p. 23	8	343	34	29	10	3	100	250
Marble Chiffon Cake, p. 219	12	411	6	57	19	6	125	189
Marble Doughnuts, p. 138	15	989	9	151	45	16	29	271

RECIPE	Servings	Calories	Protein (g)	Carbohydrates (g)	Fat (g)	Saturated Fat (g)	Cholesterol (mg)	Sodium (g)
Marinated Pot Roast with Vegetables, p. 22	8	365	32	26	15	4	90	437
Mixed Country Greens, p. 149	6	121	5	9	8	3	14	478
Molasses and Rum Baked Beans, p. 154	10	326	12	50	8	3	14	413
Molasses Hermits, p. 215	40	89	1	14	4	1	11	43
Mustard-Glazed New England Boiled Dinner, p. 29	6	590	32	50	31	10	148	2,034
Mustardy Potato Salad, p. 148	6	269	4	27	18	3	11	466
Nectarine–Raspberry Conserve, p. 176	96	57	0	13	1	0	0	1
Nectarine Sunrise, p. 46	8	142	1	24	0	0	0	8
New Potatoes with Lemon–Basil Sauce, p. 41	6	189	3	28	8	2	0	120
Nutty Coconut Macaroons, p. 214	45	43	1	6	2	1	0	4
Old-Fashioned Cornmeal Gingerbread, p. 194	9	264	5	40	10	2	73	177
Orange–Cinnamon Rolls, p. 123	24	223	4	33	9	3	28	60
Orange-Glazed Lamb Chops, p. 31	3	276	31	11	11	4	93	430
Orange Mincemeat, p. 181	10	443	2	115	1	0	0	26
Orange–Rhubarb Bread, p. 133	24	185	3	31	6	1	10	100
Pan-Fried Catfish, p. 54	4	367	27	29	16	3	72	339
Pan-Fried Trout, p. 54	4	461	36	29	22	4	89	306
Parsnip–Carrot Salad, p. 39	6	236	2	19	18	3	11	133
Peach and Watercress Salad, p. 147	6	298	3	20	25	3	0	15
Peach–Berry Pie, p. 51	8	412	5	61	18	4	0	142
Peach Cobbler with Cinnamon-Swirl Biscuits, p. 202	8	365	4	56	15	4	7	177
Peanut Butter–Streusel Coffee Cake, p. 135	9	292	6	39	14	4	25	234
Pecan Pie with Spicy Crust, p. 200	8	679	7	72	43	12	121	218
Peppy Green Tomato Chutney, p. 180	56	35	0	9	0	0	0	6
Pesto-Stuffed Turkey Breast, p. 85	6	302	34	2	17	4	74	288
Piccalilli, p. 179	112	18	0	5	0	0	0	39
Poached Salmon with Dill Sauce, p. 58	4	237	25	7	12	3	81	462
Po'boys, p. 60	4	440	18	38	23	4	141	693
Pork Crown Roast, p. 14	6	561	35	45	28	7	78	515
Pork Loin with Sausage Stuffing, p. 16	8	283	33	14	11	4	88	180
Pork Medaillons with Brandy–Cream Sauce, p. 15	6	410	36	4	28	15	143	217
Potato Soup, p. 100	4	201	8	32	5	2	15	593
Pumpkin–Hazelnut Crunch Pie, p. 197	8	512	8	56	30	8	93	3,300
Quick Sweet–Sour Pickles, p. 183	60	73	0	19	0	0	0	564
Red Beans and Rice, p. 11	5	424	22	66	8	3	28	610
Red Snapper Stuffed with Barley Pilaf, p. 56	4	272	26	38	3	1	40	415
Rhubarb Cobbler, p. 202	8	389	4	61	15	4	7	187
Rib Eye Roast with Herb-Mushroom Sauce, p. 21	12	299	31	3	18	8	94	254
Roast Goose with Fruited Stuffing, p. 84	6	805	42	78	37	11	129	816
Rosemary Lamb Kabobs, p. 32	4	297	24	19	14	4	72	82
Rosemary Roast Chicken with Stuffing, p. 73	6	316	27	20	14	4	75	453

RECIPE	Servings	Calories	Protein (g)	Carbohydrates (g)	Fat (g)	Saturated Fat (g)	Cholesterol (mg)	Sodium (g)
				PER SERVING				
Rustic Home-Fried Potatoes, p. 117	4	222	4	39	6	1	0	214
Sally Lunn, p. 127	20	163	4	23	6	1	33	176
Saucy Apple Dumplings, p. 203	12	368	4	68	10	3	22	248
Scalloped Corn, p. 163	8	186	8	23	8	4	73	425
Scalloped Oysters, p. 63	4	246	13	21	11	3	92	455
Sesame Asparagus, p. 40	6	103	4	8	7	1	0	110
Shortenin' Rounds, p. 214	18	125	2	11	9	4	14	44
Short Ribs with Sweet-and-Spicy Molasses Sauce, p. 28	4	354	38	30	10	3	115	154
Sour Cream Chicken Fricassee, p. 77	4	556	39	44	24	7	140	466
Sour Cream Country Scones, p. 226	20	125	2	17	6	2	16	175
Sour Cream Raisin Pie with Nut Pastry, p. 201	8	436	7	65	18	4	80	131
Sourdough Bread, p. 129	24	146	4	27	2	0	9	108
Southern Fried Chicken and Gravy, p. 68	4	420	34	16	24	6	103	541
Southwestern Corn Bread, p. 142	8	311	10	38	13	4	67	456
Southwestern-Style Three-Bean Salad, p. 49	8	223	8	26	10	1	0	353
Spiced Apple Wedges, p. 153	6	179	0	38	4	1	0	46
Spiced Peach Freezer Jam, p. 178	96	51	0	13	0	0	0	1
Spicy Black-Walnut Cake, p. 191	16	452	7	56	23	5	63	255
Spinach-and-Ricotta-Stuffed Meatloaf, p. 20	6	379	30	15	23	10	171	676
Steaks with Peppercorns and Mustard, p. 35	4	318	33	2	17	5	87	136
Sweet Pepper Slaw, p. 48	8	98	1	9	7	1	0	140
Sweet Pickled Beets, p. 183	20	58	1	15	0	0	0	24
Sweet Potato and Fruit Salad, p. 168	6	199	3	37	5	3	16	58
Sweet-Potato–Wheat Twist, p. 120	32	109	3	21	1	0	7	145
Tartar Sauce, p. 60	20	83	0	1	9	1	7	84
Teatime Petits Fours, p. 224	36	124	1	26	2	1	0	27
Texas-Style Beef Brisket, p. 47	8	385	34	18	18	6	105	787
Three-Cheese Macaroni, p. 155	6	462	18	41	25	12	53	716
Three-Fruit Conserve, p. 178	128	48	0	12	0	0	0	1
Tomato–Dill Bisque, p. 98	4	148	5	13	10	3	7	719
Trout with Salsa, p. 55	4	233	20	10	13	3	97	338
Turkey with Dressing, p. 89	8	633	58	34	28	8	160	693
Upside-Down Pineapple and Carrot Cake, p. 195	8	391	5	48	21	3	53	171
Vegetable Salad with Parmesan Dressing, p. 171	6	141	4	9	11	2	9	172
Whiskey-Sauced Bread Pudding, p. 211	6	383	9	41	18	6	197	273
Whole Wheat Sourdough Bread, p. 129	24	147	5	27	2	0	9	109
Whoopie Pies, p. 218	14	449	5	63	22	6	24	232
Wild Rice Bread, p. 126	24	123	3	21	3	1	18	120
Wild Rice Pilaf, p. 82	4	138	6	29	1	0	0	482
Wilted Succotash Salad, p. 147	8	79	3	14	2	0	0	224
Zucchini–Barley Salad, p. 170	6	268	5	25	19	3	11	199

C

D–F

G–K

L–N

O–Q

METRIC COOKING HINTS

By making a few conversions, cooks in Australia, Canada, and the United Kingdom can use the recipes in this book with confidence. The charts on this page provide a guide for converting measurements from the U.S. customary system, which is used throughout this book, to the imperial and metric systems. There also is a conversion table for oven temperatures to accommodate the differences in oven calibrations.

———■———

VOLUME AND WEIGHT: Americans traditionally use *cup* measures for liquid and solid ingredients. The chart above left shows the approximate imperial and metric equivalents. If you are accustomed to weighing solid ingredients, here are some helpful approximate equivalents:

■ 1 cup butter, caster sugar, or rice = 8 ounces = about 250 grams
■ 1 cup flour = 4 ounces = about 125 grams
■ 1 cup icing sugar = 5 ounces = about 150 grams

Spoon measures are used for smaller amounts of ingredients. Although the size of the teaspoon is the same, the size of the tablespoon varies slightly among countries. However, for practical purposes and for recipes in this book, a straight substitution is all that's necessary.

Measurements made using cups or spoons always should be *level*, unless stated otherwise.

———■———

PRODUCT DIFFERENCES: Most of the products and ingredients called for in the recipes in this book are available in English-speaking countries. However, some are known by different names. Here are some common American ingredients and their possible counterparts:

■ Sugar is granulated or caster sugar.
■ Powdered sugar is icing sugar.
■ All-purpose flour is plain household flour or white flour. When self-rising flour is used in place of all-purpose flour in a recipe that calls for leavening, omit the leavening (baking soda or baking powder) and salt.
■ Light corn syrup is golden syrup.
■ Cornstarch is cornflour.
■ Baking soda is bicarbonate of soda.
■ Vanilla is vanilla essence.

USEFUL EQUIVALENTS

⅛ teaspoon = 0.5ml	⅔ cup = 5 fluid ounces = 150ml
¼ teaspoon = 1ml	¾ cup = 6 fluid ounces = 175ml
½ teaspoon = 2ml	1 cup = 8 fluid ounces = 250ml
1 teaspoon = 5ml	2 cups = 1 pint
¼ cup = 2 fluid ounces = 50ml	2 pints = 1 litre
⅓ cup = 3 fluid ounces = 75ml	½ inch = 1 centimetre
½ cup = 4 fluid ounces = 125ml	1 inch = 2 centimetres

BAKING PAN SIZES

AMERICAN	METRIC
8x1½-inch round baking pan	20x4-centimetre sandwich or cake tin
9x1½-inch round baking pan	23x3.5-centimetre sandwich or cake tin
11x7x1½-inch baking pan	28x18x4-centimetre baking pan
13x9x2-inch baking pan	32.5x23x5-centimetre baking pan
12x7½x2-inch baking dish	30x19x5-centimetre baking pan
15x10x2-inch baking pan	38x25.5x2.5-centimetre baking pan (Swiss roll tin)
9-inch pie plate	22x4- or 23x4-centimetre pie plate
7- or 8-inch springform pan	18- or 20-centimetre springform or loose-bottom cake tin
9x5x3-inch loaf pan	23x13x6-centimetre or 2-pound narrow loaf pan or pâté tin
1½-quart casserole	1.5-litre casserole
2-quart casserole	2-litre casserole

OVEN TEMPERATURE EQUIVALENTS

FAHRENHEIT SETTING	CELSIUS SETTING*	GAS SETTING	
300°F	150°C	Gas Mark 2	*Electric and gas ovens may be calibrated using Celsius. However, increase the Celsius setting 10 to 20 degrees when cooking above 160°C with an *electric* oven. For *convection* or *forced-air* ovens (gas or electric), lower the temperature setting 10°C when cooking at all heat levels.
325°F	160°C	Gas Mark 3	
350°F	180°C	Gas Mark 4	
375°F	190°C	Gas Mark 5	
400°F	200°C	Gas Mark 6	
425°F	220°C	Gas Mark 7	
450°F	230°C	Gas Mark 8	
Broil		Grill (watch time and heat)	